International Taxation and Capitalism

The book introduces a novel approach to international taxation through the lens of heterodox economic and social theories, in particular Marxism.

The book argues that the radical reorganization of the international tax system that has been underway for the last few decades – initiated by the OECD and furthered by the G20 and the European Union – is a response to changes in the global structure of capitalism, especially in terms of "center-periphery". Through both normative analysis and empirical evidence, the book shows that the global tax system emerging from these changes consolidates the regulatory and tax revenue control of the central states. It also demonstrates that this consolidation and centralisation is designed to enable the dominance of multinational corporations in the global economy. This path of international taxation is explained in the book through certain general concepts of Marxian economic theory, such as the accumulation of capital and the tendency of the rate of profit to fall, along with other specific developments, such as the unequal participation of the different regions of the world in the capitalist system and a general theory of money that incorporates elements proposed by some sectors of post-Keynesianism.

This book is invaluable reading for anyone interested in global capitalism, the financial system, heterodox economics, and Marxist theory.

Andrés Blanco holds a Law and Social Sciences degree from the Universidad de la República, Uruguay (UDELAR). He teaches both undergraduate and graduate courses at UDELAR's School of Law and School of Economic Sciences and is full professor and chair of UDELAR's Public Finance Institute. He has published several books (in Spanish), including *El Impuesto al Valor Agregado*, *Tributos y precios públicos*, and *Estudios críticos sobre finanzas públicas*, as well as articles in English and Spanish in peer-reviewed journals.

Routledge Frontiers of Political Economy

Sustainable Economic Development
Perspectives from Political Economy and Economics Pluralism
Edited by Giorgos Meramveliotakis and Manolis Manioudis

The Myth of the Global Market
A Marxist Critique of Neoliberalism
Giulio Palermo

Government and Economic Growth in the 21st Century
A Classical Liberal Response
Edited by Juan E. Castañeda

Political Economy in Middle East and North-Africa
Why Institutions, Rents and Power Matter in Economic Reforms
Rachid Mira

How Economists Think
A Kantian Interpretation of Mainstream Economics
Steven Buccola

Economic Populism and Institutional Reform
Emre Ünal

Capital, Entrepreneurship and Management
A New Austrian Theory of Organizations
Thierry Aimar

Capitalism as Megamachine
A New Historical, Legal and Political Approach
Jacques Richard

A Financial Theory of the Business Cycle
Net Present Value and Fractional Reserve Banking
Fuller and Young

For more information about this series, please visit: www.routledge.com/Routledge-Frontiers-of-Political-Economy/book-series/SE0345

International Taxation and Capitalism

A Heterodox Economics Perspective

Andrés Blanco

Routledge
Taylor & Francis Group
LONDON AND NEW YORK

First published 2025
by Routledge
4 Park Square, Milton Park, Abingdon, Oxon OX14 4RN

and by Routledge
605 Third Avenue, New York, NY 10158

Routledge is an imprint of the Taylor & Francis Group, an informa business

British Library Cataloguing-in-Publication Data
A catalogue record for this book is available from the British Library

ISBN: 978-1-032-60346-9 (hbk)
ISBN: 978-1-032-60347-6 (pbk)
ISBN: 978-1-003-45867-8 (ebk)

DOI: 10.4324/9781003458678

Typeset in Times New Roman
by Deanta Global Publishing Services, Chennai, India

Contents

Figures

Preface

Lengthening prefaces is never a good idea: it is always preferable for readers to investigate the pages of the book for themselves to discover its errors and successes. Suffice it to indicate, therefore, that this book is an attempt to explain, in a theoretical framework that combines a large part of categories from Marxism with others from post-Keynesianism, the evolution of international taxation. The normative or propositional parts of the book are minor: only the final chapter contains some reflections on the matter. This is motivated by the restraints (or doubts) that I have about the possibility of taxes leaving the channel set by the capitalist system.

For the purposes of explaining taxation at the international level, I had to delve into a theoretical construction of taxation in general, whose conclusions are valid both at the domestic and international levels. Other issues of the theoretical framework (for example, the conception of money and the rate of profit) have a general scope beyond this research in particular.

Finally, I wish to express my gratitude to Andy Humphries and Yarisa Wahlang Kharbuli for their generous invitation to this task and their ongoing support, the reviewers for their work, and Laura Pérez for her invaluable help in the editing of this book.

1 Introduction

In recent years, the academic world has seen a notable growth in literature on the subject of international taxation. Such literature, however, has focused on what could tentatively be referred to as legal aspects, and consequently mainly circumscribed to an academic audience in the field of law. Nonetheless, the issue has not been ignored by mainstream economic theory, which has produced some – basically econometric – works dealing with the effects of the new global trends in taxation. However, as with all paradigms, that school of thought is limited by its own theoretical assumptions and, therefore, fails to perceive (or is unable to explain) two features of international taxation that are clearly observable: its institutional and fiscal biases. Furthermore, the rationale of the mainstream approach to international taxation has remained unchanged for about a century.

An informal, but unavoidable and effective, starting point for any comprehensive study on international taxation is the obvious fact that international tax policy design is increasingly concentrated in a small group of states, acting individually or through organizations such as the Group of 20 (G20), the Organisation for Economic Cooperation and Development (OECD), and the European Union (EU). These subjects of international taxation no longer play merely complementary roles in this matter. Rather, they issue tax policy guidelines that amount to veritable diktats that are followed by most national taxation systems. Moreover, the content of these tax policies is not determined randomly. Those subjects themselves often highlight that the main objective of these policies is to increase taxes levied on "international economic activities" and, in particular, on the activities of multinational corporations. While this is probably not untrue, there is a detail that is often omitted. At first glance, proposed designs for international taxation policies reveal a bias in favor of the very states behind the global taxation diktats, as they assign most of that additional tax revenue to them.

Moving on to the realm of explanations, and continuing in an informal tone, we can infer that an exploration of international taxation must combine two major theoretical issues: an explanation of the global economy and an explanation of taxes in general. In any writings or discussions on the "global economy", both in general and concerning a specific, related phenomenon, as is taxation, there is a risk of resorting to trite phrases such as "the consequences of the digitalization of the economy", "the growing globalization", "the new global economic order", and so on, which are heard everywhere from mass media outlets to conferences,

DOI: 10.4324/9781003458678-1

academic or popular literature, and political debates and the like. Thus, the first task at hand in an introduction to taxation from an international perspective is to show that those phrases are, almost without exception, discursive devices. This entails providing a brief preview of the book's theoretical framework, which is essential to introduce readers to the language of this work, as – echoing Ludwig Wittgenstein's *Tractatus* – its limits are the limits of the portion of the world that will be addressed in these pages.

First, the economy has not entered a new historical phase, understood as a new design – in any meaningful sense – of the social relations that underpin its fundamental structure. The global economy, in fact, continues to operate according to the pattern we call capitalism, or the capitalist system. What is more, if there is a significant aspect that characterizes the so-called globalization, it is the mass and rapid incorporation of many more regions and human groups into the global capitalist system. So that rather than transcending capitalism, this process deepens and expands it.

Second, the great ease of communications today and the speed that such ease brings to economic operations create the illusion that we are only now living in an economy in which every corner of the world is interconnected. This is an illusion because capitalism has been, since its inception, the first mode of production with global reach. After all, one of its earliest external manifestations was the European expansion of the sixteenth and seventeenth centuries. That process has only continued to grow and become more complex, given that, in addition to the specific needs of each stage of capitalism (increasing demand or avoiding the tendency of the rate of profit to fall), capital must always move forward beyond itself, even going as far as inventing "non-capital" spheres to, then appropriate them.

There is no doubt that the technical innovations seen in recent years are huge and that they entail a change in the material conditions in which the economy unfolds. But they have not exerted pressure on the social relations that characterize capitalism, at least not in any discernible way that would suggest a drastic change in them (although, as history teaches us, this could occur when least expected).

Third, a feature of the global economy that is, however, highlighted in the discourse deployed by international subjects (although, admittedly, not by economic scholars of the dominant schools) is the growing importance of multinational corporations and the ensuing global tendency toward monopolies (or oligopolies) in the various branches of production.

But what role do taxes play in all this? In general (not only in the international sphere), it would appear that, except in theories situated on the margins (where I include myself), it is assumed without much discussion that taxes supply money to states, money they would not otherwise have. Under this vision, therefore, taxes constitute the indirect prerequisite for the development of all kinds of state policies, ranging from the absurd wars that plague the world to aid programs aimed at providing assistance for all sorts of vulnerable people. Taxation is not believed to serve any purpose for the private economy (in the sociological sense of "being inherently meant for"); rather, in any case, taxes are said to have "effects", understood as secondary – and often undesired – consequences for the private sector. Their insertion in the general workings of the capitalist system, from the smallest geographical spaces to the world at large, is thus shaped by this dominant view.

This conception is the reason why the international taxation "problems" (and I deliberately use scare quotes here) that are raised by the dominant discourse, in both public and academic spheres, involve issues such as "avoiding multinational corporation tax evasion", "establishing new tax rules in response to the delocalization of production factors", "making tax collection compatible with investment", etc.

Now then, as noted above regarding the global economy, this book will propose a view of taxes that is at odds with the view usually found both in discourse and in writings. Therefore, instead of identifying solutions for the international taxation problems currently on the public agenda, or even taking a novel approach to them, different problems will be identified and addressed here. More specifically, rather than as a source of revenue for states, taxes are viewed here essentially as regulators of the quantity and distribution of money at the national and international levels, and associated with public spending, but as a consequence thereof, not as an antecedent, and even then only partially. In addition, this conception is connected with a different view of public debt: the view that holds that public debt is also a necessary element for the functioning of money. Before discussing these, I will present a theory of money different from the dominant theory.

What questions will this book attempt to answer, then? The first and more general question is: how do taxes fulfill the function of global regulators of the quantity and distribution of money? The second question, considering the answer to the first, is: why do the G20, the OECD, and the EU and its individual members propose and further new international taxation policies, and where are those policies aimed at?

The research rationale, in the terms laid out in this chapter, clearly indicates that this book falls under a theoretical framework that draws on heterodox economic theories. To begin with, the theoretical framework incorporates several central categories developed by Karl Marx and some Marxian schools of thought, namely: (a) the idea that all economic systems are "modes of production"; (b) the characterization of the current mode of production as capitalist, given that it revolves around capital as a special type of social relation with respect to the means of production; (c) the labor theory of value; (d) the concept of "capital accumulation" as an essential process of the capitalist mode of production; and (e) the profit rate, its tendency to fall, and the counter-tendencies, as explanatory hypotheses of the structural dynamics of capitalism, at both the national and international level. The theoretical framework also incorporates a theory of the state and the concept of "ideology" posited by certain Marxian schools of thought. These elements will be discussed in Chapter 3.

The tax theory applied here and its underlying theory of money are not, strictly speaking, Marxian (although neither are they incompatible with Marxism); rather, they are drawn essentially from the monetary circuit theory derived from John Maynard Keynes, Abba Lerner, and other post-Keynesian authors. I will elaborate on this theory in Chapter 4.

The theoretical framework indicated determines the epistemological assumptions and the methodological strategy adopted, so that, while I deal with these in Chapter 2, I mention them here after the theoretical framework. My first concern in this sense was that both the theoretical framework and the specific hypotheses be within the realm of science, and this required adopting a scientific demarcation criterion. Secondly, the theoretical framework adopted entails a metatheory of social phenomena, particularly those, such as taxation, in which the state plays a leading role. Indeed, without being grossly deterministic, an approach to economic phenomena that structurally accepts Marxist categories must also accept that they are subordinated to the fundamental processes of the mode of production. Roughly speaking, this means that the evolution of taxation systems, both national and international, must have an explanation based on the theory of money, given that it is a monetary phenomenon, and also on the underlying processes mentioned above: capital accumulation and the evolution of the rate of profit. For that same reason, the methodological individualism typical of neoclassical economic theory, along with its corollaries (for example, the theory of rational choice), will be avoided here.

Specifically, with respect to methodology, the hypotheses will be tested in different phases, using statistical information whenever possible. This will involve a significant difficulty, given that the data available in this sense is normally produced according to neoclassical economic theory and therefore not generally applicable when working with a Marxist and post-Keynesian taxonomy. However, that data will be used as indirect evidence with the purpose of empirically testing the hypotheses. Qualitative methods will also be used, namely, comparative descriptions of different or similar phenomena, both contemporary (to establish an association between them) or successive (to explain a current phenomenon through the change in a past phenomenon, or to identify a past connection that may be repeated today). This is a key part of the Marxian approach but also an element of any science, given that studying the past and its evolution is highly important, as science itself is based on the assumption that relations between phenomena are repeated, or, in other words, that the structural evolution of the future is similar to that of the past. Without that assumption, scientific prediction would be impossible.

Once the epistemological and methodological frameworks, as well as the theoretical framework, have been established, I will address the relationship between capitalism and space in Chapter 5. Chapter 6 will posit the book's central hypothesis regarding international taxation systems. Chapters 7 and 8 will describe the evolution of the international taxation system from antiquity to recent decades. After identifying the major institutional players involved in this evolution (including the OECD, the G20, and the European Union), both the instruments and the contents of the taxation policies furthered by them will be described and interpreted according to the theoretical framework presented. This historical reconstruction will have the methodological nature of a test of the hypothesis set out in Chapter 6.

In Chapter 9, the hypothesis will be tested with evidence stemming from the legal structures of international taxation, as well as from statistical information, to the extent that such information is available. In Chapter 10, I will try to interpret some of the main categories and solutions of the international taxation legal system (both supranational and domestic) in light of the hypothesis posited in Chapter 6 and the general concept of taxation discussed in Chapter 4. In Chapter 11, I will consider the superstructural aspects of the international taxation system, mainly in its most recent designs, as described and explained in economic terms in the previous chapters. This approach will apply the concepts of state, law, and ideology as relations or discourses that play the role of generating or reproducing behaviors and beliefs that serve a certain structure of social relations, both existing and emergent.

Chapter 12 will sum up the conclusions of the previous discussions, which will be essentially explanatory. Finally, in Chapter 13, I will tentatively suggest an alternative global taxation system, comparing it with other proposals put forward recently, but with a great uncertainty as to its feasibility, given the trends in the international capitalist system observed throughout the book.

2 Epistemological and methodological basis

2.1 Science, heterodox economic theories, and Marxism

We cannot undertake the explanation of the capitalist system or its relation with space, nor can we explain taxation at all its levels, without first explicitly stating the epistemological and methodological premises that will guide this work.

In this sense, there are a series of strictly epistemological aspects that are more important than – and must precede – the construction of a theoretical framework. I am particularly interested in addressing three issues in that regard: the demarcation of science from non-science; the paradigmatic nature of scientific knowledge; and the need for a methodology that enables the collection and processing of empirical information.

With respect to the first issue, and given that this book adopts a theoretical framework with many elements originating in Marxism, it should be noted that, historically, Marxian – economic, social, political, etc. – theorists have tended for the most part to reject the epistemology developed during the twentieth and twenty-first centuries, most likely because that epistemology is linked to other philosophical schools (particularly to analytical philosophy and recent versions of rationalism). I believe such rejection is a mistake, as contemporary epistemology primarily contains reflections derived from the enormous explanatory achievements of the so-called natural sciences. In fact, one need not delve too deeply into the literature to note that contemporary epistemology constitutes an effort to identify the factors that determined the success of modern physics, chemistry, and biology (which were largely developed without prior epistemological support), and to consolidate and expand them for other researchers and other disciplines. These achievements in no way contradict the Marxian view of science; quite the opposite. Therefore, there should be no reason to fear the adoption of concepts derived from them. We should thus start by accepting that social theories should be considered sciences, or at least something that comes close to a science. Hence, the first problem consists in determining what conditions must be met for them to be considered sciences.

To do that, we must know if the features typical of the natural sciences can be extended to the so-called social sciences and even if the latter can be called sciences. For now, I will assume that this problem has a – shall we say – cautiously affirmative answer. While we can question whether the distinctive features of the

DOI: 10.4324/9781003458678-2

natural sciences can be fully applicable to the social sciences, and also that the latter are more strongly influenced by factors that subjectivize knowledge,[1] I believe that, in essence, the criteria proposed in the last century and a half for demarcating science can also be applied to the social sciences.

Let us begin by posing the following question: what demands shall we impose on our work for it to, at least, come close to qualifying as scientific? Given that a thorough reflection on this is not possible here, I will propose answering that question with Karl Popper's criterion: for something to be considered scientific, its discourse must produce empirically refutable statements (Popper 1962, 253ff.). It may come as a surprise to find Popper's epistemology in a book with a theoretical framework that draws abundantly from Marxism. But that surprise should immediately dissipate when we consider that Marxist economic theory meets the standard proposed by Popper to a greater extent than other schools of economic thought. Indeed, Popper essentially sought to exclude from science any discourse that was supposedly explanatory but at the same time compatible with contradictory observations or experiments. The fundamental requirement for a hypothesis to be scientific is that it must inherently admit a counterexample that falsifies it. From that perspective, Marx's theory contains many hypotheses that are, in Popper's terms, highly falsifiable and, therefore, can safely qualify as scientific. The most notable of these is the tendency of the rate of profit to fall: it predicts a concrete relation between the total value of production and its costs, as well as the generation of other movements that tend to diminish those costs and bring the rate back up to a desired level. In contrast, neoclassical theory rests on a central hypothesis – that of marginal utility as a determinant of economic behavior – that cannot pass the test of falsifiability, given that it is compatible with any kind of observation or experiment (Blaug 2006, 137ff; Sen 1988, 10ff; Bunge 1989, 109ff.).

Without denying falsificationism as a criterion for demarcating science from non-science, an important clarification is in order: falsificationism, or any other conception of science, *must accept* that certain concepts of a discipline that are fundamental, insofar as they are the most basic elements of its chain of explanations, may lack – precisely because of that characteristic – conceivable counterexamples, without that entailing that the theoretical current they underpin is no longer scientific. For example, in most modern and contemporary physics, it is assumed that matter is made up of particles. One may question just how many and how elementary those particles are, but the general notion of particle is in any case considered irreplaceable. However, it is difficult to think of a counterexample of particles as the basic component of matter, at least within the physics paradigms of the last few centuries. It is such a basic concept that, strictly speaking, no counterexamples can exist, only perhaps substitute concepts, which, also because of their basic nature, would have to be foundational elements of a completely different paradigm (such as the controversial *string theory*).

It should be noted, however, that even when employing falsificationism as a boundary for delimiting science from non-scientific discourses, actual scientific practice is not limited to proposing hypotheses for others to refute or to finding evidence to refute rival hypotheses. Rather, researchers are normally focused on conducting fieldwork (observations and experiments) that will *confirm* their hypotheses. It is also true that the scientific community's acceptance of a hypothesis is associated with the accumulation of empirical evidence in its favor, and not merely with the lack of observed counterexamples. That is, scientists behave in fact (and that is how it should be) as if the strength of a hypothesis were probabilistic and as if its probability depended on the accumulation of concrete cases that confirm it (Carnap 1962, 162 ff.).

Opting for a falsificationist conception, as well as accepting a probabilistic praxis, is linked to a recurring debate in Marxism, namely: is it necessary for Marxist theory, in any of its manifestations, to test its assertions with empirical data? This discussion is obviously connected with the question of whether or not Marxism needs to adjust to the demands of the general epistemology of the twentieth century, as discussed in some paragraphs above. As noted, Marxism passes the scientificity test of contemporary epistemology with flying colors, but it remains to be seen whether it is really necessary to put it to that test.

On the one hand, the voices that oppose pursuing an "empirical Marxism" draw on the notions of science and ideology proposed by Louis Althusser. If, in line with this author, we accept that objective knowledge – understood as correspondence with facts independent from the social being of the researcher – is impossible, then the essential element for something to be scientific is that it has internal consistency in its development. And the contrasting with "facts" that appear to "be there", but are always filtered by ideology, is thus irrelevant (Amariglio and Ruccio 2017, 22–23). As we will see below, this view is similar to the constructivist conceptions of the social sciences. But there is also a reluctance by a significant portion of Marxism to accept empirical work insofar as a great deal of Marxist approaches consist in "lifting the veil" of the apparent in order to penetrate deep social processes, and it is (sometimes) assumed that empirical data are the "veil" that needs lifting (Desai 1991, 28–29).

In my opinion, on the contrary, it is not only possible but also necessary for approaches that are – either partly or wholly – connected with Marxian theory to test their hypotheses against empirical data. From a philosophical perspective, refusing to address facts and withdrawing into a purely conceptual self-reflection would entail adopting a grossly idealistic ontology, openly contrary to the philosophical materialism that is the necessary assumption of Marxism. Moreover, if an essential part of Marxism consists in lifting ideological veils, this is only possible through the contrasting of ideological discourses, not just with strong theories but also with empirical evidence that supports those theories (Blanco 2022b, 4). More precisely, ideological veils are not found in empirical data but rather in discourses (Norval 2000). While ideological discourses do skew the collection and ordering of empirical data, the answer to that cannot be to renounce observation; rather, this must be addressed by conducting observations outside the conceptual frameworks that are presented as theoretical but are instead ideologies. That is, drawing on empirical information and focusing on the factual are tools for confronting ideology, so that to reject them is to engage in ideology. Which is why one of Marx's central concerns was *denouncing* ideology, as well as dogmatism, not in order to allow other ideologies or dogmas to emerge but rather to give way to science. Marx himself, and many Marxists after him, made extensive use of empirical information to support their theses, and rather than diminishing their explanatory power, that use strengthened it (Dunne 1991).

2.2 Methods and methodological problems

Heterodox economic thought, and especially Marxism, has an initial epistemological advantage over mainstream economic thought, namely, the limited influence it has on state policies. For those interested in obtaining tangible practical results from economic analyses, this may be considered a shortcoming. But it is actually a significant epistemological advantage in that, being freed from commitments to specific economic policies, Marxian (and post-Keynesian) analyses are better positioned to formulate hypotheses, test them empirically, and adjust them according to the evidence available (Blaug 2006, 244).

Nevertheless, handling empirical information under a heterodox framework, in particular a Marxist one, presents specific difficulties that are also derived from its minority or non-official position. In this sense, I agree with the assertion that all research is developed within a paradigm (Kuhn 1982) or research program (Lakatos 1999, 8ff.), so that it is within that paradigm (and not others that may exist within the same field of knowledge) that researchers define the language and categories to be used in their work, propose hypotheses consistent with the theoretical statements of the paradigm, and design their empirical experimentation and/or observation strategy. This presents certain advantages, but also a number of difficulties.

The paradigm thus determines not only the hypotheses that can be formulated but also what Thomas Kuhn called "taxonomy" (i.e., the conceptual categories used to analyse reality), and deciding what is observed and how it is observed is based on that taxonomy. This immersion of observation within a paradigm means that much of the empirical information collected within one paradigm cannot be used, at least not directly, to confirm or refute hypotheses formulated under other paradigms. How does this circumstance affect the development of empirical strategies in heterodox and Marxist economic thought?

On the one hand, there is a set of empirical analysis methods that are quantitative, and which refer to phenomena or objects that can be measured in units (Bunge 1967, 194ff.). As stated above, I think Marxism, or any heterodox economic theory, can and should use quantitative data, as applicable. Indeed, several central Marxist categories are by definition quantifiable: the tendency to fall of the profit rate, the rate of capital accumulation, etc., are in *themselves ratios, which must be expressed in real numbers.*

But this entails a major practical difficulty, given that the statistical data that is normally available – that which can be produced by what is commonly known as *econometrics* – does not involve a merely neutral or aseptic data collection. Rather, it consists in the quantification of variables proposed by neoclassical theory (Dunne 1991, 8–10), which is only natural since – as indicated by Kuhn – those who collect and order such data are situated within that theory. There are, of course, certain magnitudes available that can cut across all paradigms – to cite an example that is pertinent here, the volume and variation in gross tax revenue, globally or by tax, are expressed in monetary units – and can in principle be used even in a heterodox theoretical framework. However, the classification of countries into low-, medium-, or high-income countries is instead built on the assumption that the situation of a country in the global economy is defined by the relation between its population and its national income, without taking into account, for example, the country's production structure or whether those who control capital are local or foreign. Moreover, certain key categories of Marxian economics that could be quantifiable, such as surplus value and capital accumulation, cannot be quantified directly because their unit of measure, which is necessary labor time, is not considered by orthodox econometrics.

The above situation regarding available empirical data poses a major challenge to anyone who attempts to work under a heterodox paradigm (particularly a Marxian one) and is not able to produce their own empirical information from scratch. In some cases, and taking due precautions, certain existing statistical data can be used as evidence against or in favor of certain Marxian hypotheses (Bunge 1967, 241ff.). This must be done with extreme caution, since it will surely require numerous assumptions and adjustments, the modification or rejection of which will naturally entail changing or undermining their validity to confirm or refute the hypothesis in question (a good example of successful adaptation of statistics to Marxian theoretical categories can be found in Freeman 1991).

In any case, all scientific explanations include *relations* between phenomena that are not quantifiable. This is a feature of scientific research that has been highlighted even in the field of the so-called hard sciences (Bunge 1967, 203). In general, it is this type of relation between categories of reality that is not quantifiable, or at least cannot be expressed in numerical *ratios*, that has been the subject of *qualitative research methods*. While qualitative methods are often likened to self-described "critical" and "constructivist" paradigms, which tend to reject objectivity and the possibility of generalizations in the social sciences (Lincoln, Lynham, and Guba 2017), such association is not necessarily true in all cases, as paradigms that admit nomothetic generalizations allow for (and sometimes require) qualitative research. Mario Bunge, for example, indicates that all sciences deal with "relational concepts", or simply with relations, which are often not quantifiable. This is the case, for instance, of the relation *x is influenced by y* or *the existence of x is determined by the characteristics of y*.

In some cases, while relations themselves are not quantifiable, the elements of those relations are. For example, let us assume that a central hypothesis of this book is that tax revenue shifts from the periphery to the center, inversely to the movement of material production. While it is not possible to establish a *ratio* between the collection that is shifted in one direction and the production that is shifted in the opposite direction, each considered separately can be the object of direct measurements or of measurements of evidences associated with the shift.

In other cases, neither the relations nor the elements of those relations are quantifiable, or if they are, their measurement is purely arbitrary (Bunge 1967, 203).

When we have phenomena that are observable but not quantifiable and there is a relation between them, verifying that relation can be done through a method known as *colligation* (Ward 1972, 164–165). This method consists in the observation of the two elements that are related to each other in the hypothesis that is being tested, with the aim of determining the presence of both, or the presence of first one and then the other, and detecting properties in one and the other that constitute signs of that relation. This method is used in Marxism, as well as in other paradigms, such as the one inspired by Max Weber (1968, 10), and it is considered epistemologically acceptable for empirically contrasting hypotheses.

A clear case in which Marxian hypotheses can be tested empirically through methods consistent with colligation is the historical approach to social phenomena. Indeed, while every social formation has its own regularities, which constitute – to put it simply – its "laws" (see below), a phenomenon cannot be fully understood if it is not placed in a temporal perspective. Thus, a very important feature of Marx's work (and also of other social theorists, such as Weber), is the emphasis placed on observing and reflecting on the historical antecedents of a given phenomenon, its relations with other phenomena contemporary to it, and the succession of changes, sometimes stretching over centuries, that shed light on the current properties of the phenomenon studied. That is the explanatory strategy that Marx put forward in the "Preface" to *A Contribution to a Critique of Political Economy*, using commodity and labor, among others, as examples (Marx 1976).

Let us look, in this sense, at the problems connected with taxes that will be addressed in this book. This is not a category built solely through the sum of certain properties of current or contemporary taxes. To begin with, we cannot understand the characteristics of taxes without at the same time delimiting money and the state, at the very least. Moreover, the state, money, and levies imposed by the state on civil society – either in money or in kind – have existed since long before capitalism became the dominant mode of production. The historical progression of mercantile economies toward modes in which money has an ever greater importance, leading eventually to capitalism, particularly in its mature form in which exchanges are exclusively monetary, explains why state levies have also become exclusively monetary. But, also, the establishment of the state as the absolute monetary authority, both in the issuing of its own money and in the regulation of the private emission of money, helps us understand the essential role that taxes play in the total quantity of money and its distribution among social groups. The way in which capitalism expands across the world, incorporating countries and regions in unequal conditions, explains, for its part, some more specific features of taxes, such as the way the global income and sales tax system is being redesigned in the twenty-first century.

This form of historical explanation gives Marxism a differential explanatory power, but it imposes additional methodological precautions on researchers. Indeed, the application of methods such as colligation must be done through the accumulation and comparison of descriptions, and when they also refer to chronologically remote events, the origin of the information must be explicitly indicated without losing sight of the filter involved in the reconstruction performed by the researcher from whom the information is drawn. As with statistical data, special care must also be taken when that information is translated into Marxist categories.

While valid, the use of historical reconstruction as a specific methodological variant of confirmation (or refutation) of hypotheses must be undertaken with extreme caution, as has been stressed by Paul Ricœur (1990, 52ff.). Briefly stated, this author observes that the apprehension of human actions in a temporal sequence (which is what historiography and history are) is a process of successive *mimesis*, that is, of assigning meanings to bare actions. The simple observation of actions is anything but simple. It requires apprehending the meaning of each act, each interaction, each intention, etc., by an observer who then uses it to create a narrative plot. That is a first mimesis. A second mimesis is produced when that sequence of acts, already articulated in a plot, is in turn resignified in a second narrative through an emplotment: the joining together of those actions, interactions, intentions, etc., in a coherent temporal whole, within a conceptual structure established by whoever produces that second grade narrative. Finally, there is a third (or fourth, or *n*) mimesis, which occurs when the narrative produced by the emplotment is used by another subject for a different purpose, for example, to confirm a hypothesis. It is crucial to bear this process of continuous resignification in mind because the method of historical reconstruction is not based on a direct observation of the past (which is, moreover, impossible), but on the use of successive narratives in which more and more interpretations are gradually incorporated by those who produce the texts.

For example, the discussion of the history of international taxation in Chapters 7 and 8 will draw on many texts that narrate past taxation structures, even from before capitalism. These texts were, in turn, built on other narrations, perhaps a long succession of narrations, going back to some that may be contemporary with the facts narrated. This means that historical reconstruction actually consists in a documentary analysis of second, third, fourth, or *n* grade narratives, which are certainly reshaped by the successive emplotments (to use Ricœur's term). That is not to say that we should renounce historical reconstruction as a method for validating any hypothesis, but we do need to see it for what it is. In any case, and given that, as noted in Section 2.1, I will follow the common scientific practice of accumulating evidence to increase the probability of a hypothesis (in line with Rudolf Carnap), the accumulation of historical narratives coinciding in the confirmation of a hypothesis leads to greater strength in the probability that such a hypothesis holds true. We will see that this is the case with international taxation.

2.3 The issue of determination and functionality

An important epistemological aspect of any analysis containing elements from Marxism is that of "determination." Indeed, from *The German Ideology* by Marx and Friedrich Engels to Marx's "Preface" to *A Contribution to the Critique of Political Economy*, and including the seminal works by Antonio Gramsci (for example, 1971, 374ff.), Marxism has been characterized by its positing that there is a necessary relation between economic production – sometimes referred to as the "base" – and other instances of social life – often grouped together under the term "superstructures" (Cohen 2001, 217ff.). This merits some discussion in this book, given that there are at least three elements that will be mentioned in it that are usually considered superstructures – namely, the state, law, and ideology – and others that are usually identified as being part of the base or of economic production, such as production itself, surplus value, the profit rate, and the accumulation of capital, among others. The inclusion of taxes as such in either the base or the superstructure also poses a problem.

To avoid having to reproduce in full the discussion on the degrees of determination of the superstructure by the base, I will assume here that the relations between, shall we say, the level of economic relations and what we call, somewhat vaguely, superstructure are one of *overdetermination* (Althusser 2005, 100 ff.; Resnick and Wolff 1987, 49–52; Blanco 2022, 5). This means, in sum, that superstructures are not passive products of the relations of production and circulation: while superstructures have a meaning that is consistent with the latter, they affect economic relations by triggering or consolidating behaviors that allow for production, circulation, and other associated phenomena to move in a given direction.

In the case of taxes, as in many other cases, there is an overlapping of phenomena that fall under what we have called the base with others that fall under the superstructure. On the one hand, what we call tax is a set of social relations directly inserted into the processes of production and distribution: money – which is a social relation necessary for capital (another relation) to fulfill its role by accumulating, moving, organizing production, etc., in order for surplus value to be realized, for classes to appropriate part of production, and so on – is partly extracted from civil society. This generates, in turn, money-holding situations for social classes that differ from those at the starting point. But in order for all of this to happen, several superstructures must be set in motion: the state, international organizations of states, legal systems, ideologies, etc.

Now then, the problem of overdetermination is, within the Marxian paradigm, part of a kind of relation of a much wider scope, which we could call *functionality*, and which occurs even among elements of the base: it consists, namely, in asserting that a phenomenon behaves in a certain way so that another will do so in a certain manner. These ways in which the different elements of the base influence each other are what have been called economic laws, which are regularities that vary from one mode of production to another. These regularities – which in Marxism, as in any paradigm, are central hypotheses or theories in the proper sense – are what can be compared more directly against empirical data.

It should be noted that this idea of functionality, which is at the core of Marxism, does not imply – at least not necessarily – a causal relation. Indeed, and as Bunge notes in general for all sciences (1979, 17–19), causality is a modality of a broader type of relation that he calls "determination", a term that the Argentine epistemologist uses in a different sense from the Marxist tradition. For Bunge, determination is simply the name of all relations of influence or incidence that one phenomenon has with respect to another.

The concept of overdetermination adopted in this book includes both causal relations and relations of determination in the broader sense proposed by Bunge. For example, this book proposes the following hypotheses: (a) the evolution of the rate of profit determines the shift in production toward the periphery, due to wages being lower there and thus enabling an increase in surplus value and, with it, of the rate of profit itself; (b) this shift in production to the periphery entails a disconnection between production and the location of the money owners; (c) tax revenue must be aligned with the place where the money owners are located; and (d) tax revenue must therefore be concentrated in the countries of the center. The relation between the wage level in the periphery and the shift in tax collection toward the central or core countries is one of determination, but it is not, strictly speaking, causal: that wage level allows for the triggering of other processes that eventually lead to a shift in tax collection, but it is not the factor that immediately causes said shift. Instead, the disconnection between material production and the location of the money owners, and the shift in taxation power and revenue toward the central countries, is a causal relation, in a broad sense, because the first phenomenon is the direct origin of the second. But the changes in the legal structures of international taxation systems and the distribution of tax revenue, stemming from the changes in capitalist production, in turn, reinforce and consolidate the core-periphery scheme of current capitalism. Those reciprocal and complex causalities show that superstructures are not passive epiphenomena of economic relations but rather operate decisively on these in the framework of a general process of adjustment to the historical needs of capitalist development.

Note

1 As we will see, Marxism and other schools of thought derived from it have played a central role in clarifying this point.

References

Althusser, Louis. 2005. *For Marx,* London: Verso.

Amariglio, Jack, and David F. Ruccio. 2017. "Epistemology." In *Routledge Handbook of Marxian Economics*, edited by David M. Brennan, David Kristjanson-Gural, Catherine P. Mulder, and Eric K. Olsen. London: Routledge.

Blanco, Andrés. 2022a. "International Taxation and the Global Structure of Capitalism: The Influence of the OECD in the Design of the International Tax System." *Review of Radical Political Economics* 51 (2): 218–238. https://doi.org/10.1177/04866134211055871.

Blanco, Andrés. 2022b. "An Ideological Critique of the OECD Beps Action Plan." *Griffith Law Review* 31 (3). DOI. 10.1080 10383441.2022.2096966

Blaug, Mark. 2006. *The Methodology of Economics. Or How Economists Explain.* Second edition. Cambridge: Cambridge University Press.

Bunge, Mario. 1967. *Scientific Research II. The Search for Truth.* Berlin-Heidelberg-New York: Springer Verlag.

Bunge, Mario. 1979. *Causality and Modern Science.* Mineola, NY: Dover Publications.

Bunge, Mario. 1989. *Seudociencia e ideología.* Madrid: Alianza.

Carnap, Rudolf. 1962. *Logical Foundations of Probability.* Chicago: University of Chicago Press.

Cohen, Gerald A. 2001. *Karl Marx's Theory of History: A Defence*. Oxford: Oxford University Press.
Desai, Meghnad. 1991. "Methodological Problems in Quantitative Marxism." In *Quantitative Marxism,* edited by Paul Dunne et al., 27–41. Cambridge, UK: Polity Press.
Dunne, Paul. 1991. "An Introduction to Quantitative Marxism." In *Quantitative Marxism,* edited by Paul Dunne, 1–26. Cambridge, UK: Polity Press.
Freeman, Alan. 1991. "National Accounts in Value Terms: The Social Wage and Profit Rate in Britain 1950–1986." In *Quantitative Marxism*, edited by Paul Dunne, 84–106. Cambridge, UK: Polity Press.
Gramsci, Antonio. 1971. *Selections from the Prison Notebooks.* London: Lawrence & Wishart.
Kuhn, Thomas S. 1982. "Commensurability, Comparability, Communicability." *PSA: Proceedings of the Biennial Meeting of the Philosophy of Science Association,* 1982 (1982): 669–688. https://www.jstor.org/stable/192452.
Lakatos, Imre. 1999. *The Methodology of Scientific Research Programmes. Vol. 1 of Philosophical Papers.* Cambridge: Cambridge University Press.
Lincoln, Yvonna, Lynham, Susan and Guba, Egon. "Paradigmatic Controversies. Contradictions, and Emerging Confluencias, Revisited. In *The Sage Handbook of Qualitative Research,* edited by Nomran Denzin and Yvonna Lincoln, 5th edition. Los Angeles: Sage Publishing.
Marx, Karl. 1976. "Preface to A Contribution to the Critique of Political Economy." In *Preface and Introduction to "A Contribution to the Critique of Political Economy,"* 1–7. Peking: Foreign Languages Press.
Marx, Karl, and Friedrich Engels. 1998. *The German Ideology.* Amherst, New York: Prometheus Books.
Norval, Aletta J. 2000. "The Things We Do with Words – Contemporary Approaches to the Analysis of Ideology." *British Journal of Political Science* 30 (2): 313–346.
Popper, Karl R. 1962. *Conjectures and Refutations.* London: Basic Books.
Resnick, Stephen A., and Richard D. Wolff. 1987. *Knowledge and Class. A Martian Critique of Political Economy.* Chicago: The University of Chicago Press.
Ricœur, Paul. 1990. *Time and Narrative.* Vol. I. Chicago: The University of Chicago Press.
Sen, Amartya. 1988. *On Ethics and Economics.* Oxford and New York: Basil Blackwell.
Ward, Benjamin. 1972. *What's Wrong with Economics?* London and Basingstoke: Palgrave MacMillan.
Weber, Max. 1968. *Economy and Society: An Outline of Interpretive Sociology.* Berkeley, CA: University of California Press.

3 Theoretical framework

3.1 Some preliminary matters

This chapter presents a number of central theoretical hypotheses regarding the capitalist economy and the state under capitalism. This theoretical framework serves to justify the explanatory hypotheses that will answer the research questions.

While the theoretical framework will primarily be composed of hypotheses drawn from Marx and Marxian schools of thought in their various branches (economics, theory of the state, etc.), hypotheses from other paradigms will also be incorporated. In particular, the core aspects of the concept of money developed under the post-Keynesian monetary circuit theory will be incorporated, as well as certain characteristics of taxation originating in that same school of economic thought. This form of theorizing aims to be, above all, non-dogmatic, which is one of the great virtues of the work of Marx and Engels, namely, being able to recognize, as Popper noted (1962, 114 ff.), that good explanations can come from anywhere, even from the most unexpected sources.

The starting point for the theoretical framework as a whole are hypotheses that refer to the capitalist mode of production, although in order to fully understand many problems, it will be necessary to repeatedly look further back to pre-capitalist economic formations.

3.2 Essential features of capitalism

While it may seem unnecessary, it is essential to explicitly outline the core properties of capitalism to then move on to the theories of money, the state, and taxation. In this chapter, I elaborate on my 2022 article, where I briefly presented my explanation of international taxation (Blanco 2022a).

The first premise is the *labor theory of value*, which posits that labor is the essential social and economic process, with labor defined as the human activity of transformation of the world. Labor is, moreover, *productive* when its results have *value – use value* or *exchange value*. *Capitalism* is a specific mode of production in which: (a) the owners of the labor force (i.e., the workers) do not apply such force for their own benefit, and rather sell that force to capitalists (the owners of capital); and (b) *capital* organizes and controls production and the economic process as a whole, appropriating the value generated in the labor process. A *commodity*

DOI: 10.4324/9781003458678-3

is any material or non-material object of exchange. *Wages* are the portion of the value appropriated by workers as remuneration for the sale of their labor force, and the difference between wages and the total value is the *surplus value* (Marx 1995–1996: 127 ff.). Therefore, the value of a commodity is determined by the labor it incorporated (Marx 1995–1996: 30–33). The quantity of labor incorporated in a commodity can only be expressed in working hours, which is why monetary prices are not a measure of value but rather the expression of the rate of exchange of a commodity (see below Section 3.3).

Capital is the part of the surplus value not meant for the capitalists' consumption (Marx 1995–1996, 410ff.). Nevertheless, capital is not a set of objects, but a social relation (Wright 1975, 6). For example, a machine, in itself, is a piece of the inanimate world with technical functionality; what turns it into capital is that there is a social relation of ownership that allows a person to make others operate that machine, using it to transform other objects, and that the new objects that are generated belong to that owner and not to the operators. Capital has a tendency toward incessant and increasing accumulation. *Accumulation* means that capital cannot simply replace the equivalent of its normal depreciation; it needs to increase constantly its net amount (Marx 2008, 298ff.). A formula to express capital accumulation and the rate of accumulation (i.e., the growth percentage of new capital over existing capital) will be proposed below in Section 3.4. With these concepts, we can already begin to see a problem with the Marxian explanation of capitalism.

When Marx speaks of capital accumulation, replenishment, depreciation, etc., it would appear that he does so in monetary terms, although simultaneously – sometimes in the same sentence – they appear in terms of value understood as volume of labor incorporated into commodities and measurable in units of time. This duality or confusion is all the more significant when Marx discusses whether *money-capital* – that is, money that remains in the form of liquid money or credit instruments – is a real form of capital accumulation (Marx 1959, 343 ff.). This confusion is even more problematic when Marx analyzes profit. Indeed, in the third volume of *Capital* (published posthumously by Engels), Marx introduces several new categories for analyzing the capitalist economy, different from those included in volumes I and II. One of those categories is *profit*, understood as the difference between the total value generated by a capitalist or a group of capitalists and the costs of constant capital (the goods that the capitalist acquires from other capitalists) and of variable capital (the remuneration for labor, that is, wages). Closely linked to profit as a magnitude is the *rate of profit*, which is the ratio of surplus value to the cost of constant capital and variable capital (Marx 1959, 28ff.). The difference with the theses proposed in the first two volumes of *Capital* lies in that in capitalist production both the results (commodities) and the social relations it generates (capital and labor) are no longer expressed in terms of value as volume of work, but as *costs*, that is, as *monetary magnitudes*. This means that the formulas that Marx implicitly or explicitly proposes to describe profit and the profit rate are unsuitable, as they contain terms that represent *value* (surplus value) and terms that represent *money* (capital costs). Let us see this below:

If P is profit as a magnitude, V is the total value, s is surplus value, p is the rate of profit, c is the cost of constant capital, and v is the cost of variable capital, we have the following formulas:

Profit

I) $P = s$

Profit rate

$$II)\ p = \frac{s}{c+v} \text{ or}$$

$$III)\ p = \frac{V-(c+v)}{c+v}$$

The rate of profit has a natural tendency to fall (Marx 1959, 33, 153ff.). Since such tendency to fall is caused by the increase in the cost of constant capital, it has been linked to the continuous process of accumulation of capital (Norton 2017, 199–201). As a rule, accumulation cannot stagnate or decrease; the only case of reduction in the net amount of capital occurs when the countertendencies of the tendency of the profit rate to fall are activated, given that one such countertendency is the destruction of capital (Kliman 2012, 25–27).

The formula for expressing the tendency of the profit rate to fall, where t_0, t_1, …., t_n, are successive moments in the development of a capitalist economy, would be as follows:

$$IV)\ \frac{s}{c+v} = pt_0 > \frac{s}{c+v} = pt_{1,} > \ldots \frac{s}{c+v} = pt_n,\ ct_0 < ct_{1,} < \ldots ct_n$$

In a historic perspective, from the early and mid-twentieth century, capitalism evolved into a monopolistic scheme (Kalecki 1971, 105ff.), which is still the main feature of material production. Over the last decades of the past century and in the current century, the financial sector gained a dominant position in the internal composition of global capital, in a process commonly known as *financialization* of capitalism (Bryan and Rafferty 2017[1]). Although some Marxian authors highlight as an attribute of "financial capital" its constant conversion and mutation into non-financial (industrial or other) capital and vice versa (Resnick and Wolff 1987, 219 ff.), that is not, in fact, an exclusive feature of recent capitalism: Marx's traditional scheme of money-commodities-money (*M-C-M*) reflects perfectly the permanent role of money in the production circuit.

As can be seen above, upon presenting the key concepts of the Marxian explanation of the economy, we encounter a major theoretical and methodological problem, namely: the difference between monetary prices and value. If it is true that value is derived solely from the application of labor and monetary prices do not necessarily represent that value, what does the labor theory of value mean when commodities are exchanged in monetary terms, which is an objectively different parameter from the amount of work incorporated? This problem is of the utmost theoretical importance: if the core categories of Marxism refer to value (surplus value is the value in excess of that which is appropriated by workers, capital is the part of the surplus value that is not consumed, etc.), none of them should be interpreted in monetary terms. However, we have just observed that profit and – above all – the rate of profit, which play a central role in the explanation of the major historical internal developments of capitalism, are presented – even if incompletely and inconsistently – in monetary terms. Moreover, as briefly noted above, taxation – which is the focus of this book – is by definition a monetary phenomenon, so that no discussion, whether Marxist or non-Marxist, that seeks to explain taxation can be presented purely in terms of value. We therefore have a general theoretical problem as well as a specific theoretical problem: we need to provide an explanation that is consistent with the general Marxian theory of a phenomenon that is entirely monetary, as is the case of taxation.

This theoretical difficulty is reflected in the methodological domain. Indeed, in the previous chapter we saw that, with some exceptions, the statistics that are available are produced based on neoclassical theory categories that do not take labor value into account and, thus, only consider and process monetary prices. Therefore, while these statistics are, in any case, only indirect elements for corroborating or falsifying this book's theses, even that limited or oblique use would be invalidated if we did not first determine the relations between value and price.

3.3 Value, price, money

It would be impossible, in a work of this length, to list all the ways proposed under Marxist theory to bridge the gap between value and price, so I will only mention a few here. For example, one theoretical approach argues that despite the conceptual difference between value and price, prices are, generally speaking, determined by the quantity of labor that is *socially necessary* to produce a commodity, so that there is an observable correlation between the two: the commodities that incorporate a greater quantity of socially necessary work are exchanged at higher prices, and those that require less socially necessary labor are exchanged at lower prices (Farjoun and Machover 1983; Shaikh 2016, 221ff.). Another explanation of the relations between value and price is closely linked to the conceptions that offer a quantitative solution to what is known as the transformation problem, that is, the conversion of the labor value of a commodity to production prices, as this problem is a special case of the equivalence or non-equivalence of labor quantity and price. Along this same line, there is a reciprocal interaction between values and prices, which influence and determine each other sequentially (Kliman and McGlone 1988; Freeman and Kliman 1998). An alternative way of dealing with the difference between value and price is to posit a qualitative relation between the two, arguing, for example, that the core concepts of the capitalist economy can only be expressed in monetary terms, and that the labor theory of value is merely meant to illustrate the phenomenon of exploitation and the unequal appropriation of production under capitalism (Sheppard and Barnes 2015, 54–56). A solution that has also been suggested rests on the *dialectic* aspect of Marx's oeuvre, arguing that capital in abstract adopts diverse concrete forms, such as the price form or the value form (Robles Báez 1997).

As I understand it, while some of these solutions have their merits, they all err in that they fail to go beyond the production and circulation of commodities, when the problem actually falls outside those spheres. What distinguishes value from monetary price is, without a doubt, the absence or presence of money. Therefore, the answer to the difference between price and value – and to many other problems that Marxism has been unable to resolve satisfactorily – depends on the introduction of a general theory of money.

There are many reasons for reformulating the theory of money and for inserting it into the Marxist explanation of the economy. To begin with, we need to address the problem that we have already identified: the discrepancy between value and price. Indeed, the difficulty in aligning the two notions derives from the fact that none of the authors that address this can see that monetary prices are a fraction of a much larger element, which is, precisely, the total volume of money. There is a failure to understand that the difference between value and price is a strong indication that money is an object distinct from commodities in the strict sense, and that the social process through which it is generated is different from the processes of production of commodities. The same can be said of money-capital, which Marx develops in volume III of *Capital* and which is disconnected from labor value if, again, we lack a concept of money that is both general and consistent.

As for the specific subject of this book, it can be intuitively observed that what we currently call "taxation" is a social relation with a fundamentally monetary content: it entails a continuous flow of money from civil society to the state, so that it is hard, if not impossible, to understand its properties through the concept of labor value or through a theory of value. The same can be said of the other components of public finances, such as public spending and public debt, which are also exclusively monetary phenomena: the explanations put forward by Marx and some Marxist economists – in many cases satisfactorily – are, however, disconnected from the labor theory of value due to the lack of a theory of money that explains the latter in a way that is consistent with the former.

First, let us list the external differences between price and value. The idea put forward by Marx (and Adam Smith and David Ricardo before him) that value, in an economic sense, originates in labor marks the most basic level of the explanation of the sphere of social life that is called economy. Both Marx and his predecessors were primarily interested in understanding why certain objects (and here the word "object" does not necessarily denote a physical entity and rather includes behaviors as well) have economic significance, while others do not. The assertion that the difference is in the application of labor means that portions of reality do not spontaneously generate anything that has in itself economic value. Nothing is "naturally" economic; rather, economic significance is a human invention and, more specifically, one of the results of the actions of human beings on their non-human and human environment. The relevance of the labor theory of value lies in that it explains why those objects give rise to a special set of social relations that we call "economic". In primitive communities there are no, or almost no, exchanges, so that human activities generate *use value* only. With the emergence of the social division of labor and the birth of commodities, as a result of the introduction of exchange, the transformative activity of human beings generates *exchange value*. Which is to say that anything, and even any human conduct, can be exchanged for another thing or another human conduct. This action that turns anything into something endowed with some kind of value is *labor*.

Let us see an example. If a thirsty person simply goes to a river or a lake and drinks from its water, there is no labor of any kind involved, and neither the conduct nor the water has any economic significance. If a person carries water to their community and distributes it among the people there without obtaining anything in return, there is labor: the water now has economic significance and it has use value. And if that person appropriates the water and takes it to another community that has no water and exchanges it for fruit that their own community lacks, there is labor: the water has an economic significance, but it now has, for that person (and perhaps for their community), exchange value, which is different from use value.

If we take the labor theory of value to its ultimate conclusion and admit, as Marx did, that commodities have different values in terms of the different quantities of labor they have incorporated, those values must necessarily be measurable. The quantity of labor incorporated in a commodity can only be expressed in working hours, so the exchange value of a commodity is the total working hours needed to produce and deliver it to consumers (Marx 1973, 64–65; Wright 1975, 7–8; Farjoun and Machover 1983, chap. 4). The material dimension of commodities is, in turn, equal to their physical volume. Now then, the relation between the amount of labor incorporated in a commodity and the physical amount of commodities is not linear and rather depends on other historical and technological factors. That is what the idea of the *socially necessary amount of labor* refers to. The amount of labor that is needed to produce a certain commodity given the available technology, the skill of the workers, the environmental conditions, the cultural conditions, etc., in a given time and place, *vary*, and, therefore, those different production contexts entail that different gross amounts of labor (hours worked) are needed to produce the same commodity (Marx 1995–1996, 29; Sheppard and Barnes 2015, 56–58). Thus, the magnitude of value of a commodity is the volume of worked hours pondered by factors that determine that more or less time is necessary to produce the commodity and take it to a certain point in the circulation circuit.

Once a specific commodity is, shall we say, fully formed, it is evident that it can be exchanged for many possible prices. At a given time it can be sold at a price P; a few days later, it might be sold, for example, at P+1; if instead of being sold locally, it is exported, it might be sold at P+2; if we were to wait two weeks to sell it, the price might be P-1; etc. (Farjoun and Machover 1983, chap, 4). What is the reason for this? Prices represent quantities of money, so the answer to this question is simple: it is due to buyers of commodities having different quantities of money depending on the place and time. This tells us that money is something that operates independently from value, since for the same amount of socially necessary labor incorporated in a commodity, the money given and received for that commodity can vary significantly.

That is why Marx (as well as some, but not all, Marxian economists) insisted on asserting that monetary prices are not a measure of value but rather the expression of the rate of exchange of a commodity (Marx 1973: 64–65; Wright 1975: 7–8). This eliminates the "value of money" problem in many Marxian approaches that confuse value and money (for example, de Brunnhof 1976: 26–30; Hein 2002), a confusion that certainly arises from some pages in Marx's writings where he unsuccessfully addresses the subject (Graziani 1997: 37–40). Money, on its own, has no value, but it does have a price for passing from hand to hand (interests).

We can generalize this thesis. If we argue that in a particular case the value of a commodity is independent from the quantity of money given for it, we can then state in general that money, or more precisely, the *money stock* (without having yet defined these terms), is not the expression of the total value. We then need to explain what money is and how it is inserted into the economic process.

We cannot do this by drawing on Marx alone, because while he provides elements that are enormously valuable for that purpose, he does not develop, as noted above, a complete theory of money. Our attempt at building a theory of money that is consistent with the labor theory of value could begin with a few concepts put forward by Keynes and some of his theoretical successors, which form what has come to be known as the "monetary circuit theory" (see, among many others: Keynes 1930, 3ff.; Lerner 1947, 312–317; Bell 2001, 157–158; Parguez 2002; Bougrine and Seccareccia 2002, 61–67). I will take certain central hypotheses from this theory (while implicitly discarding others), as well as some of its ancillary hypotheses, without discussing them, so as to not stray from the object of this article.

According to this approach, money is essentially an incarnation of a specific social relation, which we can call "debt/credit" (Ingham 1996, 517). Its source and origin are to be found not in a value-creating relation but in several social relations that allow certain social actors to create – literally from nothing – a credit, that is, an obligation toward another, which is (in principle) unlimitedly transferable. For example, let us analyze a bank credit. First, the bank opens a credit line, which means the debtor (a company, for instance) is authorized to give third parties (other companies, workers, shareholders, etc.) certain symbols (checks, transfers for credit in an account, etc.) for canceling a debt. Those third parties, in turn, use that money, expressed by similar symbols, to cancel their own debts, and so on. At the same time, the beneficiary of the credit line acquires a debt with the bank for an amount equal to the portion of the credit line used to pay third parties. Why can the bank grant such a credit? Only because it has been authorized by a public authority (the central bank) to do so, up to a limit. Even though the bank receives deposits from companies and individuals, the granting of credit is creational in nature, given that there is an arbitrary relation between deposits received and credits granted.

The same occurs with state money. When the central bank issues money, in whatever form, it is creating purchasing power that is initially in the hands of the state itself. The state is theoretically in the same position as a bank client that applies for credit. That state money starts circulating through diverse forms of public spending (purchases of goods, payment of wages, etc.), and it has the same properties as bank money.

Thus, the typical (though not the only) forms of money are relations between the bank and whoever applies for a credit, or between the state and whoever receives state money in payment: the essential feature of that relation is the creation of a power to cancel obligations, a power that circulates from hand to hand, and has at its origin a debt counterpart with banks. When money circulates, it is inserted into other social relations different from those that gave rise to it. Money has already been turned into pure symbols: a piece of paper, a bit of metal, a record in a computerized system, etc. These symbols confer a power to those who hold them, a *power that consists of appropriating a commodity* that someone else has, thereby transferring that purchasing power to the other in exchange. These properties are extended to all the functions of money: commodity exchanges, capital accumulation, public spending, etc. This is where this conception differs from other Marxian approaches that adopt a post-Keynesian (or Keynesian) conception of money only for certain functions, such as money-credit (for example, Hein 2002, 10).

When that purchasing power of the money holder can be used right away, we say that it is *liquid money*. Thus, liquid money is a social relation that links its holder to an unknown number of persons: all those who have accepted the canceling effect of money on debts. The exchange of commodities is, therefore, the appropriation of a commodity by a money holder, and the acquisition of money, and its corresponding purchasing power, by the now former commodity holder. It should be noted that while the bulk of commodities are the result of production processes (extraction, industry, services, etc.), anything can be turned into a commodity. The typical example of this is labor force when the worker sells it. Money can also confer a purchasing power that is not immediate, as is the case with deposits or bonds. But even then, at a certain point in the future, those forms must be convertible into liquid money, thus conferring an immediate purchasing power. So those are the two essential properties of money: a social relation of credit and the entailing power to appropriate a portion of production by purchasing commodities.

Having described its features, we can now understand why money is independent of value. This independence emerges from the separation of money producers, that is, the financial sector (in particular, banks), and the state, with respect to the rest of the "departments" of the economy, to create – as Luxemburg very perceptibly foresaw – a "Department III" specialized in producing money, in addition to a "Department I" (capital goods) and a "Department II" (final consumer goods), which would constitute another stage in the social division of labor (Luxemburg 2003, 65ff.).

If we combine this theory of money with the Marxian labor theory of value, we have that all production and circulation relations have a *monetary dimension on the surface* and a *value dimension at a deeper level*. The value dimension includes production, as a process of application of the labor force, and the appropriation of different portions of production (i.e., the value generated by the labor force). Money is the vehicle for appropriating portions of production: value can only be expressed in worked hours, and it can only be realized if the commodities are exchanged for money. When capitalists, workers, etc. purchase commodities, they appropriate such commodities by means of money. For the same reason, wages have a monetary expression since they must lead – by means of appropriation of commodities – to the workers' consumption in order to ensure the reproduction of the labor force. There are certain economic relations that do not involve the exchange of commodities, involving instead the exchange of money. In order for them to occur, what Marx called "money-capital" (which will be discussed in the next section) must appear.

Given that commodities only have one end, namely, exchange, and that exchange can only be done by means of money, there has to be a constant flow of money for exchanges to be possible. As we will see below, the relations between quantity of money and increasing production are crucial for understanding the trajectories of capitalism in both time and space.

Money created by banks or by the state circulates from hand to hand to fulfill its purpose, but it is a circuit that has to have a reflux phase: if there were no mechanisms to extinguish money, its stock would grow indefinitely and the price system would go out of control (this point will be discussed in greater detail in Chapter 4). These mechanisms are mainly the repayment of credits by bank debtors, and the collection of taxes by the state. This outlines the main hypothesis that will be developed in Chapter 4: taxation is first and foremost a mechanism for regulating the money stock.

A feature of money that is particularly interesting for understanding the role of taxation is its inextricable connection to the state. Indeed, historical studies (summarized by L. Randall Wray with abundant bibliographic references) leave no doubt as to money having appeared with the first mercantile economies and simultaneously with the emergence of the state structures that accompanied the end of primitive communism and gentile society. In particular, by demanding payments in money, first as penalties and, not much later, as taxes, the state imposed the use of money on civil society and, also, established account money, that is, the monetary units and the types of money that, because they are acceptable for payments, are also acceptable for all private exchanges (Wray 2000, 4; Wray 2010, 40–42). As a result of the changes in capitalist production on a global scale and the emergence of state structures that are above the nation-state (the "supranationality" that will be discussed in Section 3.5), there are at least two phenomena that transform the traditional framework: (a) in many countries, especially in the periphery (see Chapter 5), national currency coexists with the currency of core countries (generally US dollars), or is directly eliminated and replaced by it (as is the case of Ecuador or Panama); and (b) in Europe, the nation-states have ceded the power to establish account money and the general criteria for regulating money to a supranational entity, which is the European Central Bank (Wray 2010, 43).

The adoption of the general definition of money put forward by Keynes and some of his theoretical successors, notwithstanding, the post-Keynesian theory of money also strongly supports the endogeneity of the money supply. This means that the amount of money is determined by the credit demand made by companies to banks: it is not, as the quantitative theory of money argues, that all money is determined by decisions made by the monetary authority; rather, it is the economy's private sector that pushes *the financial sector* to create money through credit. This, however, does not mean that the demand for money is in turn circumscribed to the immediate needs of companies for the purchase of fixed assets, current assets, and payment of wages. What determines the demand for bank credits and, with it, the creation of bank money are *company expectations* (Wray 1992, especially 1156). This means that we can add Keynes's "propensity to liquidity" to the motives for generating a demand for money, which is not translated into investment or consumption, but is instead accumulated (Wray 1992, 1157 ff.).

An important caveat to the endogenous conception of money is that it holds true for money created through bank credits, but not for state money. The volume of public spending, which requires the creation of state money, is in fact not determined by a demand from the economy's private sector, but by political decisions that are the result of more complex conflicts of social forces. This entails that that portion of money, which is far from insignificant, is not part of the "expectations → credit demand → money creation" chain.

As for empirical evidence on the influence of bank credit demand on the money supply, there are several studies that have shown that endogenous relation (see, for example, Moore 1983; Lavoïe 2005; Nayan et al. 2013). With respect to these studies, it should be noted that the "money stock" variable used in them is a defined variable and, therefore, its content is statistical. This is typical of the orthodox theory and not of the post-Keynesian theory. Whether or not they adopt the definitions commonly labeled M1, M2, etc., they all have in common the inclusion of liquid money or money easily convertible to liquidity, in addition to – depending on the case – different types of deposits and/or reserves in the banking system. Now then, we have observed that the post-Keynesian theory (at least the circuit theory) not only posits the endogeneity of money but also challenges the traditional (or monetarist) definition of money itself. That is what is meant when it is stated that money is a credit-debt social relation, from which it must consistently follow that *any such relation that is transferred is, in essence, money*. If that is so, then the traditional definitions of money (M1, M2, etc.) do not match the scope of money in the post-Keynesian theory. This does not mean, however, that variables defined and measured according to the orthodox theory cannot be used as indirect indications of the relation between money in the post-Keynesian (or circuitist) sense or of any other variable.

Finally, it is essential to keep in mind that money is purely a social relation, not a physical object. This means that to locate money, for example, in a place according to, for instance, the place where a bank account is registered is a serious theoretical error. Money is located where the human being who decides the use given to that relation is located. This will be of crucial importance for understanding the evolution of international taxation.

3.4 Interpretation of capital accumulation and profit as value or money, and statistical projection

We can now reconstruct some concepts that were briefly outlined before and which are crucial for understanding the spatial evolution of capitalism and the phenomenon of taxation. The first aspect that must be clarified is that capital is an *a posteriori* phenomenon with respect to commodities. While chronologically capital and commodities follow each other reciprocally in a continuous circle (commodities generate capital, which is used to generate commodities, which generate capital, and so on), commodities can exist without capital (as was the case in pre-capitalist economic formations), but capital cannot exist without commodities. Capital is the result of a very special form of production of commodities, in which the total value (i.e., the labor incorporated for its production) *as a rule exceeds the value consumable in an immediate or near future time*, with consumption understood as the consigning of the commodity to private use. Consumption would thus occur when the economic object no longer has – at least for an indefinite time – exchange value and only has use value. Given that this excess is repeated over and over again, capitalism is a mode of production that invariably generates more value than it can consume. Part of the value is consumed by workers and consists of the commodities they acquire to subsist and continue working. The value exceeding the commodities consumed by workers is what Marx captured with the concept of surplus value. Part of the surplus value is consumed by capitalists. It is on the remainder – that is, on the excess value not consumed by anyone (neither capitalists nor workers) – that the social relations we call "capital" are established. For simplicity purposes, the commodities produced and not consumed can be referred to as capital, but without losing sight of the fact that what turns those commodities into capital is the social relations established around them, and not the material properties of the object. What turns a social object into capital is that, around it, its owner establishes production relations and not consumption, affective, family, or other relations. Let us look, as an example, at the production of chairs. If a worker or a capitalist purchases a chair to use it in their home, that chair has been "consumed", as it is no longer used to produce anything. A chair exactly like the one consumed that is purchased by a company for a worker to sit on while performing their task is capital because it is being used to produce other commodities.

Capital, insofar as it is excess *value in the true sense* of the term, can only be expressed in volume of commodities and in the amount of socially necessary working hours that those commodities contain. In terms of value, the accumulation of capital is equivalent to the *value not consumed by workers or capitalists, which is converted into commodities that are again applied to production* (Marx 1995–1996, 407ff.), as fixed assets, exchange goods, raw materials, services incorporated into production, etc.

We have also observed that all capitalist processes are impossible without money. Money is what enables the transferring of commodities that are consumed, but, above all, money is what enables the acquiring and transferring of capital for production. Whoever has money and can transform commodities into capital decides what, when, where, and how much is produced. Moreover, the process of production of commodities, their circulation, and the generation of capital are increasingly rapid, besides being continuous. All of this means that Department III of the economy (formed by banks and the state) must always produce a quantity of money that exceeds the exchanges in the short and medium term, because there must always be money available to increase or redirect production. In other words, *there must always be a surplus of money that is not immediately used to purchase consumer goods or constant capital goods (fixed and current assets), but remains as pure money*. This effect was identified by Marx: while again confusing capital as value with the money required to purchase capital goods, in the chapter – scarcely cited by subsequent literature – in which he examines the relation between the capital turnover period (which is actually the period of production) and the quantity of capital (actually the amount of money necessary to produce), Marx notes that if the aim sought is to maintain or increase the scale of production, and not to reduce it, a larger volume of money than that obtained through the sale of commodities is required (Marx 2008, chap. 15).

Marx's idea that money must always exceed the immediate needs of investment and consumption coincides with the post-Keynesian thesis that the money supply is determined by expectations, including the propensity to liquidity (see Section 3.3).

That money that exceeds investment and consumption, which Marx called *money-capital* (perhaps an inaccurate term, but one I will use here for the sake of clarity), generates the illusion that it is an excess value or a value reserve, as production capitalists (those in Departments I and II) often obtain, through the sale of commodities, more money than they need to purchase constant capital and pay wages. But if we consider that masses of money *that find no commodity through which to be exchanged* are constantly appearing, we must conclude that the money not destined for the immediate purchase of commodities does not correspond to a value reserve or accumulation. In any case, and as Marx sensed (1959, 336), money-capital is a set of securities against future production.

This necessary and structural misalignment of money and current production has to be reflected in the behavior of Department III. The financial sector of the economy does not operate as a mechanical response to simple investment and consumption demand. The clearest evidence of this is that if the money supply were to adjust automatically to the demand for investment and consumption, monetary savings would not exist, nor would financial instruments such as debentures, forwards, options, etc., and neither would public debt. Similarly, the work by Hyman Minsky (1992) on crises caused by the over-indebtedness of production sectors can be interpreted as evidence that when the financial sector, or Department III of the economy, generates money, there will necessarily be a dual adjustment, regardless of medium-term production capacity: on the one hand, Department III will appropriate an excessive part of production by judicially foreclosing on its credits or forcing business operators to sell their assets, thus accelerating the reflux of money and affecting investment and consumption; and on the other, a mass of credit will become uncollectible, so that, in the absence of state intervention, the size of Department III of the economy will be reduced through the bankruptcy of banks and other financial companies.

All of this indicates that the accumulation of capital, understood as the accumulation of unconsumed value, does not include money-capital. This is necessary for the process of accumulation to continue, but the quantification of capital accumulation cannot include money-capital.

Let us consider, at least conceptually, a possible measure for capital accumulation in a given period. Assuming value measured in socially necessary labor time (*nl*), we have that it is a concept applicable to the total production of a country, a region, or the world, which we will call (*P*). A portion of that production consists of commodities consumed by the workers and constitutes the part of the total value that they appropriate (*Cw*) and the commodities consumed by the capitalists (*Cc*), all in a given period of time (*t*). By definition, capital accumulation (*KA*) is equal to the socially necessary labor for all production minus total consumption:

$$V)\ KA_t = P(nl)_t - \left[Cc(nl) + Cw(nl) \right]_t$$

This formula has several assumptions, similar to those made by Emmanuel Farjoun and Moshé Machover (1983, 504–506): (a) that there is no destruction of pre-existing capital, given that the obsolescence or uselessness of capital goods must reasonably be reflected in a decrease in their value in terms of socially necessary labor, which is to say that the formula reflects gross capital accumulation; (b) that the pondering of labor as socially necessary is uniform, which is obviously unreal both in time and in space (on this, see, Sheppard and Barnes 2015, 56–58). To overcome this last weakness, we should have a criterion to ponder the necessary labor according to the place where it is performed and the technological developments introduced throughout the period, in addition to establishing a depreciation criterion for pre-existing capital that is not monetary but based on labor. In any case, however, the formula, *as with all formulas that measure magnitudes of value in a strict sense*, requires knowing the number of worked hours, which is information that, at best, is only fragmentarily available.

In short, with the statistical information available, *it is not possible to measure capital accumulation in the form of labor value*. Farjoun and Machover's hypothesis that monetary prices are generally aligned with values in terms of labor and that therefore, according to the law of large numbers, worked hours can be replaced with costs in money (1983, 468, among others), is not convincing, given the structural and necessary misalignment of total value with money stock, posited and substantiated above. This does not at all mean that value and concepts expressed in value are not observable and measurable. They certainly are, but that would require an econometrics totally different from mainstream econometrics, and based only on categories of labor value.

We can nevertheless try using prices as an indirect approximation to the accumulation of capital. For that, we first need to assume a constant ratio between prices and value, even though we know that is not true (Freeman 1991, 87). With this assumption, we can provisionally take GDP as an indicator of value, and then, through successive approximations, we can approach something close to an indicator of capital accumulation, always in monetary terms and, therefore, indirect.

There is a strictly monetary phenomenon that does not respond to value generation: tax revenue. As observed above, taxation entails, in general, taking an amount of money out of circulation so that, as it is not exchanged for commodities, that money is canceled or destroyed. We also know that GDP includes an element that is not representative of value in Marxian terms: interests and other financial benefits, and land rents. Therefore, if we subtract from GDP the amounts corresponding to tax revenue, interests and land rent, we will have a better indicator of value with the remaining monetary amount (Freeman 1991, 87–88).

At the other end, we know that what appears in statistics as "final consumption" is equal to the sum of the monetary prices of commodities that are not converted into capital, that is, which are not used to continue the production process. Again, as it is a monetary expression, final consumption is not necessarily equivalent to the value of those commodities. But, with the same caveats noted for GDP, we can assume that *the monetary expression of final consumption is an indication of its value*. At this point, we can provide two further approximations.

First, consumed commodities must be equal to total wages – assuming, in line with Michal Kalecki, that workers consume all they receive (Kalecki 1971, 78) – plus the consumption of capitalists, which is a part of the surplus value. Therefore, apart from final consumption, commodities can only be constant capital in terms of value. Given that we have already subtracted tax revenue, interests, and land rents from GDP, the monetary expression that results from also subtracting final consumption is equal to the total price of the new constant capital plus savings in a broad sense (financial assets of all types). The hypothesis of decreasing money-capital responds to cases where the money created in the period is less than the money destroyed in the same period. The increase or decrease of the money stock exceeding the sum of other elements complete the scheme.

Consequently, the price of the accumulation of capital (PKA) must be equal to GDP, minus final consumption (fc), minus tax revenue (T), minus interests and other financial returns (i), and minus land rents (lr), minus savigs (SA). all for a given period (t):

$$VI)\ PKA_t = GDP_t - \left(fc + T + i + lr + SA\right)_t$$

As it is a monetary formula, it is not an alternative way of expressing capital accumulation, which, strictly speaking, can only be expressed in pondered labor time. However, it can be an indicator of the level of material accumulation.

The internal inconsistency of the formulas for profit and the rate of profit is solved by replacing surplus value in the strict sense with a monetary expression: the difference between the total monetary price of production and the total cost of variable capital, that is, the total money wage bill, plus the cost of constant capital. The reason for this is that, as noted in the previous paragraph, profit – according to Marx – is disaggregated into purely monetary flows, so that it is reasonable to argue that it must be measured only in monetary terms both as a magnitude and as a rate. Thus, we could replace surplus value with the difference between monetary income (*I*) and the monetary costs of constant and variable capital (*c* + *v*):

$$VI)\quad P = I - (c + v)$$

$$VII)\quad \frac{I - \left(c + v\right)}{c - v}$$

The next step is to determine if it is possible to measure profit and the profit rate with the statistics available. The fact that they are monetary expressions puts us in a more favorable scenario than with capital accumulation, since there is a lot of statistical information of a monetary nature. As for monetary income, we must avoid the temptation of equating it with each country's GDP. Indeed, this concept includes income from the financial sector as well as income from rent, both of which are concepts that, according to Marx, are derived from profit, and therefore cannot be added to quantify it. Here we encounter a difficulty, as in some countries it will not be possible to separate the income of the financial sector and rents from GDP. As for variable capital, there should be no difficulties: it would be equivalent to the total wage bill, so that if that magnitude is available for a country or a region, we can safely include it in the formulas.

Finally, in order to include the cost of constant capital, the acquisition prices of current assets and fixed assets in a given period should be taken into account, along with – in principle – other associated expenses, such as repairs, cleaning, transportation, etc. Thus defined, while we would not be able to calculate the cost of constant capital perfectly, we could obtain a rough calculation. First, the statistical concept of added value is very similar to the difference between the gross operating income of companies in productive sectors and the costs of acquiring raw materials and goods. Moreover, the cost of fixed capital is, in broad numbers, equivalent to gross fixed capital formation, which reflects the costs of acquiring fixed assets, and which is generally available in the national accounts of countries. While, as noted above, this magnitude is not suitable for measuring capital accumulation in the Marxian sense, given its monetary nature, we can include it in indirect formula V, and in profit and profit rate formulas VI and VII.

The above position differs from the one held by Andrew Kliman, who asserts that there is no such thing as a Marxian profit rate. He instead posits that the concepts proposed by Marx should be replaced with different formulas that, in substance, measure yields according to neoclassical parameters (Kliman 2012, 94–97). One of the most interesting aspects of Marx's concepts of profit and profit rate is that they provide evidence that monetary flows are subordinate to the generation of value, and that, while money does not originate in the productive sector of the economy, it is in this sector that we find the basis from which money is distributed among the different social classes. This characteristic is captured by the components of profit and the profit rate, in particular constant capital. By definition, this is a concept that only makes sense with respect to the productive sector of the capitalist economy because: (a) in the financial sector, or department III, the income-generating asset – money – is completely independent from labor and is self-generated by banks; (b) rents depend on a product of labor (commodities), but it is a past and "coagulated" labor, to use Marx's terms; and (c) tax collection is notably independent from human activities and all capital. Thus, the conversion (which is, strictly speaking, distribution) of profits into earnings of productive capitalists, financial returns, taxes, and rents reflects the fact that the heart of the capitalist mode of production is – at the risk of being redundant – production, as in all modes of production, and it also reflects the subordinate nature of the sectors of the economy not involved in the production of commodities, such as banks, the state, and real estate owners. This explanatory richness is lost if we consider, together with neoclassical theory, that the profit rate can be equal to *n* measures of monetary return.

3.5 Elements of the theory of the state and supranationality

If one of the defining features of taxation is its monetary nature, its other, even more invariable defining feature is its connection to the state. Therefore, a general theory of taxation requires the adoption of a general conception of the state, which I will develop here within the general framework of Marxian theory.

Marx himself did not develop a comprehensive theory of the state (Miliband 1969, 5–6), although the premises of the theoretical framework proposed by him suggest a way to address the problem of that entity. Specific variations notwithstanding (some of which will be examined in this chapter), there are certain elements that are common to all Marxian views of the state and can be traced back to the works by Marx and Engels. The most notable of these can be expressed as follows: the activities of the state are prompted by, and aimed at, the conservation, reproduction, or transformation (as the case may be) of the prevailing social structures, at least as far as economic production is concerned, without prejudice to the state also participating actively in other types of production (cultural, scientific and technological, family, etc.). This entails some points of consensus, both theoretical and epistemological, namely: (a) the state cannot be studied as an autonomous entity; rather, it must be studied as part of the prevailing mode of production; (b) consequently, both its dynamic aspects (historical evolution) and its static aspects (forms of organization, specific actions, etc.) are neither the result of chance nor totally independent and self-determined; rather, they are guided by its social conservation and reproduction functions; however, debatable the degree of autonomy of the state may be with respect to the social relations it reproduces, as well as the bearing that each social class has on the state, the struggle between classes, etc.; and (3) as a result of 1 and 2, it is impossible for the state to be neutral.

In order to outline the foundations of a Marxian theory of the state, and with respect to what interests us here, we again need to begin with one of Marx's key epistemological contributions: the historical perspective (see Section 2.2) for understanding any social phenomenon.

The first step to do that is to reconstruct its birth, as Engels did (2004, 108ff.). Engels noted that the state was born when, following the destruction of the ancient communities and the transition away from the so-called gentile regime, mercantile economies fully emerged with the first forms of division of labor. The remains of the gentile political structures thus became a structure that *detached itself from civil society, like a separate body*. This is the first major finding of the Marxian theory of the state: the segmentation of the state and what the state encompasses (the military apparatus, the bureaucratic organization, the legal administration through the judicial system, etc.), with respect to the social and economic structures, in contrast with the pre-mercantile formations, where the political, the social, and the economic formed a single whole. The idea of the state as a result of a split from the rest of social life is, essentially, similar to the idea posited by Pierre Bourdieu, who conceived the state as a field distinguished by certain special characteristics (2014, 14, 159–160).

This obviously does not mean that the state does not participate in social life, quite the contrary. The separation of the state entity from the rest of civil society occurs because, with the division of labor and the emergence of social classes, large groups of people *become subordinated to other groups of people*. Therefore, the emergence of economic domination renders impossible the adoption of common decisions by the whole of civil society as such: first, because at the core of civil society there are no longer common interests; and second, because entire categories of people who are dominated must be excluded from participating in political, military, judicial, and other forms of power, which are subordinated to economic power. Significantly, women are the first social group to be excluded: their marginalization from private property and from the control of certain economic activities is the first form of social division of labor, and runs parallel to their marginalization from the state.

The separation of the state from civil society continues even under a fully democratic organization. Even when it reaches its most advanced stage and allows for the broadest participation of all interest groups, the plurality of interests leads to conflict, and there must be an instance that is above civil society in which that conflict can be resolved. Only that way can decisions be made authoritatively and enforced coactively, even through active violence and against the will of those involved.

Engels noted that the four essential features of the state are the monopoly of social coercion and violence, translated into the formation of special bodies of force-bearers; the delimitation of a territory; the creation of a body of special officials who exercise authority outside civil society; and the existence of taxes as a mechanism for collecting resources from civil society to – initially – maintain that bureaucratic and military apparatus (Engels 2004, 270–272). Both the monopoly of force and the forming of a bureaucratic apparatus are features also identified by Weber (1968, 44) and Bourdieu (2014, 16).

The essential features of the state indicated at the start, and the basic constitutive elements proposed by Engels, still leave ample room for discussion on numerous issues. To begin with, in what way and how much does the economic instance of the mode of production influence the actions of the state? And conversely, to what extent do the actions of the state influence the economic instance of the mode of production?

Regarding these questions, in the late twentieth century a now classic debate on the state took place within Marxism between Ralph Miliband and Nicos Poulantzas (Miliband 1969, 68ff.; Poulantzas 1978, 126ff.). That debate was ultimately an epistemological and methodological discussion: while Miliband proposed a set of empirically verifiable factual hypotheses regarding the characteristics and functions of the state in capitalist society, Poulantzas argued that the characterization had to be purely conceptual and limited to the identification of "the political" as one of the "instances" of each mode of production, in clear alignment with Althusser.

From the methodological point of view, in this book I adopt a position that is much closer to Miliband's than to Poulantzas's. With respect to the state, the starting point will be certain theoretical concepts (in the case of the state, the concept used will be almost exclusively Marxian in origin), as well as pre-existing hypotheses or hypotheses developed in this research, contrasting them empirically.

In this sense, Miliband's reflections (1969, 72 ff.) are interesting in that he notes that the state operates on the basis of a commitment to the capitalist system assumed by everyone who exercises or can exercise authority. This commitment is realized, on the one hand, through the intersection of activities and individuals between the state and the private sector and, on the other – and primarily – through *ideology*. Ideology is understood as a system of beliefs that, whether false or not, play a role that is functional to the mode of production, insofar as they reproduce the behaviors necessary for it to develop (Marx 1976, 4ff.; Mannheim 1979, 50–53; Blanco 2022b, 4). The actions of all the individuals who adopt decisions in the state are imbued with a set of convictions, normally not conscious, but adopted as natural and obvious descriptions, which entail that: (a) the capitalist system as a whole cannot be breached; and (b) in each of the areas in which the state acts regulating private activities, the purpose of those regulations is, directly or indirectly, favorable to the permanent or transitory needs of the capitalist system. This does not mean that social groups that are not part of capital are systematically neglected, but it does mean that the broad lines of action of the state underpin the major processes of the mode of production indicated above: the production of commodities, the realization of value, the accumulation of capital, and, when necessary, the recomposition of the rate of profit and, as we shall see in the next chapter, the regulation of the money stock and its distribution through the complex of public spending and taxation.

What may be debatable is the extent of such functionality. State actions are frequently the result of class struggle, both of labor against capital and of the different sectors of capital against each other, but they also generally reflect each historical phase of development of capitalism, which determines a general framework from which it is not normally possible to escape. That general framework is established as a result of a concrete dispute within the state, which is not visible to the general public but can be observable. In this sense, Bourdieu conducted remarkable fieldwork on the reconfiguration of housing regulations and policies in France, showing at a micro-social level and step by step the sequence of movements (changes in the composition of state bodies, meetings between business organizations and government decision-makers, generation and dissemination of ideological discourses originating in academic institutions, press media, etc.) that shifted control from the industrial capital sector connected with construction to the financial sector through loans to individuals and companies (Bourdieu 2005, 15ff.).

Once the general framework of activity of the state has been established, that historical mode of configuration of capitalism will hold all the smaller struggles, during the time it prevails. For example, in a general phase of predominance of financial capital, there may be disputes that define more or less contractionary wage policies, but it seems unlikely that severe restrictions on financial operations will emerge, such as a large tax on currency exchange operations, financial derivatives, futures, etc. (a sort of increased Tobin tax).

The global evolution of the capitalist system poses specific challenges to the Marxist theory of the state, particularly with regard to supranationality, that is, organizations that group together states and, especially, those that are not merely discussion forums for its members, but are beginning to take on authority roles that were formerly found only at the nation-state level.

The *Open Marxism* school of thought has developed a theory of supranationality that emphasizes the need of nation-states for the survival of capitalism. This school convincingly posits that a constituent feature of capitalism is its international nature and its tendency to expand spatially, so that the so-called novelty of globalization as an economic system is completely false. This scenario of constant expansion of capital does not lead, however, to a weakening of national states; rather, it leads them to compete among themselves to appropriate part of a surplus value in constant movement as a result of the also constant movement of capital (see, among others, Clarke 1991). The argument of this internal school of Marxism is that while capitalism, as a mode of production, is from its origins global and international, the national states are like nodes that try to attract capital toward their territories, each providing differential advantages for production. In other words, global capital triggers a differentiation between states that compete to grant better conditions for production, so that capital has a wide range of options of where to go.

The empirical evidence, however, contradicts this assumption of the proponents of Open Marxism. The emergence of an "embryonic structure" of "global governance" (Tsolakis 2010, 402) must be understood as a new dimension of the state in a broad sense, whose formation and growth can be explained by the new characteristics of the spatial expansion of capitalism. Given that production chains, and also financial capital, tend to concentrate in globally identifiable ownership groups, slowly but inexorably displacing local expressions of capital, the functions of national states must also, slowly but inexorably, move to international bodies. Thus, for example, banking regulations (from the definition of crimes to credit ceilings and reserve requirements) can no longer be left to decisions by local authorities, but must be planned and established as global guidelines that states then merely implement.

Public finance, for their part, are also an eloquent example of this emergence of a new international dimension of the state. The European Union has already consolidated a consistent and long-term policy for the restriction of public spending through the Stability and Growth Pact (Larch 2014). In tax matters, both the OECD (on a global scale) and the European Union (first in Europe, but progressively also on a global scale) have become centers for the design of policies that are increasingly more specific and more coercive in their application, including (and primarily) with respect to states that are not members of such organizations. This point is included in the central hypotheses of this book, so it will be addressed in Chapter 6.

It is true that globality has been an intrinsic feature of the capitalist mode of production since its birth (not just since the twentieth or twenty-first century), and that that expansion requires disparity, not uniformity, in local conditions of production. That is precisely one of the central theses of this book. However, this disparity should not be confused with a multiplicity of centers of political power: increasingly, inequality must be centrally regulated in order to globally establish who and what things must or can, depending on the case, be unequal.

Thus, supranationality is but another phase in the development of the state under capitalism, adjusted – as with previous phases – to new conditions of production. Given that production acquires a global scale not only in the exchange of commodities but also in production itself, the distinguishing features of the state must be projected far beyond the traditional nation-state. The state does not disappear, but it does gradually relinquish its functions to international bodies, of which the European Union, the United Nations, and the OECD are the most prominent examples (Miliband, 14; Mandel 1976, 196).

Note

1 Marxian (and non-Marxian) literature on the expansion and predominance of financial capital in recent capitalism is so vast as to be unmanageable. I have made a brief selection of references that are useful for my purposes here.

References

Bell, Stephanie. 2001. "The Role of the State and the Hierarchy of Money." *Cambridge Journal of Economics* 25: 149–163. https://doi.org/10.1093/cje/25.2.149.

Blanco, Andrés. 2022a. "International Taxation and the Global Structure of Capitalism: The Influence of the OECD in the Design of the International Tax System." *Review of Radical Political Economics* 51 (2): 218–238. https://doi.org/10.1177/04866134211055871.

Blanco, Andrés. 2022b. "An Ideological Critique of the OECD BEPS Action Plan." *Griffith Law Review* 31 (3): 333–360. https://doi.org/10.1080/10383441.2022.2096966.

Bougrine, Hassan and Mario Seccareccia. 2002. "Money, Taxes, Public Spending, and the State Within a Circuitist Perspective." *International Journal of Political Economy* 32 (3): 58–79. https://doi.org/10.1080/08911916.2002.11042876.

Bourdieu, Pierre. 2005. *The Social Structures of the Economy.* Cambridge, UK: Polity Press.

Bourdieu, Pierre. 2014. *On the State. Lectures at the Collège de France, 1989–1992.* Cambridge, UK: Polity Press.

Bryan, Dick and Michael Rafferty. 2017. "Financialization." In *Routledge Handbook of Marxian Economics*, edited by David M. Brennan, David Kristjanson-Gural, Catherine P. Mulder, and Eric K. Olsen. London: Routledge.

Clarke, Simon. 1991. "The State Debate." In *The State Debate*, edited by Simon Clarke, 1–69. London: Palgrave.

de Brunhoff, Suzanne. 1976. *Marx on Money.* New York: Urzen Books.

Engels, Friedrich. 2004. *The Origin of the Family, the Private Property and the State.* Chippendale, Australia: Resistance Books.

Farjoun, Emmanuel and Moshé Machover. 1983. *Laws of Chaos. A Probabilistic Approach to Political Economy.* London: Verso.

Freeman, Alan. 1991. "National Accounts in Value Terms: The Social Wage and Profit Rate in Britain 1950–1986." In *Quantitative Marxism*, edited by Paul Dunne, 84–106. Cambridge, UK: Polity Press.
Freeman, Alan and Andrew Kliman. 1998. "Simultaneous and Temporal Valuation Contrasted." *Munich Personal RePEc Archive*. https://mpra.ub.uni-muenchen.de/52805/1/mpra_paper_52805.pdf.
Graziani, Antonio. 1997. "The Marxist Theory of Money." *International Journal of Political Economy* 27 (2): 26–50.
Hein, Eckhard. 2002. "Money, interest, and capital accumulation in Karl Marx's economics: A monetary interpretation." *The European Journal of the History of Economic Thought* 13 (1): 113–140. https://doi.org/10.1080/09672560500522868.
Ingham, Geffrey. 1996. "Money is a Social Relation." *Review of Social Economy* 54 (4): 507–529. https://doi.org/10.1080/00346769600000031.
Kalecki, Michal. 1971. *Selected Essays on the Dynamics of Capitalist Economy*. Cambridge: Cambridge University Press.
Keynes, John Maynard. 1930. *A Treatise on Money. Vol. 5 of The Collected Writings of John Maynard Keynes*. Cambridge: Cambridge University Press.
Kliman, Andrew. 2012. *The Failure of Capitalist Production*. New York: Pluto Press.
Kliman, Andrew and Ted McGlone. 1988. "The transformation non-problem and the non-transformation problem." *Capital & Class*, 12 (2): 56–84. https://doi.org/10.1177/030981688803500106.
Larch, Martin. 2014. "The Stability and Growth Pact of the European Union." In *The New Palgrave Dictionary of Economy*, edited by Steven N. Durlauf and Lawrence E. Blume. London: Palgrave-Macmillan.
Lavoïe, Marc. 2005. "Monetary Base Endogeneity and the New Procedures of the Asset-Based Canadian and American Monetary Systems." *Journal of Post Keynesian Economics* 27 (4): 689–709. https://doi.org/10.1080/01603477.2005.11051462.
Lerner, Abba P. 1947. "Money as a Creature of the State." *The American Economic Review* 37 (2): 312–317.
Luxemburg, Rosa. 2003. *The Accumulation of Capital*. London: Routledge.
Mandel, Ernest. 1976. *Late Capitalism*. London: NLB.
Mannheim, Karl. 1979. *Ideology and Utopia. An Introduction to Sociology of Knowledge*. London and Henley: Routledge and Kegan Paul.
Marx, Karl. 1959. *Capital. A Critique of Political Economy*. Vol. 3. New York: International Publishers. https://www.marxists.org/archive/marx/works/download/pdf/Capital-Volume-III.pdf.
Marx, Karl. 1976. "Preface to *A Contribution to the Critique of Political Economy*." In *Preface and Introduction to "A Contribution to the Critique of Political Economy*," 1–7. Peking: Foreign Languages Press.
Marx, Karl. 1995–1996. *Capital. A Critique of Political Economy*. Vol. 1. Moscow: Progress Publishers. https://www.marxists.org/archive/marx/works/download/pdf/Capital-Volume-I.pdf.
Marx, Karl. 2008. *Capital. A Critique of Political Economy*. Vol. 2. Moscow: Progress Publishers. https://libcom.org/files/Capital-Volume-II.pdf.
Marx, Karl. 1973. *Grundrisse. Foundations of the Critique of Political Economy (Rough Version)*. Harmondsworth, Penguin Books in association with New Left Review.
Miliband, Ralph. 1969. *The State in Capitalist Society*. London: Weidenfeld and Nicolson.
Minsky, Hyman P. 1992. *The Financial Instability Hypothesis: Capitalist Processes and the Behavior of the Economy*. Levy Economics Institute Working Paper, No. 74. The Levy Economics Institute of Bard College, Annandale-on Hudson, NY. https://www.levyinstitute.org/pubs/wp74.pdf.
Moore, Basil J. 1983. "Unpacking the Post Keynesian Black Box: Bank Lending and the Money Supply." *Journal of Post Keynesian Economics* 5 (4): 537–556.

Nayan, Sabri, Norsiah Kadir, Mat Saad Abdullah, and Mahyudin Ahmad. 2013. "Post Keynesian Endogeneity of Money Supply: Panel Evidence." *Procedia Economics and Finance* 7: 48–54. https://doi.org/10.1016/S2212-5671(13)00217-7.
Norton, Bruce. 2017. "Accumulation." In *Routledge Handbook of Marxian Economics*, edited by David M. Brennan, David Kristjanson-Gural, Catherine P. Mulder, and Eric K. Olsen. London: Routledge.
Parguez, Alain. 2002. "A Monetary Theory of Public Finance: The New Fiscal Orthodoxy: From Plummeting Deficits to Planned Fiscal Surpluses." *International Journal of Political Economy* 32 (3): 80–97. https://doi.org/10.1080/08911916.2002.11042882.
Popper, Karl R. 1962. *Conjectures and Refutations*. London: Basic Books.
Poulantzas, Nikos. 1978. *Social Classes and Political Power*. London: Verso.
Resnick, Stephen, and Richard Wolf. 1987. *Knowledge and Class. A Marxian Critique of Political Economy*. Chicago: The University of Chicago Press.
Robles Báez, Mario. 1997. *On Marx Dialectic and Genesis of the Money Form*, edited by Marx, Keynes and Money. Paul Mattick Jr. ed. New York: ME Sharpe.
Shaikh, Anwar. 2016. *Capitalism. Competition, Conflict, Crises*. New York: Oxford University Press.
Sheppard, Eric, and Trevor J. Barnes. 2015. *The Capitalist Space Economy*. London: Routledge.
Tsolakis, Andreas. 2010. "Opening up Open Marxist Theories of the State: A Historical Materialist Critique." *The British Journal of Politics and International Relations* 12 (3): 387–407. https://doi.org/10.1111/j.1467-856X.2010.00414.x.
Weber, Max. 1968. *Economy and Society: An Outline of Interpretive Sociology*. Berkeley, CA: University of California Press.
Wray, L. Randall. 1992. "Alternative Approaches to Money and Interest Rates." *Journal of Economic Issues* 26 (4): 1145–1178. https://doi.org/10.1080/00213624.1992.11505365.
Wray, L. Randall. 2000. *Money and Inflation*. Pennsylvania State University Working Paper No. 12. Pennsylvania State University. https://citeseerx.ist.psu.edu/document?repid=rep1&type=pdf&doi=66fc9c6aea6cb3824f98c636fd04738730fe48f5.
Wray, L. Randall. 2010. "Alternative Approaches to Money." *Theoretical Inquiries in Law* 11 (1): 29–49. https://doi.org/10.2202/1565-3404.1235.
Wright, Erik Olin. 1975. "Alternative Perspectives in Marxist Theory of Accumulation and Crisis." *Critical Sociology* 6 (1): 5–39. https://doi.org/10.1177/089692057500600102.

4 Taxation

4.1 Introduction

The theoretical framework for taxation, like the spatial characteristics of capitalism, merits a separate chapter, as both matters are at the heart of this book.

The most frequent Marxian approach to taxation posits that taxes are forms of appropriation of surplus value and, therefore, of worker exploitation (Marx 1995–1996, 37; Preobrazhensky 1967, 89–90; Yaffe 1973, 218). However, this traditional Marxist thesis must be amended in light of the theory of money discussed in Chapter 3, and the ensuing difference between value and prices and the money stock.

The main hypothesis about taxation stemming from the theoretical premises stated above is that it is a mechanism for regulating the money stock. This hypothesis is divided into two specific hypotheses: first, in mature capitalism, taxation systematically destroys quantities of money, thereby stabilizing the price system; and second, the distribution of the tax burden generates unequal endowments of money between social classes, between groups within classes, and between geographic areas at the national, regional, and world level.

The strategy I will adopt to justify these hypotheses involves, in the first place, the historical reconstruction method (which can be seen as a form of colligation, as defined in Chapter 2), starting with the oldest forms of state levies imposed on civil society, to eventually arrive at contemporary public finance and, within it, taxation. As discussed in Chapter 2, the historical inquiry strategy for analyzing social phenomena is very typical of Marxism, but it is also grounded in scientific methodology in general. Science is based on the admission of regularity: what happened in a certain way many times in the past will tend to happen in a similar way in the future, and if changes occur in successive descriptions of a phenomenon, the key to understanding the present and predicting the future lies in discovering the pattern of changes (Bunge 1967, 85ff.). In the following paragraphs, I will propose empirical justifications of the hypotheses, using, as far as possible, the statistical information available for the last decades.

4.2 The historical perspective

Since I will be applying the historical reconstruction method in this chapter, it will be useful to briefly review Ricœur's concept of mimesis discussed in Chapter 3,

DOI: 10.4324/9781003458678-4

now with respect to the successive texts that I will draw on for my historical reconstruction of taxation. The following observations are also valid for the discussion on strategy in Chapters 7 and 9.

When I say that I will use historical reconstruction as a form of colligation – that is, as a qualitative method for contrasting a hypothesis – I do not mean that I will be carrying out an actual observation of past events, as that is, obviously, impossible. Adopting a historical perspective involves gathering historical or historiographical texts that, with rare exceptions, are not even historical sources in the strict sense of the term. This poses two methodological problems. First, it means we have to place our trust in the descriptive content of the text we are working with. This problem can be mitigated by using reliability techniques (for example, checking whether it is consistent with other related information that we know to be undoubtedly true). It can also be addressed through volume: if we are able to gather different texts that point in the same direction, their volume will strengthen the validating force of that evidence. Second, we need to bear in mind that any text we use is the product of one or more emplotments, to use Ricœur's terms. That is, it is the result of an ordering of events that is made by the author of that text, and not the events themselves, and which is further most likely imbued with some theoretical assumption other than those we have adopted. It is impossible to entirely escape the emplotments that came before us: at most, we can only hope to identify the most theoretical elements in the text and filter them from it (for example, the causalities it suggests). Let us now move on to our historical reconstruction.

Building on the assumption that the state was born as an entity that broke away from civil society to better perform certain functions required by mercantile production (see Section 3.5), it follows that any economic relation between the state and civil society, such as the relations that currently embody taxation, public spending, and public debt, was impossible prior to that split. Taxation, thus, like public spending and public debt, is a phenomenon typical of mercantile economies and impossible in primitive communities. Consequently, once the state separated from civil society, economic relations necessarily had to be established between the two, and those relations also had to be colored by a differential feature of the state: the monopoly of coercion and the regulation of social violence.

In studying the phenomenon of taxation from a historical perspective, I will focus predominantly on its evolution in pre-capitalist Europe, as well as on the birth and the different stages of capitalism, which are also events centered first in Europe and spreading later to the rest of the world. It may seem that this explanatory strategy unfairly neglects similar phenomena occurring in other parts of the world and in other human groups. Such comparative analyses of taxation in other societies, which followed paths that differed from that of the European world, are certainly very relevant, but I cannot lose sight of my research questions. These questions clearly refer to the international taxation system as it appears in the late twentieth century, which is an object that belongs exclusively to mature (or late) capitalism, and capitalism is itself a mode of production that originated in Europe and later expanded to the rest of the world. As a result, a general study on the forms of taxation in history must certainly take into account the specific features of taxation in various times and places, but a study on current international taxation must focus on the specific origins of this phenomenon, which are European.

In primitive communities, whether European or not, taxation did not exist. In this book, I have adopted a specific definition of taxes as monetary levies imposed by the state on civil society. Therefore, if there is no money or no state as an entity separate from civil society, there can be no taxation. Taxes cannot be confused in any way with the solidarity contributions in the form of both objects and activities that existed in primitive communities and still do in the few remaining pockets where such communities survive. Indeed, the separation of the state with respect to civil society and the emergence of money, which are both phenomena that are completely impersonal and alienated from social relations in primitive communities, mean that taxation cannot be described as the result of an evolution of the reciprocal collaborations of communities that preceded mercantile economies. That is so even in modes of production that apparently transcended the primitive community because of the existence of individuals invested with despotic authority (ancient Egypt, Peru, etc.), but that essentially continued in a communal phase of production, without commodities and without money as such (Marx 1964, 69–71).[1]

Studies on the birth of primitive European states (mainly Greece) show that both phenomena (the emergence of the mercantile economy and the emergence of the state) run parallel to the appearance of money (von Reden 2002, 152ff.). The most primary forms of money were generated by individuals, with state money appearing later, but always with the same characteristic: it is a purchasing power that allows for the acquisition of commodities, but that as such is independent of those commodities, as discussed in Section 3.2. Some centuries later, bank money appears, with modalities very similar to those it has today (von Reden 2002, 147).

These evidences show that, since its origins, the state has played a central role in the creation and control of money, and – contrary to mainstream theory – that money is not a spontaneous creation of the market meant to replace "mass barter", which is historically false (Keynes 1930, 4; Wray 2000, 4; Wray 2010, 40–42). In line with the above, since the beginning of the state, taxation has had an evolution parallel to that of money.

While non-monetary personal contributions existed in these primitive states, very quickly monetary taxes also appeared: money flows that the state received as a result of coercive unilateral decisions. The hypothesis posited by Engels and Bourdieu that the existence and collection of taxes have a foundational role in the emergence of the state holds true (see Section 3.5). The consolidation of the state as a social subsystem separate from (and in opposition to) civil society entails not only that the state absorbs functions previously spread among the community (the administration of penalties, armed conflict), but also that it is equipped with goods with which to carry out those functions. State officials, soldiers, and whoever exercises authority (with whatever title they may have) must reproduce their material lives just as those who participate in production do, but since, by definition, they are removed from production, there is no way for them to reproduce their lives other than through the forced absorption of part of production. State money, which emerges at this time, was not, however, the only money. Besides issuing money, states allowed for the existence of other private moneys, as occurs today with banks. For this reason, in these early stages the state used private money extracted from civil society to appropriate part of the production.

States at this time did not yet regulate money on a large scale and in a complex way, through the application of multiple instruments (interest rates, public debt, taxes, etc.), as it does in mature capitalism. However, even at these very early stages, tax revenue and public spending were decisive factors in the money supply. In the first place, the fact that the state allowed for the payment of taxes in one or various forms of money, but not in all, had a major effect: the account money with which it was possible to pay taxes displaced the other forms of money, since people were forced to form their money endowments in the denominations that the state established as the appropriate forms of payment of taxes. Second, taxation and public spending already played a role in the unequal distribution of money and, therefore, produced different economic effects depending on the situation deriving from that distribution. Thus, the archeological findings of different kinds of coins in different places that were part of the Roman Empire are explained by the transferring of currency issued in "rich provinces" to "poor provinces", as a result of the collection of taxes and the payments by the state to individuals for various reasons (von Reden 2002, 160).

In the feudal Middle Ages, a change in the mode of production can first be observed, with the emergence of a new mode in which commodities and exchanges had a more limited role than in the ancient world. The feudal mode of production in its European form was the result of the dissolution of the ancient economic system, unified under the Roman Empire, and the simultaneous dissolution of the communities within which the economies of the invading peoples developed. European feudalism is, then, the result of the assembling together of the remains of two modes of production that were at different stages of evolution, although some of their characteristics are similar to modes of production observed in other regions of the world (for example, Japan). In addition to the general decline in trade, the other element that is of interest to our analysis is the fragmentation of state structures originating in Rome. The separation between the state and civil society did not disappear, but it became less pronounced. First, in rural areas, where feudal production developed fully, "state functions" were performed directly by the social class (the feudal nobility) that directed production. Second, the cities, where traces of non-feudal production and limited commodity exchanges remained, consistently had forms of organization that were more similar to those of the state in the strict sense, but, in any case, because of their fragmentation and dispersion, they could not form a political unit.

Consequently, the issuance of money to enable commodity exchanges, state control over that issuance, and the existence of taxation persisted, but in a limited way. On the one hand, money issuance continued, and what was left of the states, despite their relative weakness, continued to control it through specific regulations (Sabatino López 1953). On the other hand, taxation also persisted, under the form of "assistance" (monetary levies) to the still rudimentary state apparatuses, and it was generally justified for military reasons. The differences with this view that

Karl Polanyi points out are no doubt due to his focusing strictly on rural production (Polanyi 1973), which in the Middle Ages had a comparatively greater relevance than in the Roman Empire, and in which commodity exchanges were scarce or non-existent, as labor was not yet a commodity *per se*. In feudalism, as in previous modes of production, commodities are not present in the production process as such, which is something that occurs in capitalism with the conversion of the labor force into a commodity. But this does not imply that there are no commodities and exchanges outside the production process (Marx 1964, 104–106). On the contrary, such exchanges were made with money, and, as we observed in the ancient modes of production, taxes strictly speaking played their normal role: extracting money from civil society for state purposes, and distributing and regulating the money stock. In the Middle Ages, the latter functions were almost imperceptible due to the minor relevance of exchanges and the extreme smallness of the money stock, but that did not mean they were completely absent.

However, as the Middle Ages progressed, the separation of the state from civil society became again more pronounced, and, at the same time, regular and depersonalized taxation systems emerged, which began to resemble modern taxes (Hoyt 1950; van Schaïk 1993). This stage and the one immediately following it, which is the earliest phase of capitalism, are crucial for understanding the role of taxation.

The birth of capitalism consisted, in the first place, in the destruction of the relations of production in which laborer and labor were not separated, so that those who directed production owned the persons of the laborers, just as they owned the means of production, as was the case with feudal serfdom. This type of social relation is extinguished through the action of money, which came from the cities and mercantile activities, generating a mass of free workers and turning the labor of those individuals into another commodity, in what was an unprecedented development in history. Moreover, money transformed the means of production into capital, insofar as it took those means out of the private sphere of small producers and made them available to large-scale production (Marx 1964, 107–108).

At the beginning of capitalism, money took on a different role from the one it had in previous modes of production. Its function as a generator of exchanges, and therefore of commodities, remained, but money was also the instrument that enabled the creation of capital. If money is defined as a social relation through which those who have one or more means of production organize production by buying labor, it follows that the monetary compensation of labor (wages), which was previously scarce or marginal, now occupies the central place in production, thus entailing an unprecedented expansion of the money stock. And this is where taxes play a special role.

Both Marx (1995–1996, 97–98) and Wray (2010) have highlighted that the expansion of the money stock, and, therefore, the emergence of capital, was possible because states introduced broad scope taxes, establishing also that they could only be paid with certain account money and not others. These measures created the need to have money with which to pay taxes and, therefore, scaled up the production of money (Marx 1995–1886, 97–98). That state policy led to a significant increase in the money stock, which was, in turn, the requisite for the initial capital accumulation. Indeed, the expansion of money stock allowed for: (a) the separation of the means of production (land, instruments of labor, etc.) from the laborers; and (b) the disappearance of the laborer as producer and their conversion into another bearer of a specific commodity – the labor force – to be exchanged for money like any other commodity.

We can say, therefore, that taxation was the instrument that enabled the true birth of the money stock and the emergence of capital in its true sense, and also ensured its central position in the mode of production.

That was a crucial moment in the history of taxation: as a monetary phenomenon it always functioned as an unconscious regulator of the money stock, but with the birth of capitalism, taxation fully deploys that function, both in qualitative terms, since its money stock growth effect enabled the fundamental and typical relations of capitalism, and in quantitative terms, given the scale of such growth.

The above interpretation differs from that proposed by those who associate modern and contemporary taxation structures with the emergence of various forms of "democracy", a term that actually denotes any form of intervention by those affected by taxes in the approval of those taxes (Kiser 2021, 17–21). While it is true that the complexity and sophistication of the taxation system occur alongside the evolution of political institutions toward their current forms (although it would be a complete exaggeration to use the word "democracy" to refer to the tax approval mechanisms of the Modern Age), these are two parallel phenomena and not a relationship of dependency of taxation with respect to participating institutions. Both movements are associated with diverse stages of the birth and process of maturity of capitalism, so they are consistent phenomena, but with a common origin in the evolution of production and, in the case of taxation, with features typical of the growing importance of money. A pre-capitalist, but entirely valid, example of how democratic legitimacy is not necessarily associated with tax collection efficiency is the Roman Empire, which succeeded in establishing a reasonably efficient tax collection system without any semblance of popular participation.

The narrative of the evolution of the economy until the birth of capitalism provides a series of corroborations for the hypothesis of taxation as a regulator of money. In this sense, we saw how humanity went from a society without levies, before the existence of money, to societies in which money emerged and where levies also emerged, and then on to a third stage in which the importance and volume of money decreased but without disappearing, and where levies and their relevance also diminished but not completely. This evidence is important but not conclusive. The fact that the variation in the relevance of money matched the variation in the relevance of levies constitutes, indeed, solid evidence of the dependence of taxation on money, and therefore the radical disconnection between personal contributions typical of pre-mercantile societies, or even later societies (such as feudalism), and taxation. However, the hypothesis of the monetary circuit theory adopted here – namely, that taxation is a regulator of the money stock – is stronger. The historical observations cited thus far in this chapter are compatible with this hypothesis, but again, not conclusive, as they do not rule out alternative hypotheses.

Somewhat more categorical in this sense is the evidence provided by the inflation observed in the Roman Empire as of the late second century, for which I will consider a 2009 article by Prodromos Prodromidis. During that period, the Roman Empire saw a continuous rise in prices, with the following monetary and taxation conditions: (a) the existence of state money identified with the effigy of the ruling emperor; (b) a gradually increasing tolerance of other non-state currencies; and (c) the fact that taxes could only be paid with state money and there were no relevant changes in their design. This situation is compatible with the hypothesis of money as a regulator of the money stock: while money is allowed to expand beyond state-issued money, tax revenue is still tied to state money and it does not change its normative structure. The rise in prices, then, can be explained by the absence of a mechanism for canceling non-state money, as is predicted by the hypothesis of the post-Keynesian circuit theory.

I should note that, in order to arrive at this conclusion, I had to eliminate from Prodromidis's text the author's own emplotment (again, in Ricœur's terms). Indeed, the author's narrative seems to posit the monetary nature of inflation, but fails to see any relationship between the flexibilization of the issuance of account money, the rigidity of the account money of tax revenue, and inflation.

4.3 Contemporary taxation: its function as regulator of the money stock and its relationships with public spending and public debt

In contemporary capitalism, taxation perfected its features in conjunction with the following developments: (a) the strong regulation of the issuance of money, both private and public, by the state, through central banks; and (b) the expansion of monetary public spending and public debt.

As noted, taxation performs money-stock-regulating functions, which initially entailed consolidating account money and later, under capitalism, accelerating the monetary nature of the mode of production by forcing individuals to be money holders. But it also fulfills another function, namely, that of regulating the volume of money available: ensuring the reflux phase of the monetary circuit through the destruction or cancellation of money. This point is worth examining in detail.

The direct effect of any tax is the withdrawal of masses of money that are in the hands of companies or individuals. There is normally the illusion that states "use" that money for public spending and that public spending is a consequence of tax revenue. But that is false: if the state spends money, and at the same time has the power to create money, that means that public spending is not necessarily tied to anything, not even tax revenue. Generally, states try to correlate their tax revenue with public spending using the public budget as a planning tool. Therefore, the question we should ask ourselves is the following: why does the state generally correlate tax revenue with its spending if the latter is independent from the former?

The most plausible answer is that taxes systematically destroy amounts of money previously put into circulation by banks or the state itself (Parguez 2002; Bougrine and Secareccia 2002). Since the state has the power to create its own money through its own banker (the central bank), it generates its "income" by issuing money that allows it to pay for commodities, public wages, and repayments of public debt. At the end of the circuit, the money refluxes into the state through tax collection. That is, briefly stated, the core explanation of public finances, and of taxes in particular, proposed by the post-Keynesian circuit theory. An aspect noted by some, but not all, proponents of the post-Keynesian theory of money is that the role of taxation as "eliminator" of circulating money holds true not only for state money but also for money represented by bank credit, given that states accept without restrictions the payment of taxes with, precisely, bank money (Wray 2010, 47).

Let us now connect this conception of taxes with the labor theory of value. As we saw above, value is divided into two components: wages and surplus value. While created out of nothing, money makes sense, first, as an instrument for appropriating shares of production and value, by means of commodity exchanges, and second, as an instrument for converting a portion of the surplus value into capital, and with that capital initiating and regulating production (i.e., determining when, where, and what is produced) and purchasing labor force. When the state collects taxes, it does not obtain a purchasing power that would allow it to appropriate production, as a company owner or a lender would, because, like banks, states generate their own money and, with money, states create their own purchasing power. What tax revenue does, instead, is eliminate purchasing power in the private sector and reduce the scope of money functions, as described above.

Taxes, therefore, do not entail a "socialization" of value in any sense, but simply an adjustment in the volume of money available in the economy. That adjustment can nonetheless have a relevant overall effect: if money is the condition for the exchange of commodities and the formation and accumulation of capital, any increase in taxes that entails a lasting net reduction of money will result in a potential restriction of production. This typically happens when the fiscal deficit is lastingly reduced, or when fiscal equilibrium is achieved (Parguez 2002, 15–16). The only way to avoid that effect is through an increase in the private elements of demand (investment, consumption, external demand), which can be done through local banking money or (in the case of external demand) by foreign money.

An evident conclusion that can be drawn upon completing the state portion of the money circuit is that money cannot be homogeneously endogenous. The endogenous hypothesis of money is developed under the post-Keynesian theory focusing only on the private circuit, which begins with banks, followed by consumption, investment, and – in my opinion – hoarding, and ending with reflux, through the repayment of credits. This part of the circuit is indeed determined by money demand. However, that does not happen with state money, which is put into circulation through the different avenues of public spending.

Public spending is not determined by a demand in the traditional sense, but by the struggle between different social sectors, which converge in pressures on both the executive and legislative branches of government in the preparation of public budgets (O'Connor 2002, 203ff.). On the one hand, different sectors of capital seek to channel parts of public spending directly or indirectly to them through state purchases so as to continue with their profit generation and capital accumulation processes. On the other, different social groups, like state employees, retirees and pensioners, private-sector workers' unions, the unemployed, healthcare system users, and so on, also exert pressure on the state for it to channel sums of money to this or that group of people, in the form of wages, pensions, subsidies, etc. This constellation of social groups does not produce any public spending that is stable in volume or homogeneous in its distribution. Although public spending and, consequently, state money, are the result of private requirements, they are much more linked to processes of social struggle, and have a discretionary component, which does not make them "infinitely complacent" with the demand for investment and consumption, as is the case with bank credit. In other words, state money is not perfectly endogenous, as bank money is.

Now that we have identified the place of taxation in the monetary circuit, let us specify its effects on capitalist production as a whole. While in most cases higher public spending entails an increase in demand and production, an increase or reduction in tax revenue, with public spending remaining unchanged, will have as a consequence a reduction or an increase, respectively, in the possibilities for investment and consumption, so that tax revenue conditions production, as commodities can only be commodities when they are exchanged for money. Nevertheless, those effects of public spending and taxation may vary due to other factors.

On the one hand, the global development of capitalism has led to unequal production structures between the different regions of the world and between countries, and this has had an effect on the reaction to the increase in state money derived from public spending. To give a simple example, the productive sector's reaction to public spending in a core country with a great diversification of production cannot be the same as that of the productive sector in a country with a predominantly agricultural production and with a weak or virtually nonexistent industrial sector. Even in core countries, production structures are the result of processes played out over long periods, resulting, for example, in different dimensions of Departments I (capital goods), II (consumer goods), and III (financial sector).

A second element that is also often overlooked in standard post-Keynesian analyses, and which is crucial in periphery countries, is the presence of foreign state money, primarily dollars issued by the United States and – to a lesser extent – euros, from exports, direct foreign investments, and other international flows. Therefore, in much of the world, the money stock is not made up solely of state money and bank credits; it also includes money from abroad.

Therefore, the effects of public spending on production may be different from those generated by bank money. In particular, an increase in state money can lead to an increase in production, but it can also push prices up if the installed production structures fail to react to the increase in public spending with an increase in production. Generally, such an increase does occur, and public spending drives a country's output up. But it may not happen that way, in which case it is possible that the increase in state money will cause inflation, not for the reason given by orthodox theory (the expectation of the sustained increase in public spending and the loss of the "unpredictability effect" of its sudden increase), but because of the factors listed above. That is, while inflation is not an exclusively or primarily monetary phenomenon, a monetary-based inflation can certainly exist.

However, both taxation and public debt can be the subject of political decisions that take them out of alignment with the creation of money in all its forms, in the same way that we observe with respect to public spending. So its regulatory role of the money stock should not be interpreted as endogeneity or absolute dependence on the flow of money.

The consequence is that tax revenue, together with money's other "reflux points", has a stabilizing effect on the price system. In general, tax revenue, and all forms of money reflux, prevent the money stock from growing indefinitely. Assuming that, from a certain point on, the capitalist production system no longer responds to an increase in money (especially in public spending) with an increase in production, then such uncontrolled growth of the money stock would generate inflation. But inflation is not a permanent situation because, among other instruments, the state is constantly destroying money through tax revenue.

This forces us to analyze the remaining form of money reflux, besides the repayment of bank credits and tax revenue: public debt. Its other functions notwithstanding, the immediate effect of the issuance of public debt is to eliminate a mass of money that is in the hands of individuals, in an amount equivalent to each issuance of public bonds. However, there is a significant difference between tax revenue and the issuance of public debt in terms of how they are managed.

The creation and regulation of taxes today fall under the jurisdiction of parliaments (although the scope of that parliamentary competence varies from country to country). Public debt, instead, has traditionally been managed discretionally by administrative authorities and central banks. But, in any case, both tax revenue and the issuance of public debt, for various reasons, are not rigidly determined by public spending and the issuance of state money, which means that they are not endogenous and also reinforces the lack of endogeneity of state money.

4.4 Evidence for taxation hypotheses as a component of the reflux phase of money

In order to support the above hypotheses regarding the role of tax revenue – together with other elements – as a component of the reflux phase of money and a regulator of its volume, we must provide empirical evidence. With respect specifically to tax revenue, empirical observation of its reflux function may be obscured by several factors: first, the fact that it shares that function with other elements; and second, its rigidity, derived from its legal structure, which suggests that its magnitude must be less sensitive to the variations in the quantity of money. The only – indirect but compelling – sign that taxation is a regulator of the money stock would be the case of an economy that has public spending and, therefore, produces state money, in addition to bank money, but in which neither taxation nor public debt exist, and in which taxation is reintroduced at a second moment. If my hypothesis is correct, in that case we should be able to observe an inflationary explosion at an initial moment (issuance of state money without reflux) and a frank reduction of inflation at a second moment (issuance of money with the reestablishment of taxation).

That case existed in the immediate aftermath of the October Revolution in Russia. Initially, the novel Soviet government abolished several taxes, and adopted many measures to reduce the rest, after an initial brief period of broad decentralization of taxation power in favor of local Soviets. The consequence of this was the reduction of tax revenue to almost zero. On the other hand, and despite the revolution, a net of monetary exchanges and payments persisted throughout the Russian economy, for which state money originating in public spending was used (Shmelev 1931). The combination of a lack of tax revenue and the existence of monetary public spending led to an unprecedented inflationary process, until the New Economic Policy, implemented as of 1921 at the urging of Grigory Sokolnikov (the People's Commissar for Public Finance), restored monetary taxes. Price volatility quickly subsided to normal levels (Rheingold 1931). Whether aware of it or not, the architects of this policy produced the proof – categorical, in my opinion – that taxation is indeed an essential regulator of the money stock, and, in addition, that state money is not strictly endogenous, that inflation is not necessarily monetary, although it can be, and that therefore taxation also has a stabilizing effect on the price system. We have here another case of the use of the colligation method based on historical narratives. However, I believe that the compelling force of these narratives is stronger than in other cases, given that, despite being produced in a context of great theoretical and political commitment, the tone of these authors is completely devoid of any theoretical reference, and their work is limited only to the accumulation of information and details.

That extreme case notwithstanding, we must test the circuit theory as a whole, and taxation functions according to that theory's framework. To do that, we must translate the circuit theory into categories that, to the extent possible, can fit into the statistical data available. If we put together all the pieces outlined, we have that in the money flux (or creation) phase there are two sources: financial credit and public spending. In the reflux phase, there are three "end points": repayment of financial credits; tax revenue; and public debt issuance, net of its repayments. Between the origin and the end of the circuit, there should be a money stock composed of circulating state money, plus all kinds of bank deposits and other financial assets, such as negotiable bonds, stocks, and the like. International money movements are reflected in the balance of payments. Now, in order for some kind of measurement of these elements to be possible, we generally need to consider the difficulty posed by the distortion caused by foreign-produced money that is in the country in question. The only case in which we could have a relatively clean observation of all the elements is that of a country in which all the elements of the flux, reflux, and intermediate phases are expressed in local currency. This is, naturally, the case of the United States.

The first graph shown (Graph 4.1) is a line graph, provided for illustration purposes, and it breaks down the elements of the reflux phase and the intermediate phases of the monetary circuit for the United States. In all cases, only dynamic factors are taken into account, so that for public debt and the "intermediate phases", only annual growth is considered. For the "intermediate phases", only money supply growth is considered, which according to the orthodox theory only measures

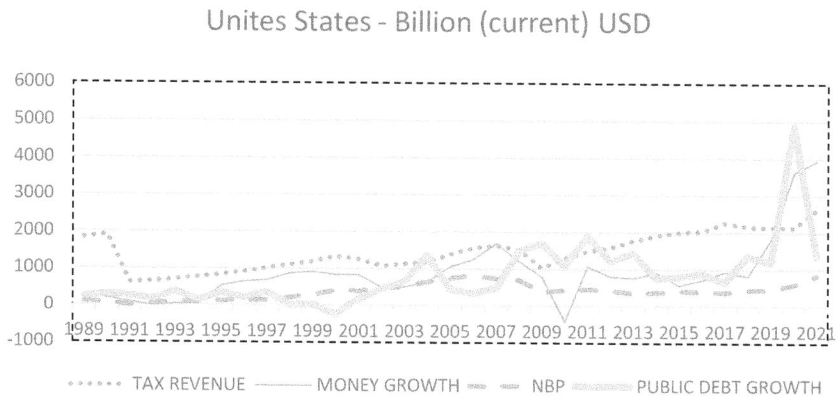

Graph 4.1 US – Money flux and reflux indicators (line graph).

Source: Direct data and author's calculations based on direct data from the World Bank (GDP, money growth, banking credit and public debt growth) and the International Monetary Fund (tax revenue). Available respectively at data.worldbank.org/indicator and www.imf.org/external/datamapper/rev@FPP/USA.

the positive difference, from year to year, of circulating state money plus bank deposits. Also added to the graph is the negative balance of payments (NBP), which, being consistently negative, indicates the net outflow balance of dollars from the US economy, and, therefore, complements the money supply. Financial assets are not included in the graph due to lack of information. The graph has, from the post-Keynesian point of view, many important defects. First, it does not consider the balance of bank credit, which in this theoretical framework constitutes money to the same extent as circulating state money. Second, it does not reflect the other source of money, which is public spending. In any case, it is worth trying to test my hypothesis with that statistical information from another theoretical framework (Graph 4.1).

According to the epistemological concept of paradigm stated in Chapter 2, Graph 4.1 does not shed light on my hypothesis since the statistical information stems from a different theoretical framework and, consequently, shows data organized according to a different taxonomy. Incidentally, a careful examination of the graph indicates an insufficiency of the mainstream concepts of money and taxation: how is the origin of money used to pay taxes explained? If the answer were "through the issuing of money by the state", we would be within the post-Keynesian theory. In any case, these inconsistencies notwithstanding, the images show a chronological correlation between "mainstream-defined money" and tax revenue.

Graph 4.2 is more interesting, as it is a scatter plot that correlates the elements of the flux and reflux phases under the form of a simple regression. Bank credit growth and annual public spending are added as parts of the money flux phase, while the other variable is integrated with all the forms of reflux and the intermediate phases of the circuit that were already included in the previous graph, plus the balance of the balance of payments (always negative, and which, therefore, has an effect similar to that of the withdrawal of money from circulation). Tax

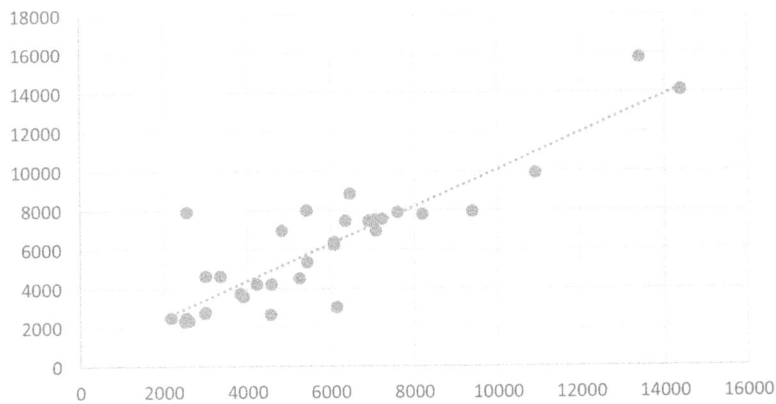

Graph 4.2 US – Money flux and reflux indicators (regression).

Source: Author's own calculations based on data from the World Bank (GDP, net growth of domestic credit to private sector, circulating money, and banking deposits) and the International Monetary Fund (tax revenue and public spending). Available respectively at data.worldbank.org/indicator and www.imf.org/external/datamapper/prim_exp@FPP/USA).

revenue includes federal taxes, social security contributions, and state and local taxes. If the hypotheses regarding money formulated under my interpretation of the post-Keynesian circuit theory are correct, we should have that, in a certain period (Graph 4.2):

Flux = Reflux + Money in intermediate phases

More extensively stated:

Public spending +/- Increase/decrease of banking credit = Tax revenue +/- Increase/decrease of public debt + Circulating state money + Bank deposits + Other financial assets

The banking credit and public debt data were simplified by including only the respective net balances on either side of the equation.

US – Money flux and reflux phases (regression)

Graph 4.2, the regression equation, and the coefficient do not include the other financial assets, due to the lack of information. They are as follows:

$y = 0.9494x + 595.04$
$R^2 = 0.7837$

In a regression, we can never overlook the fact that the relationship between the two phenomena that are compared is presupposed, that the quantitative variables are constructed based on theoretical assumptions that are also presupposed, and, therefore, that the relationship indicated by the graph and the coefficient merely show the degree in which the concomitant variation of the variables is produced. In

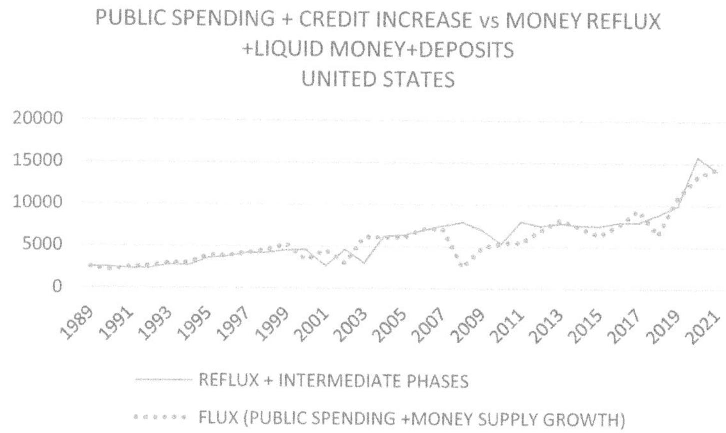

Graph 4.3 US – Money flux and reflux phases (line graph).

Source: Author's own calculations based on data from the World Bank (GDP, net growth of domestic credit to private sector, circulating money and banking deposits) and the International Monetary Fund (tax revenue and public spending). Available respectively at data.worldbank.org/indicator and www.imf.org/external/datamapper/prim_exp@FPP/USA).

particular, the regression assumes the post-Keynesian methodological conception that tax revenue is in principle a variable dependent on the money stock.

The result of the regression, with all of these limitations, is reasonably consistent with the hypotheses formulated. The difference in the coefficient can be explained by the absence of a measurement for the financial assets not included in the intermediate phases of the circuit. The two groups of variables are shown (not disaggregated) in Graph 4.3 (a line graph):

I stated that tax revenue is "in principle" a variable that is dependent on the money stock because, as posited above, money flux and reflux movements dependent on the state (public spending and taxation) are not endogenous. Therefore, deliberate policies aimed at reducing the deficit by increasing taxes should be reflected statistically in a gap between the money stock and tax revenue. That is another advantage of the statistical information from the United States, since in that country there were no policies of this nature in the period considered.

Let us now consider a regression with public spending as an independent variable and tax revenue as a dependent variable, both corresponding only to the central government of the United States. This regression is less realistic than the previous one, as we are leaving out a very important portion of tax revenue (namely, social security contributions and the tax revenue of the individual states that make up the Union), as well as other components of the flux and reflux phases. While we have posited that tax revenue, like the other components of the reflux phase, absorbs both bank money and state money, given that the latter is scarcely or not very endogenous, its variations should have a clearer impact on tax revenue. Therefore, if the post-Keynesian hypothesis is correct, a regression that only correlates public spending with tax revenue should, at least in the United States, show a stronger sensitivity of the latter with respect to the former.

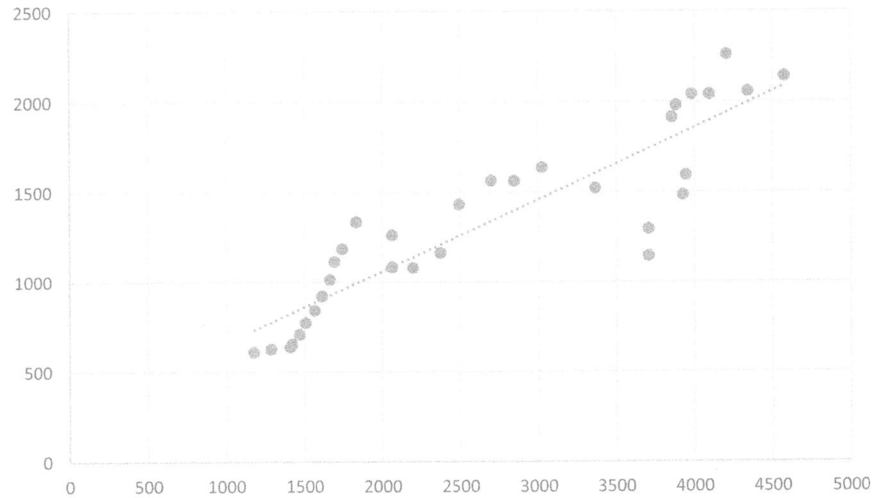

Graph 4.4 US (only central government). Money flux and reflux phases excluding public debt (regression).

Source: Author's own calculations based on data from the World Bank. Available respectively at data .worldbank.org/indicator

US (only central government). Money flux and reflux phases excluding public debt (regression) (Graph 4.4).

$R^2 = 0.8076$

If we add the net increase of the public debt to the central government's tax revenue, excluding the private components of both phases, we will still have a favorable correlation:

US (only central government) Money flux and reflux phases excluding private components (regression)

$R^2 = 0.7191$

The lower value of R^2, as compared with the previous cases, is consistent with the circuit theory because US public debt is subject to greater influences from non-state money or money located outside the country. Indeed, and while tax revenue still has a predominantly local component (without prejudice to what we will observe in Chapter 10), the issuance of public debt by the United States has the ability to capture money originating in bank credits and money in the hands of non-residents, so that it is natural for it to be less sensitive to variations in public spending. However, the fact that, despite these "contaminations", the variation of public debt maintains a strong correlation with public spending significantly reinforces the circuit theory as a whole.

While these last two regressions are less descriptively rich than the first, the fact that all three evidences yield results that are consistent with the post-Keynesian

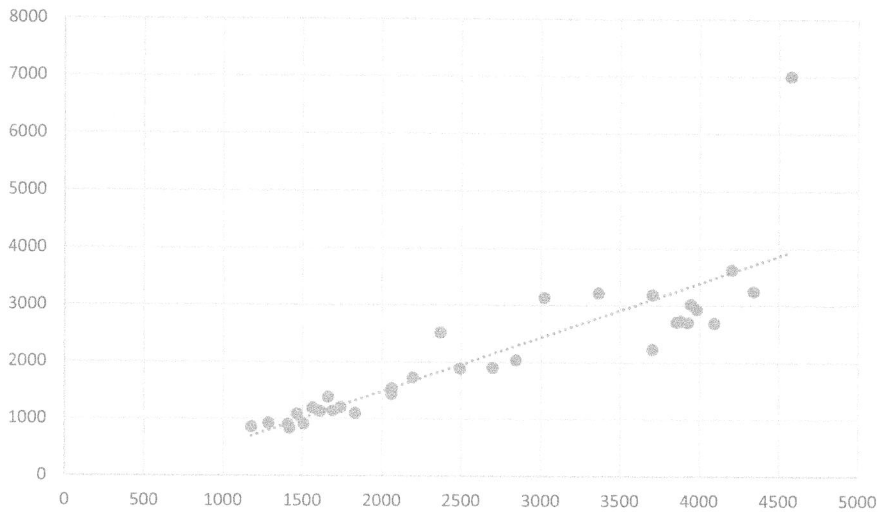

Graph 4.5 US (only central government). Money flux and reflux phases excluding private components (regression).

Source: Author's own calculations based on data from the World Bank. Available respectively at: data.worldbank.org/indicator.

circuit theory, both in its original version and in the non-endogenous version posited in this book, is of significant value. Indeed, variations notwithstanding, with respect to public finances, the essential point of the circuit theory is that public spending is not at the end but at the start of the cycle of public finances, and that tax revenue and – in part – public debt are not at the start but at the end of that cycle. The fact that the three evidences put forward go through very different stages in terms of monetary, public spending, and taxation policies in the United States and yet are persistently consistent with the post-Keynesian hypotheses renders such hypotheses extremely robust.

4.5 Taxation effects: tax shifting, tax incidence, surplus value, capital accumulation, profit, and the profit rate

The monetary conception of taxation and the ensuing hypotheses force anyone working within a theoretical framework that is essentially Marxist to reinterpret the effects of taxation on the basic categories of Marxian economic theory.

The usual focus in Kalecki-inspired works on the effects of taxation tends to be on the consequences of taxation on investment and the extent to which it reduces corporate profits. This approach (Mott and Slattery 1994; Laramie and Mair 2000, 64ff.) reproduces three errors made by Kalecki in his famous paper on the effects of taxation (1971, 35ff.): (a) assuming balanced public finances, so that any increase in tax revenue translates into higher public spending, which we know is usually false under mainstream-oriented fiscal policies; (b) detaching the effect of taxes from the theory of price formation, which was developed by Kalecki himself; and (c) assuming that investment depends on monetary profits alone, when Kalecki himself argued that the future profitability of investment was also a determinant. This approach should be changed to one that combines Kalecki's assumptions on price formation and investment decisions with the assumptions of the monetary circuit theory.

As stated in the previous section, taxation has a stabilizing effect on prices. While that is a general effect of taxation, we must bear in mind that taxation acts on a society divided into classes, which are in turn subdivided into subclasses, and which participate in production by exchanging commodities. This applies both to the capitalist who sells a good or a service and to the worker who sells their labor force. Furthermore, class and subclass divisions determine: (a) unequal endowments of money; and (b) different degrees of power in setting the prices of commodities. The conclusion that can be drawn by linking those premises consistently is that taxation is likely to cause a redistribution of money endowments through a rearrangement of the price system. This is what is known as the phenomenon of tax shifting and tax incidence, as explained below.

While inflation can have a monetary origin, it is a multi-causal phenomenon, as observed above (basically in line with Wray). This, which is true in general, is reflected at the individual level of a company, a sector of activity, or the relations between social classes. At the core of the price system are companies, which is where capitalist production happens and, moreover, where the essential part of the distribution of value in capitalism occurs: workers' wages, on the one hand, and surplus value, on the other.

Assuming that price is the amount of money exchanged for commodities, its dimensions are determined – in addition to the total money stock and the money endowments of each social class and subclass – by the different degrees of power of the buyer and seller, and the possibility that the buyer or seller (as the case may be) has of rejecting the price offered or asked by the other party, as well as the possibility of seeking a different buyer or seller. This is what we could call *degree of monopoly* (Kalecki 1971, 44–45).

At the center of the price system, then, are companies, which concentrate capitalist production. Companies with high degrees of monopoly generally have large amounts of money endowments and are in a position to impose sale or purchase prices (in the case of purchase prices, it would be degree of *monopsony*) on their counterparts. These companies have the capacity to react to the withdrawal of money caused by a tax imposed on them as taxpayers, by increasing their prices, or by pressuring their supplier to lower their prices. This involves not only companies but also workers, who are the suppliers of the leading commodity that capital acquires – labor – and its price – monetary wages. This is what is known as tax shifting. If a price increase and shift by one company is followed by a price increase and shift by another company, and then another, the tax shifting spreads along a chain of companies and activities, and even from country to country. When it reaches a company or individual that lacks the ability to increase its prices, that is when tax incidence occurs. That conclusion is stated in a highly abbreviated form in the final part of the paper by Tracy Mott and Edward Slattery (1994, 403), but in an incidental way, when it should be the central point of any theory of the distribution of the tax burden.

Occasionally, tax incidence will affect a company or a group of companies, reducing – as will be shown below – the share of the profits that the capitalists appropriate. This can happen either for companies whose prices are fully demand-driven, or with income or asset taxes in the expansionary phases of economic cycles, since the expansion of their profit caused by their own activity can offset the new tax burden without an extraordinary increase in prices. But it is more often the case that tax incidence impacts workers, directly or indirectly (O'Connor 2002, 203ff.). This can happen openly when new taxes on wages are created or existing ones are raised. It also happens when many companies can unload the burden of the taxes they pay, or the indirect impacts they suffer through other companies' shifting, onto their workers' wages by lowering them or through layoffs or workforce reductions. In other cases, taxation affects workers by increasing consumer prices and reducing the amount of goods they can buy with their wages in money if those wages remain unchanged while consumer prices increase. In such cases, taxes literally lower wages, which are the workers' share of production (Wright 1975, 26–27).

If we incorporate this wage reduction into the fundamental concepts of the Marxist theoretical framework, we have that a pure increase in taxes normally entails:

(a) an increase in surplus value, as by reducing the amount of money available to workers, these taxes reduce the share of production that can be appropriated by workers and, therefore, increase the share of production appropriated by capitalists, which is, precisely, surplus value;
(b) an increase in the profit rate as a monetary ratio, because of the decrease in variable capital, which, according to formula VI, is added to the denominator and subtracted from the numerator of the division (compare with Jankowski 1987); and
(c) an internal redistribution of profit: if profit increases as a consequence of the increase in surplus value, that increase will be divided in different proportions according to – once again – the degree of power of the groups that appropriate that profit (production capitalists, financial capital, lessors, and the state).

In the case of a lack of increase in surplus value, when in response to a pure tax increase companies neither raise their prices nor lower the wages they pay, the increase in taxes has the effect of reducing the share of the profit that is appropriated by subjects other than the state, which appropriate profit as a monetary magnitude (again, the capitalist who runs the company, financial capital, or lessors).

The role of taxation as a tool for lowering wages, proposed by Erik Olin Wright, is consistent with one of the post-Keynesian hypotheses regarding inflation. Indeed, one of the causes of inflation proposed by post-Keynesianism is the increase in wages above productivity (Wray 2000), so that their reduction through an increase in taxes has a concrete anti-inflationary effect, which is an individual manifestation of taxation's overall effect of controlling the money stock.

These conclusions are valid not only for the so-called consumption taxes (where tax shifting is usually considered uncritically as invariable), but also for corporate income taxes. For example, a study focusing on Germany provided solid empirical evidence that, in addition to the transfer via prices, companies transfer the burden of corporate income taxes internally to the salaries of their workers, even in a context of intense wage negotiation (Arulamparam, Devereux, and Maffini 2010; Dwenger, Rattenhuber, and Steiner 2013). It is, however, plausible that firms with tax-shifting capacity may be able to do so more quickly in the case of sales taxes, and with some delay in the case of income or asset taxes (Mott and Slattery 1994, 404). But, in the long run, almost all of the tax burden of corporate taxation impacts workers, as arises from the empirical works mentioned above in this paragraph. In other words, we can confirm the hypothesis that, as a whole, the increase in tax collection increases surplus value by decreasing wages, as posited by Wright.

In any case, we have identified here a complementary function of taxation, specifically associated with Marxist theory, that is consistent with, but different from, the regulation of the money stock: *the lowering of wages and the increase in surplus value, profit, and the profit rate, when that is necessary in a certain instance of the trajectory of capitalism.*

As for capital accumulation, taxation is less important than public spending for these purposes. Besides being a form of variable capital costs (social wages), given that it is a component of aggregate demand (in fact, the only component directly managed by the state), public spending boosts production, thus tempering the economic cycle. As a consequence, (non-financial) public spending favors capital accumulation (Mandel 1976, 485–486). Nevertheless, taxes play an important role in the process of accumulation of capital. As stated above, the lowering of wages and the increase in surplus value are phenomena that are necessary, from time to time, in the trajectory of capitalism. That need consists, precisely, in increasing capital accumulation in the short term, since, as discussed in Chapter 3, capital emerges from surplus value, so that by increasing surplus value, the "fund" from which capital is born is objectively increased. However, that effect is by definition limited in both its material and temporal scope, since any increase in taxes, without a corresponding increase in public spending, operates against demand by contracting the money stock and, ultimately, acts against the process of accumulation.

This last conclusion has a crucial corollary: it is a mistake to theorize about the effects that taxation alone has on investment and consumption, as mainstream economics and even sectors of post-Keynesianism do. Instead, it is necessary to analyze the effects of tax revenue and public spending combined, based on the following rules: in principle, the fiscal deficit is expansive of investment and consumption, while the balance and the fiscal surplus are actually or potentially recessive.

At this point, it is worth remembering that taxation as a monetary phenomenon has effects that are actually monetary in the immediate term but are translated into instances of value, such as surplus value and capital accumulation. For example, when we say that taxes increase surplus value, such increase happens because, by increasing the amount of money that is obtained from the sale of commodities and not transferred to workers, workers appropriate a share of production that contains less labor-value, while the other subjects can appropriate a share of production that contains more labor-value. Similarly, saying that taxes can enhance capital accumulation means that by increasing their money endowments derived from the sale of their production, capitalists have a greater possibility of appropriating commodities that they then turn into capital. It is important to remember that money is only a mediator between commodities and social relations that are built around production.

When the essential functions of taxation are combined with the (Marxist-inspired) conception of the state proposed in Section 3.5, taxing rights and the power to tax exercised by states and supranational entities acquire a whole new meaning. States are formations functional to capitalism, as they must create the conditions for the continuation of the essential processes of the mode of production, namely, production itself, the generation of surplus value, the accumulation and reproduction of capital, and the counter-tendencies that offset the tendency of the profit rate to fall.

4.6 Taxation and the distribution of money among social classes

The standard post-Keynesian circuit theory (with the exception of the Kaleckian tradition, which inherits the Marxian class conception) presupposes a social structure with two agents: firms and households. But that assumption is unrealistic: firms are production units in which unequal relations exist; those relations entail that individuals cannot be considered homogeneously as households, but as members of classes, with different behaviors and needs; and even the relations between firms are unequal, due, for example, to the size of their territorial scope. Marxian theory has the tools to adjust the circuit theory of money applied to taxes to take into account the social substrate of the capitalist economy. This will be discussed in the following paragraphs.

First, although taxes are a way to eliminate circulating money, that elimination has differentiated effects on the various social groups because money endowments are unequally distributed among these groups (financial sector, industrial capitalists, workers, etc.), and cause effects beyond the reduction of general demand.

This entails a change with respect to the traditional Marxian concept of taxes, as well as to the standard circuit conception of taxes. Taxes are not a form of appropriation of surplus value; rather, in immediate terms, they are a form of suppression of money. But that suppression of money has effects throughout the chain of money: directly (when taxes are imposed on wages) or through the price system, which makes subsequent changes to the money available to subjects and their purchasing power, with workers coming last in that process. It is in this sense, then, that taxes do not negatively affect surplus value and rather usually increase it, and with it, they increase the exploitation of workers.

We could think of taxes as having re-distributive effects insofar as, for example, they comparatively reduce the money endowment of the financial sector, or that of capitalists, without affecting workers (similarly, Parguez 2002, 10–11). However, this is not likely to happen on a significant scale, given the system of monetary prices in any capitalist economy, and also the essential role played by taxes in systematically eliminating circulating money. Indeed, the simplest way to fulfill the latter function is by focusing tax revenue on the business sector by means of a corporate tax, a value-added tax (VAT), or similar taxes since that sector concentrates much of the money stock, and this can be easily controlled by tax authorities. A different tax structure is not unthinkable: it is (conceptually) possible, for example, to restore the integral progressivity of personal income taxes, and to create personal property taxes and financial transaction taxes, like the Tobin tax. But the complexity of such a personalized taxation structure makes its adoption unlikely in the short or medium term, thereby consolidating the reinforcement of existing inequality in the shares of production appropriated by workers in comparison to other social groups (see the final chapter).

4.7 Taxation and public debt

The relations between taxation and public debt merit special consideration. Let us begin with Marx's traditional interpretation: the role of public debt is to absorb the portion of money-capital (which, as we saw, is an inappropriate name for the excess of money after meeting capital accumulation and consumption demands) that cannot be placed either as deposits, private bonds, or the like in the financial system. The state, therefore, covers that gap by providing the portion of money-capital gains that enables the continuation of the general system of money circulation. Public debt is in essence a security to be satisfied by future production, as it allows for the appropriation of a share of material production upon maturity. The credit right represented by public debt has a higher degree of certainty than that of private debt, due to the state's coercive power, which ensures liquidity. As any other share of production that is not wages, public debt essentially entails an appropriation of surplus value, and a form of exploitation of labor (Marx 2008, 535–536; Forges Davanzati, and Patalano 2017, 50–51).[2]

Regarding the latter aspect, in Marxian approaches, public debt is often viewed as a form of indirect exploitation of workers through taxes. Assuming that the state uses tax revenue to pay debt holders and that taxes are a form of appropriation of surplus value, it follows that the public debt/taxes set is an indirect and veiled way of appropriating a larger share of surplus value (Michl and Georges 1996; Bin 2015). However, if we combine the theory of money with the theory of value, this view changes.

First, and as noted in the previous chapter, the issuing of public debt has an immediate effect similar to that of tax revenue: it eliminates circulating money. Therefore, public debt is also a regulator of the money stock, and consequently of the price system, with an advantage over tax revenue: historically, public debt has been managed discretionally by governments so that it can be quickly expanded or reduced (especially through short-term bonds, such as treasury bills). The regulation of the money stock through public debt includes cases in which the exchange rate of the local currency with respect to the dollar or the euro is managed, a tool that is sometimes used by the governments of periphery countries (see, for example, Neaime 2009).

Second, for public debt holders, they are forms of appropriating production, directly or through their conversion into liquid money. For example, public debt can operate as capital contribution in a production company of any kind. Public debt can be sold at any time, with the holder receiving liquid money in exchange, which can be used immediately to realize value and accelerate capital accumulation. But in all cases, public debt itself retains its essential property of being convertible into liquid money after a certain term, and not immediately. It thus fulfills the function of all debt securities: given the difficulty, or impossibility, that money-capital has of being used right away to realize value and increase physical capital, it must be guaranteed a way of being converted into a profitable asset of a particular kind. When it reaches maturity, the debt is replaced with liquid money provided by the state, and that liquid money allows for the appropriation of a share of production.

A consequence of this conclusion is, on the one hand, that a state's degree of indebtedness does not depend solely or primarily on that state's decisions or needs, but on the needs and pressures of money-capital, which forces public indebtedness whenever opportunities for profitability cannot be found in the private financial sector (Forges Davanzati and Patalano 2017, 59 ff.). On the other hand, while public debt is a starting point for increasing surplus value and for the exploitation of workers, and this effect is associated with tax increases that affect wages, this does not happen because taxes generate a flow of repayment of public debt.

To redeem the principal of the public debt and pay interest on it, the state must give holders liquid money upon maturity. Therefore, the only condition for public debt to be paid is that the state must have money available for it. If public debt is expressed in the state's account money, and there are no political restrictions for increasing total money stock (as is the case in the United States), there are no major problems in meeting debt payments while maintaining all other public spending at the desired level. If a state instead becomes indebted in a foreign currency (as occurs in periphery countries), in order to repay the debt, it will have to exchange the money it issues for foreign currency. Most likely, it will have to exchange that money in the country, as it is difficult to imagine, for example, a Latin American state exchanging pesos (or reais) for dollars or euros in the United States or Europe. If the foreign currency thus obtained is insufficient, the state will have to contract new debt in foreign currency in order to pay its previous debt in foreign currency.

The state ultimately increases public spending to repay public debt, so that the volume of public spending does not depend on tax revenue, and repaying public debt does not depend on that revenue either. Repayment of the debt is another form of public spending, which is done by issuing money or acquiring foreign currency. If that state has internalized the concept of budget constraint and is also functional to the financial sector of the economy (which is the sector that directs money-capital to acquire public debt), it is very likely that public spending in wages, subsidies, and direct purchases will be cut if the repayments of public debt increase, so that the level of total public spending will be maintained without increasing spending, or even by reducing it.

The reduction of non-financial public spending diminishes the possibilities of selling production and, if there are no other sources of demand, it causes a contraction in production, and obviously an increase in unemployment and/or a reduction in wages. If the government decides to increase tax revenue instead of, or simultaneously with, reducing public spending, such an increase will likely affect wages and increase surplus value. That is, what probably causes an increase in surplus value and a reduction in wages is not public debt *per se* but the concept of budget constraint. While Thomas Michl and Christophre Georges also argue that public debt is a way of exploiting workers under the principle of budget constraint (Michl and Georges 1996, 52), what I posit here differs with them in that the flow for repayment of the debt is not obtained through tax revenue but through the issuing of money, through the over-indebtedness of the state, or through privatization of public activities or assets. For that same reason, improving wages does not depend on the replacement of tax revenue with public debt issued to finance public spending (Michl and Georges 1996, 54ff.), but rather simply on the reduction of tax revenue.

4.8 Taxation, law, ideology, state

As with all types of social relations, taxation must be translated into a set of legal norms. This is because, first, the adoption of a legal form has the function of explicitly stating and detailing the ways in which state coercion will be exercised to enforce the behaviors involved in that social relation. Second, legal norms conceal the social relation underlying the situation (in this case, the power to extract money from civil society) and make their mandatory nature seem as if it were a result of its legal nature, when it actually derives from their social necessity. That is, legal norms have a mystifying effect on social relations (Pashukanis 2003, 73ff.).

While the difference between mystification and ideology within Marxism has never been very clear, under the mystifying function of tax law we can include the dissociation between what the law establishes as a taxable event and what the tax materially affects. If one reads the letter of a law, or legal scholarship on taxation, it would appear that taxes apply to multiple objects that are distinct from each other: income, sales, assets, etc. But if we look beyond the legal text and interpret each tax as a purely monetary phenomenon, such beliefs evaporate. Taxes, insofar as they are a monetary phenomenon, invariably affect the money endowments of those burdened with the tax and, as a material phenomenon, are always expressed in the collection of the corresponding amounts of money. Obtaining an income, selling a good, and owning an asset are all events that determine whether or not tax collection applies, but in terms of satisfying that collection, it does not matter where the money comes from. For example, in the case of a tax on assets, the taxpayer must pay a sum of money regardless of whether it is a monetary asset or not, and regardless of whether or not it generates a monetary income for the taxpayer. The adjacent or derived material phenomena are tax shifting and tax incidence. Therefore, the legal structures that proclaim other "taxed events" merely define the opportunity in which collection must occur; the rest is mystification.

But there is also a more far-reaching effect, which is what occurs when the legal system takes over a social relation and turns it into a "state institution": the ideological effect. Ideology is an extremely controversial concept, but it is also rich in explanatory insights. I will provide a more in-depth analysis of the ideological connotations and effects of the international taxation system in Chapter 11, but some general observations are in order here.

Ideologies are discourses that are functional to the preservation and reproduction of the prevailing social structure, often altering the "real" properties of social phenomena (Marx and Engels 1998, 41ff.). There are two functions of ideology that are relevant to what will be further discussed in the final chapter. First, ideology has a *legitimation* function: it creates the belief that a type of social relation – for example, the state or private property – does not only exist, but that it is beneficial (Ricœur 1986, 226ff.). Second, in the same way capital constantly generates ways to reproduce itself, in order for the system to continue working smoothly, it is also necessary for the behaviors that contribute to such smooth working to be constantly reproduced. So ideology generates the belief that a type of social relation must be maintained, and the behaviors it involves must be repeated again and again (Althusser 2014, 232ff.).

Even before it becomes a legal norm, and much more so after, the taxation system of a country or a group of countries needs to justify and protect itself by generating ideological discourses that characterize it as something positive and good. Thus, legal scholarship, ethical and political discourses, and even theories purported to be descriptive refer to taxation as something endowed with "justice", or as the embodiment of "social solidarity", etc., and tend to overlook or ignore its actual material effects (Laramie and Mair 2000, 39).

The different functions of taxation analyzed in this chapter provide, moreover, an excellent way to test the Marxian explanations of the state, irrespective of theoretical variations.

The state, through its taxation system, deploys a wide range of effects that are essential for the mode of production to continue operating. The first, which is the regulation of the money stock, is crucial: if there were no end point in the monetary circuit, the effects would be completely negative. If not done by the state through tax increases, the reduction of wages and the reconstruction of surplus value would lead to a discrediting of the status quo and the risk of social conflicts, which capitalists would have to deal with directly; if done by the state and through an instrument such as taxation, which ideological discourses surround with a halo of "solidarity" and "socialization", these problems dissipate or are mitigated. Incidentally, the ideological legitimation of the taxation system discussed above in this section also extends its effects to the social system as a whole, which, in that way, also appears to create spaces of solidarity and socialization of wealth.

That functionality of the taxation system is naturally intertwined with the functionalities of the other two components of public finances, which are public spending and public debt, aspects that have already been examined, and which revolve around money, the constituent element of all mercantile modes of production, since it constitutes commodities and, especially, capitalism. All the illusions that may be derived from the separation of the state with respect to society are thus shattered: such separation does not entail the creation of an entity unconnected with the mode of production; rather, it is a consequence of mercantile economies, it is strictly functional to them, and it lasts as long as they last.

Finally, the set of functions performed by the taxation system – from the regulation of the money stock to the distribution of money endowments and the dissemination of ideologies – shows us in practice the overdetermination that Althusser and Resnick and Wolff speak of: as a whole, those functions come from a system that is outside production (the state), but they trigger phenomena that are directly associated with production.

4.9 Differences with the mainstream

While for the reader it will be evident that this approach to taxation differs radically from the mainstream approach, it may be useful to provide an overview of the differences between the two. The normal mainstream theoretical approach combines pseudo-theoretical issues with regulatory proposals that align themselves with such issues, so I will briefly analyze the former, with the latter also consequently critiqued, based on the work by N. Gregory Mankiw et al., which summarizes in a simple way the positions of the neoclassical theory of taxation (2009).

The general assumption of the mainstream approach is that the function of taxation is to provide resources for the state so that it can carry out public spending. In the theoretical framework adopted here, taxation – or rather tax revenue, which is the relevant material phenomenon – is instead at the end of the monetary circuit, and it performs a money stock stabilizing function. Public spending, given the state's money-creating power, is in itself independent of tax revenue. Tax revenue thus plays a role of permanent regulator of the money stock, without which short-term regulators (such as short-term public debt or bank credit restrictions) would be pointless.

As for the effects of taxation on society, the mainstream assumption is of a society formed by individuals, not social groups, with such individuals interacting based on their preferences and the convergence of those preferences determining an optimal social state – the famous Pareto optimality (Pareto 2014, 72ff.) – so that, consequently, it is assumed that the main goal of taxation is to avoid altering that supposed optimality, although it is conceded that there can be solutions that deviate from that goal for reasons of "equality", that is, due to the existence of deep-rooted social convictions that demand a tax treatment that does not harm the most disadvantaged.

Under the theoretical framework adopted in this book, society is instead seen as divided into classes, and those classes into subclasses, with each of those social groups having different degrees of social power derived, primarily, from the position they occupy in the system of production. That power, and consequently money endowments, which are what taxation acts on, are unequally distributed, so that, outside the regulation of the money stock, taxation reproduces that inequality, reducing, as a rule, the money endowments of the most disadvantaged, although there could be cases where this does not happen in that way.

There is also a significant epistemological difference with the mainstream approach, namely, that the mainstream assumption is that the selection of the legal structures, the revenue volumes, and – to a large extent – the medium-term effects of tax revenue can be voluntarily regulated by states. Instead, under the theoretical framework adopted here, taxation cannot escape the functionality that is inherent to it by virtue of its insertion in the prevailing social system, and any changes in its course do not depend on the mere will of those in charge of the state. Rather, they depend on complex social processes that are ultimately the product of conflicts between different social classes with opposing interests.

Notes

1 In several passages of that book, Marx uses the word "state" as a noun or an adjective to refer to collective social organizations (tribe, community, etc.) that preceded the mercantile mode of production. Whether or not such use was deliberate, here I will assume that those social organizations *are not states nor do they have the characteristics of a state*, and that the state only appears when its bureaucratic and coercive apparatus begins to emerge as a separate entity with respect to civil society.

2 Marx conversely posited that public debt securities do not constitute capital accumulation (2007, 312).

References

Althusser, Louis. 2014. *On The Reproduction of Capitalism. Ideology and Ideological State Apparatuses*. London and New York: Verso.

Arulampalam, Wiji, Michael P. Devereux, and Giorgia Maffini. 2010. "The Direct Incidence of Corporate Income Tax on Wages." *European Economic Review* 56 (6): 1038–1054. https://doi.org/10.1016/j.euroecorev.2012.03.003.

Bilbao, Luis María. 1991. "Haciendas forales y Hacienda de la Monarquía. El caso vasco (siglos XV-XVIII)." In *Historia de la Hacienda Pública Española (siglos XV-XVIII). Homenaje a Don Felipe Ruiz Martín*, edited by Hacienda Pública Española, 43–58. Madrid: Ministerio de Economía y Hacienda.

Bin, Daniel. 2015. "Fiscal Superstructure and the Deepening of Labour Exploitation." *Capital & Class* 39 (2): 221–241. https://doi.org/10.1177/0309816815581774.

Bougrine, Hassan, and Mario Seccareccia. 2002. "Money, Taxes, Public Spending, and the State Within a Circuitist Perspective." *International Journal of Political Economy* 32 (3): 58–79. https://doi.org/10.1080/08911916.2002.11042876.

Bunge, Mario. 1967. *Scientific Research II. The Search for Truth*. Berlin-Heidelberg-New York: Springer Verlag.

Dwenger, Nadja, Pia Rattenhuber, and Viktor Steiner. 2013. "Sharing the Burden? Empirical Evidence on Corporate Tax Incidence." *German Economic Review* 20 (4): 107–140. https://doi.org/10.1111/geer.12157.

Forges Davanzati, Guglielmo, and Rosario Patalano. 2017. "Marx on Public Debt: Fiscal Expropriation and Capital Reproduction." *International Journal of Political Economy* 46 (1): 50–64. https://doi.org/10.1080/08911916.2017.1310474.

Hoyt, Robert. 1950. "Royal Taxation and the Growth of Realm in Medieaval England." *Speculum* 25 (1).

Jankowski, Richard. 1987. "The Profit-Squeeze and Tax Policy: Can State Actively Intervene?" *Review of Radical Political Economics* 19 (3): 18–33. https://doi.org/10.1177/048661348701900302.

Kalecki, Michal. 1971. *Selected Essays on the Dynamics of Capitalist Economy*. Cambridge: Cambridge University Press.

Keynes, John Maynard. 1930. *A Treatise on Money*. Vol. 5 of *The Collected Writings of John Maynard Keynes*. Cambridge: Cambridge University Press.

Kiser, Edgar. 2021. "Premodern Taxation." In *Handbook of Politics and Taxation*, edited by Lukas Hakelberg and Laura Seelkopf. Cheltenham, UK: Edward Elgar Publishing.

Laramie, Anthony J., and Douglas Mair. 2000. *A Dynamic Theory of Taxation*. Cheltenham, UK: Edward Elgar Publishing.

Mandel, Ernest. 1976. *Late Capitalism*. London: NLB.

Mankiw, N. Gregory, Matthew Weinzierl, and Danny Yagan. 2009. "Optimal Taxation in Theory and in Practice." *Journal of Economic Perspectives* 23 (4): 147–174.

Marx, Karl. 1964. *Pre-capitalist Economic Formations*. New York: International Publishers.

Marx, Karl. 1995–1996. *Capital. A Critique of Political Economy*. Vol. 1. Moscow: Progress Publishers. https://www.marxists.org/archive/marx/works/download/pdf/Capital-Volume-I.pdf.

Marx, Karl. 2008. *Capital. A Critique of Political Economy.* Vol. 2. Moscow: Progress Publishers. https://libcom.org/files/Capital-Volume-II.pdf.

Marx, Karl, and Friedrich Engels. 1998. *The German Ideology.* Amherst, New York: Prometheus Books.

Michl, Thomas, and Christophre Georges. 1996. "Debt and Taxes in a Marxian Growth Model." *Review of Radical Political Economics* 28 (3): 50–56.

Mott, Tracy, and Edward Slattery. 1994. "Tax Incidence and Macroeconomic Effects in a Kaleckian Model When Profits Finance Affects Investment and Prices May Respond to Taxes." *Journal of Post Keynesian Economics* 16 (3): 391–409.

Neaime, Simon. 2009. "Sustainability of Exchange Rate Policies and External Public Debt in the MENA Region." *Journal of Economics and International Finance* 1 (2): 59–71.

O'Connor, James. 2002. *The Fiscal Crisis of the State.* New Brunswick, NJ: Transaction Publishers.

Pareto, Vilfredo. 2014. *Manual of Political Economy.* Oxford: Oxford University Press.

Parguez, Alain. 2002. "A Monetary Theory of Public Finance. The New Fiscal Orthodoxy: From Plummeting Deficits to Planned Fiscal Surpluses." *International Journal of Political Economy* 32 (3): 80–97. https://doi.org/10.1080/08911916.2002.11042882.

Pashukanis, Evgeny B. 2003. *General Theory of Law and Marxism.* New Brunswick, NJ: Transaction Publishers.

Polanyi, Kar. 1973. "Trade, Markets and Money in European Middle Ages." *Norwegian Archeological Review*, 11 (2).

Preobrazhensky, Evgeny. 1967. *The New Economics.* Oxford: Clarendon Press.

Prodromidis, Prodromos. 2009. "Economic Environment, Policies and Inflation in the Roman Empire Up to Diocletian's Price Edict." *The Journal of European Economic History* 38 (3): 567–605.

Rheingold, I. 1931. "The New Economic Policy." In *Soviet Policy in Public Finance, 1917–1928,* edited by Gregory Y. Sokolnikov and Associates. Stanford: Stanford University Press.

Ricœur, Paul. 1986. *Lectures on Ideology and Utopia.* New York: Columbia University Press.

Sabatino López, Robert. 1953. "An Aristocracy of Money in the Early Middle Ages." *Speculum* 28 (1): 1–43. https://doi.org/10.2307/2847179.

Shmelev, K. 1931. "Public Finance During the Civil War, 1917–1921." In *Soviet Policy in Public Finance, 1917–1928,* edited by Gregory Y. Sokolnikov and Associates. Stanford: Stanford University Press.

van Shaïk, Remi. 1993. "Taxation, Public Finances and the State-Making Process in the Late Middle Ages: The Case of the Duchy of Guelders." *Journal of Medieval History* 19 (3): 251–271. https://doi.org/10.1016/0304-4181(93)90016-6.

von Reden, Sitta. 2002. "Money in the Ancient Economy: A Survey of Recent Research." *Klio* 84 (1): 141–174. https://doi.org/10.1524/klio.2002.84.1.141.

Wray, L. Randall. 2000. *Money and Inflation.* Pennsylvania State University Working Paper No. 12. Pennsylvania State University. https://citeseerx.ist.psu.edu/document?repid=rep1&type=pdf&doi=66fc9c6aea6cb3824f98c636fd04738730fe48f5.

Wray, L. Randalph. 2010. "Alternative Approaches to Money." *Theoretical Inquiries in Law* 11 (1): 29–49. https://doi.org/10.2202/1565-3404.1235.

Wright, Erik Olin. 1975. "Alternative Perspectives in Marxist Theory of Accumulation and Crisis." *Critical Sociology* 6 (1): 5–39. https://doi.org/10.1177/089692057500600102.

Yaffe, David S. 1973. "The Marxian Theory of Crisis, Capital, and the State." *Economy and Society* 2 (2): 86–232. https://doi.org/10.1080/03085147300000009.

5 Capitalism and space

5.1 Theoretical framework

In order to understand, at its highest level of abstraction, why capitalist production is fundamentally mobile in space, in contrast to pre-capitalists' modes of production, we must consider again two theoretical concepts analyzed in previous chapters.

From a dynamic perspective, we have seen that the capitalist system has two relevant phenomena: the accumulation of capital, which naturally tends to grow, and the profit rate, which periodically exhibits a tendency to fall. Intuitively, it is easy to see how these two phenomena can work against each other: the accumulation of capital requires a permanent increase in constant capital, given that it is the surplus of production over consumption, while the profit rate falls, at least to a large extent, as a result of the increase in the monetary cost of constant capital. This means that the accumulation of capital is likely to make the profit rate fall, and the tendency of the profit rate to fall can compromise the accumulation of capital because restoring it can trigger a reduction in the money that goes toward the accumulation of capital. If, in line with Wright (1975), we know that capitalism without accumulation is – metaphorically speaking – a "sick capitalism", the profit rate must, sooner or later, recover so that the accumulation of capital may continue. That explains why Marx posited the existence of forces that counter the tendency of the profit rate to fall without affecting the accumulation of capital (1959, 165–167). While the conflict can no doubt be resolved by curbing the accumulation of constant capital, which constitutes one of the forms of crises (Kliman 2012, 22–27), the countertendencies proposed by Marx are, so to speak, preventive of the crises described by Kliman. In any case, that curbing of capital accumulation, if it is to occur, must be brief.

The crucial force for countering the tendency of the profit rate to fall is, most likely, what Marx calls "increase in surplus value" (Marx 1959, 165–167). In Chapter 3, we noted that if profit, and by extension the profit rate, must be reinterpreted in monetary terms instead of in terms of value, what in Marx's profit rate equation is called "surplus value" should actually be changed to the "difference between productive monetary income and monetary wages (I-v)". Therefore, the force that counters the tendency of the profit rate to fall is the increase in that difference, as a result either of the increase in the monetary income of productive companies or of the reduction of monetary wages.

DOI: 10.4324/9781003458678-5

Therefore:

(a) Increasing capital accumulation causes the profit rate to fall, which can in turn curb the process of accumulation.
(b) This anomaly must be resolved in such a way as to allow the accumulation of capital to continue, for which the tendency of the profit rate to fall must be periodically reverted without destroying the constant capital already accumulated.
(c) This reverting of the tendency to fall entails, among other things, a reduction in monetary wages and an increase in monetary income.

5.2 Translating the theoretical framework into the spatial evolution of capitalism

Based on these theoretical premises, we can now interpret the spatial trajectory of capitalism. Capitalism has been, since its very birth, the only mode of production with global aspirations. The spatial expansion of the capitalist mode of production varied qualitatively over the centuries. Initially, it took on the form of the military conquest of territories from which resources were extracted and to which a part of production was sold. This first stage of the incorporation of the non-European world into the capitalist system was precarious: on the one hand, the conquering of territories did not hinder the subsistence of pre-capitalist modes of production in broad sectors of activity, both in Europe and elsewhere. Moreover, non-European societies had a limited importance as demanders of production. At any rate, in this initial phase (which stretches until the end of the eighteenth century or so) capitalism had yet to come into maturity and, therefore, had not fully developed all of its distinctive features.

When, gradually and in a process spanning from the late eighteenth century to the early twentieth century, depending on the country, capitalism did reach maturity, two forces that we have already identified as distinctive of this mode of production emerged, giving a much greater impulse to the global expansion of capitalism, as well as completely different features.

Capital accumulation alone triggered the absorption by capital of activities previously carried out through non-capitalist dynamics, in a process that continues to this day. First, that process converted agriculture from family production to mass and concentrated production, and created artificial "social needs" to be satisfied with new kinds of commodities (Harvey 1975, 11). Second, the accumulation of capital led to an improvement in production capacity (technical progress). Such processes had already taken place within the countries where capitalism was born, but these countries could no longer satisfy the level of accumulation required. So, in order to reach its objective, capital needed to expand *territorially*, and thus the rest of the world had to be absorbed. Capital accumulation therefore required the absorption of new spaces in which activities previously carried out under other modes of production had to be converted to capitalist production, and where technical developments could be introduced to allow capital to carry out new activities. Thus began the industrialization of non-European territories, accompanied by the transition of extractive activities from plundering to capitalist forms in those territories, even if plundering did continue in other areas.

The global expansion of capital, which has been decisive since the mid-twentieth century, is also driven by a "running away" from the tendency of the profit rate to fall through the expansion of the difference between monetary income and monetary wages. While this countertendency to the tendency of the profit rate to fall is observed even within core capitalist countries, a simple way to reduce wages is by locating production in structurally low-wage countries. Here one can observe the connection between the profit rate and the accumulation of capital as a consistent and worldwide process. Although the accumulation of capital can work against the profit rate, the mobility of capital that accumulation itself prompts makes it possible to find places with lower wages in which to produce, and to restore and maintain the profit rate. Incidentally, this process can be interpreted as a manifestation of dialectics understood as the succession of opposites that repel each other while at the same time reciprocally generating each other: the accumulation of capital causes the profit rate to fall, but at the same time generates the conditions for it to recover.

During the nineteenth century and the beginning of the twentieth, capital expanded spatially mainly by capturing new markets to which it could export manufactured goods and from which it could import raw materials (Luxemburg 2003, 108). But, at the same time, the process of exporting capital began, whether to produce commodities at lower costs, or under the form of credit to obtain benefits through interest and other capital gains (Harvey 1975, 14ff.).

In order to meet its own accumulation needs, as well as to counteract the tendency of the profit rate to fall, that expansion of capital requires a shifting of the production of goods to new territories. Historically, in some significant cases, money holders settled in the new territories conquered. This was particularly so in the British colonies in North America, which later became the United States. In the late nineteenth century, Japan underwent a state-led local capital accumulation process similar to the one experienced by Europe three centuries earlier. In this way, Japan reached an advanced level of capitalist development within a short time.

But all other territories were incorporated into the capitalist system in a way that entailed a distorted integration. This distorted or unequal integration created two great areas: a *core*, formed by the regions where capitalism developed to a certain level of maturity; and a *periphery*, encompassing the regions that were incorporated into the capitalist system at a later time and precariously.[1] Both categories are simplifications: some countries or regions cannot be easily classified in one or the other, and some features, although prevailing in one category, are also present in the other. This classification is, however, a useful theoretical device for describing the global capitalist order. Given that these categories are the main elements in the description of capitalism as a global system, we must pause here and look more closely at these terms to then describe the way in which this spatial restructuring of capitalism occurred and continues to occur.

To begin with, we need to provide a general definition for each concept. The term core refers to regions where we tend to find the people with decision-making power over money, capital, and, consequently, production on a global scale. The term periphery refers to regions that have only a weak accumulation of local capital and where activities conducted by capital are still controlled from the core capitalist countries, mainly through what is known as direct investment (Sassen 1999, 18–19, 96). The periphery is also defined by the imposition on these regions of certain types of production, almost always preventing the development of Department I (capital goods) by focusing trade on primary and consumer goods, thus hindering both production diversity and local accumulation of capital.

Some of the visible features that characterize the periphery are thus the shifting of export-oriented manufacturing processes to the periphery, along with export-oriented, large-scale agriculture, or the concentration of production in only one kind of goods, preventing production diversity and forcing a growing and exaggerated indebtedness (Harvey 1975, 14–15). The shifting of production activities to periphery countries also entails a conversion for individuals, who go from being subsistence workers to being wage workers. The other side of that process entails that management, financial activities, and decision-making are maintained in the core countries.

As a side note to this definition, we need to highlight that money is a social relation that involves human beings, so that considering money as a good entails a *reification*: i.e., treating as a concrete thing (*res*) something that is materially not a thing. But reification also involves a real effect because the people who direct social relations of production (the "owners" or "directors of money") are governed by the same relation, which thus operates as an invisible social actor.

These clarifications are important because the "location" of money (for example, the country where the bank in which an account is opened for payment and collection) is completely irrelevant: that "location" is a fiction, as there is nothing tangible in a bank account. Therefore, what is relevant is the place where the people with decision-making power over money are located and who, through that power, can order and direct most economic relations.

Let us now examine how this process took place and continues to take place. In Chapter 3, we saw that capital "organizes" production. Here we have a concrete example of that: capital determines the incorporation of new regions to capitalism, as well as what is produced and where it is produced. There is a current feature of capital that is key for this process: its mobility. Let us look more closely at this feature.

The introduction of the monetary approach clarifies how capital located in the core countries controls the process. As shown above, and in line with Marx's *M–C–M'* formula of the production process, any decision regarding production depends on the possession of money. Money, which results from the sale of production, is used – as we saw – either for consumption, or for the accumulation of fixed capital or inventories, or it remains as liquid money (money-capital, which is not strictly capital since it is not actually assigned to the production of commodities). When we say that money allows for the accumulation of capital, what it means is that it can be used, for example, to purchase a preexisting company, establish a new company, acquire the concession to operate a mine, purchase land to carry out some form of agricultural production, devote land to mass agriculture production, convert a rural area into an industrial zone, etc. If there are no legal or physical restrictions that prevent money from conducting such operations anywhere in the world, we have that the organization of production can be done on a global scale. The decision to produce a good or provide a service, and where to do it, is no longer limited to a country or a region, and rather can be done anywhere in the world.

Therefore, the mobility that characterizes capital takes the form of *mobility of money*. Such mobility is the result of a continuous process that began with Bretton Woods and became particularly pronounced in the 1960s (Simmons 2003). The question that follows is: are there patterns that determine the location of the people who make those decisions and the direction in which that mobility of capital operates?

Most money holders are located in the core countries, because that is where the capital holders, which control production, are located. The term holders refer to persons who have the power to decide where money goes. The traditional concept of capitalist – understood as an individual who decides over capital and appropriates the benefits exclusively for themselves – must be revised: ownership of capital is now diffuse, but decisions regarding capital are concentrated in identifiable individuals (directors, managers, etc.).

Consequently, the fact that money holders are located in core capitalist countries means that decision-making concerning all crucial aspects of global economic processes takes place in those countries and not in the periphery.

The process observed up until this point starts at the value level (production in the core countries leading to the accumulation of capital and the formation of money-capital) and results in a monetary process (the mobility of money across the world) to generate many value processes outside core capitalist countries, but without changing the place where money holders are located. In other words, while production shifts to the periphery, money holding remains at the core.

The above-mentioned features are what distinguish the core from the periphery: not a country's gross domestic product (GDP) or its growth rate, or its "institutional stability", or mass access to certain services, etc., but the independence or dependence of its production from decisions made abroad and implemented by means of money, as well as a non-diversified and external demand-driven production (both in kinds of goods and in prices).

David Quentin and Liam Campling eloquently describe the global capitalist system (in line with what is stated here) as two "chains" (2017, 45–47). One is the value chain, formed by all the material production processes, with the application of labor force and the generation of commodities and, precisely, value, in Marxian terms. The other is the wealth chain, which is essentially a *money chain*: a system of possession of money that allows money holders to decide what is to be produced and where it will be produced, as well as to appropriate the value generated in the other chain.

But we must introduce an additional element in the monetary approach to the structure of the global capitalist system: if money must have global mobility, there can only be one account money (or a limited number thereof). This term covers not only the denomination of money and the account units of money, but also the subjects authorized by the state or states to create that money. Now, the power to issue money and authorize the issuance of money is none other than the power to create and regulate the money stock. With which we arrive at the central point of our explanation: the current structure of the global capitalist system is only possible if there is a money stock relatively unified and controlled on a global scale. This means that the new global capitalist system requires the centralization of the state's money-stock-regulating activities in the hands of some states or of one or more supranational state structures, but on the condition that any of those entities must have material authority over money matters.

That explains the global function of the dollar and – to a lesser extent – the euro. Both are the account money of states where the vast majority of the world's money holders reside, so that the global money stock must necessarily be made up of dollars and – to a lesser extent – euros. It thus follows that money stock-regulating functions must be in the hands of the United States and the European Union, and particularly of the former. Indeed, when the government of the United States decides, for example, to increase public spending, facilitate bank credit, or exchange circulating money for money tied up in deposits by adjusting interest rates, it is deciding over the money endowments not only of its own residents but also of the entire world. In the following chapters, we will see that this is what explains the concentration of taxation power in the United States and the European Union, as taxation is also a monetary instrument.

Core and periphery are concepts, however, that cannot be considered rigid categories, for several reasons. First, the countries of the capitalist periphery naturally have local capital, and the indirect control that international capital has over that local capital admits degrees. Second, largely as a result of the migration of capitalists and the actions of national states, the makeup of local capital across the countries of the periphery is far from uniform, and cannot at all be considered a homogeneous whole. It is not unthinkable even for a national economy to transition from the periphery to the core. On the other hand, there are geographical areas and human groups within the territories of the core countries that behave, so to speak, in a peripheral manner. Nevertheless, despite these caveats, core and periphery are instrumentally useful categories for illustrating two different modes of insertion in the global capitalist system: areas where groups of people who control a globally mobile capital and impose their conditions on the rest are located, and toward which monetary flows are directed (as we will see below); and areas where people (workers and also capital holders) who, generally speaking, produce, sell, and work according to terms dictated from outside are located.

5.3 Comparison with other theoretical approaches

Having broadly set out the theoretical framework of the spatial structure of capitalism, we can now contrast it with other approaches that share conceptual elements but differ in their theoretical framework and certain crucial explanations. The core-periphery analysis no doubt calls to mind the dependency theory posited by Raúl

Prebisch, who even coined the terms core and periphery (1950). However, the theoretical framework proposed here has an essential difference with that theory, as Prebisch's focus was on the existence of unequal terms of trade, so that it had to do with what in Marxist terms we would call the sphere of circulation or exchange of goods, and not with production. Indeed, unequal terms of trade were and are one of the forms of core-periphery relations, but such relations are not, by far, limited to that phenomenon, as in Prebisch's analysis the underlying division remains hidden. The division of the world into these areas is determined by capital, which unequally incorporates areas outside its original sphere, through trade, but increasingly more so through production, and at the same time through monetary control, an issue that we will address here as it concerns, among other things, taxes. Therefore, it is not merely a matter of inequality in terms of trade, but a general inequality in the terms of incorporation into the global capitalist system. And neither is the inequality an anomaly; rather, it is perfectly consistent with the needs of that capitalist system.

Moreover, I believe that the theoretical framework set forth above can overcome the objections lucidly raised by Charis Vlados regarding Marxist and neo-Marxist approaches to economic globalization (2019). In the first place, the view – which originated with Vladimir Lenin – of the economic divisions of the world as problems between "nations/states" is explicitly discarded: under a political and legal overdetermination, national states are only one instance, which today is subsumed in another broader instance formed by many international bodies (the OECD, the United Nations, the European Union, etc.), with other modes of political and legal instances potentially emerging in the future. What is relevant is that these (accessory and circumstantial) modes of the political and legal instances in all cases overdetermine (act on and are influenced by) the two essential dynamic phenomena of the capitalist system: the accumulation of capital and the tendency of the profit rate to fall, whose protagonists are multinational corporations and not states or supranational bodies, even if these formally appear as the decision-makers.

The theoretical framework set out, and the hypotheses proposed, are even more far removed from the models posited by the neoclassical theory (e.g., Fujita, Krugman, and Venables 1999). While the empirical data used by these models essentially coincide, none underscores the conformation of two structurally disparate types of economic spaces, nor, obviously, the fact that such disparity arises from the different conditions in which they were incorporated into the global capitalist system. The causes of the shift of production to the periphery that the neoclassical models propose also differ in that, because they work outside the categories of Marxian analysis, they do not take into account the needs of capital accumulation nor the tendency of the profit rate to fall, and consider other factors instead, such as the lower costs for commercial exchanges (in the case of Fujita, Krugman, and Venables). But, above all, these mainstream theory models all fail to take into account the fact that the mobility of money entails greater ease for relocating capital, or the organizational properties of production that capital has, or the efforts to expand surplus value.

However, the predictions (although it would be more accurate to call them *ex ante* observations, given that the phenomena were observable before the corresponding articles and books were written) match those made by Marxian economic geography: the shifting of production, particularly of finished goods, to the periphery (Meyer 2004, 5). That is, the observable facts are not refuted, at least for the most part, by these models.

5.4 Multinational enterprises

An examination of the global expansion of capitalism in the twentieth and twenty-first centuries is not complete without a theoretical analysis of its leading protagonist: multinational enterprises (MNEs). Indeed, the capitalism that emerges in the twentieth century is, on the one hand, a mode of production dominated by large-sized firms that tend to eliminate the multiplicity of small and medium-sized production units, as in every sector of activity a few big companies control production directly (concentrating as such most production and sales) and indirectly (setting the conditions of production and circulation even for smaller-sized companies). But these large-sized companies are also, for the most part,[2] international in scope, and very often global. The phenomena observed above, regarding the commercial dominance both of the supply of raw materials and of markets, but especially the ease in shifting and the mobility of production, are possible because these large companies operate in multiple countries in multiple ways (Baran and Sweezy 1968, 14ff.; Suwandi and Foster 2016).

The actions of MNEs contributed – and continue to contribute – to shape the core-periphery relations described above. These are the companies that defined the various phases of integration of the periphery countries into the global capitalist system, as in an initial moment it was then that imposed on such countries their status as raw material producers and complementary consumer markets, and that later – and to this day and most likely into the future – led the changes in productive processes in the periphery. On the one hand, the periphery countries are still raw material producers, largely under the direct ownership of MNEs, particularly in the agricultural and extractive sectors. On the other hand, the growth of industrial production in many periphery countries is a result of the establishment there of countless entities owned by MNEs that operate in manufacture, mostly of final consumer goods.

Moreover, when we delve into the analysis of international taxation, we will find that MNEs are the central players in the phenomenon of tax avoidance: the adoption of practices that, using explicit taxation benefits or loopholes in national taxation systems, deliberately reduce the taxes they pay. Such practices are the ones that have been adjusted, and continue to be adjusted, through the new taxation policy designs furthered by the OECD, the European Union, and the G20. It is important to clarify, however, that both tax avoidance practices and anti-tax avoidance policies are phenomena that are functional to the capitalist system, which are necessarily sealed with a compromise solution, as we will see in due course.

5.5 Statistical evidence

Thus far, we have set out the theoretical construction, which, as noted above in line with Kuhn, precedes all fieldwork. This construction has, moreover, led to several assertions that are refutable in Popper's terms. The shifting of production to the periphery and the dominance of periphery production by capital controlled from the core countries are, for example, perfectly falsifiable factual hypotheses. The challenge consists therefore in testing them with empirical data.

Here we again face the issue derived from the inadequacy of the statistical information available at the national, regional, and international levels when it comes to reflecting Marxian categories of analysis. In general, as we saw in Chapter 3, the greatest difference is between money and value: the difference between price and value at the individual level is translated at the general level (national, regional, and global) into a difference between total value and total amount of money circulating during a given time. To this we must add that, even when Marxian theory uses monetary theoretical elements (such as profit and the profit rate), there is no previously prepared information with which to complete the monetary components of those elements (for example, the cost of inventories that make up constant capital).

Thus, the strategies for empirically evaluating – as we will attempt to do here – the mobility of money, the new tendencies in capital location, and the international structure of capitalist production must employ monetary indicators (because there are no other indicators available), not as direct measurements but as indications, with all the corresponding adjustments in those cases in which a monetary magnitude contains elements that are incompatible with a Marxian analysis. It should be noted that this strategy is not unusual. As observed in Chapter 2, it is normal for a hypothesis to be empirically corroborated using indirect evidence, presupposing one or more causal chains with the phenomena included in the hypothesis.

In very general terms, unequal development was identified as a symptom of the difference between core and periphery. Roughly speaking, we can equate what we have called core with what are classified as high-income countries, and periphery with countries classified as middle or low income, although admittedly these are by no means equivalent concepts. Let us first compare their respective share in gross world product and their percentage of world population (Graphs 5.1 and 5.2).

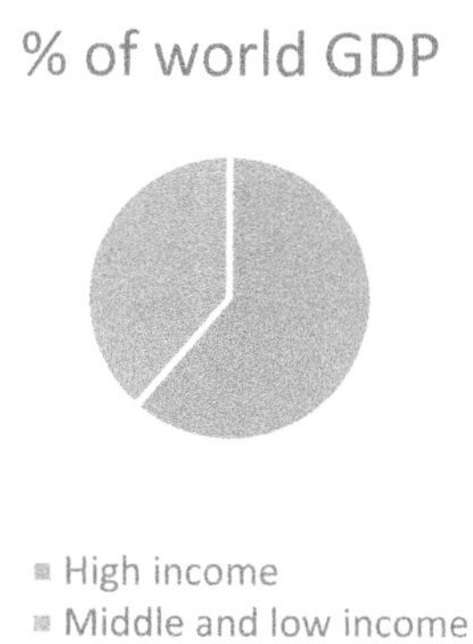

Graph 5.1 Distribution of World GDP and world population (middle- and low-income countries vs. high-income countries).

Source: Author's own calculations based on data from the World Bank available at: https://data.worldbank.org/

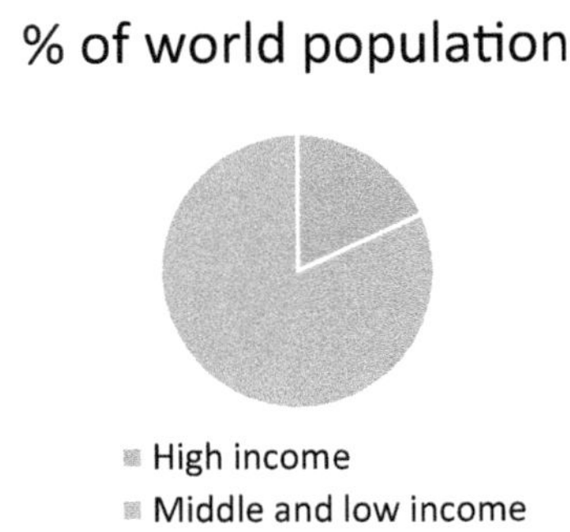

Graph 5.2 Distribution of world population (high-income countries vs. middle- and low-income countries).

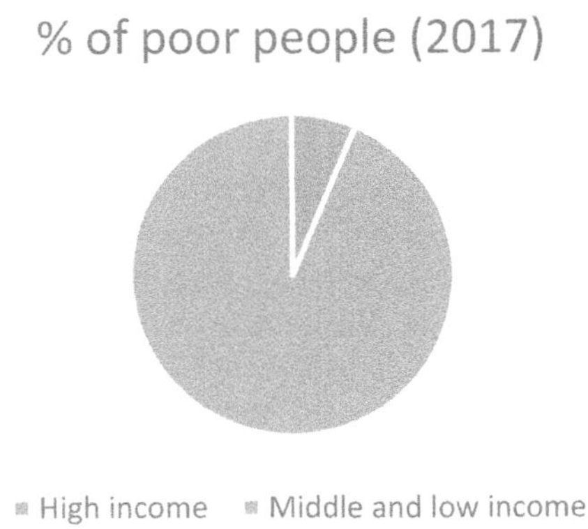

Graph 5.3 Distribution of poor people and final consumption (middle- and low-income countries vs. high-income countries).

Source: Author's own calculations based on data from the World Bank available at: https://data.worldbank.org/

Let us now compare the distribution of the population below the poverty line between the two groups of countries, measured purely in monetary terms (daily income of less than US$2.15), along with the distribution of final consumption (Graphs 5.3 and 5.4).

The above data prove that there is a clear difference in the ways the two groups of countries participate in monetary income. The concepts of core and periphery used here entail not so much a difference in the share of income and welfare as a difference in situations of power and dominance in production. But the profound inequality in the share of world monetary income is a relevant element in asserting that such inequality exists in the control of production. If we have argued that preponderance and subordination are derived from the fact that some people in core countries have control over money endowments that are much larger than those

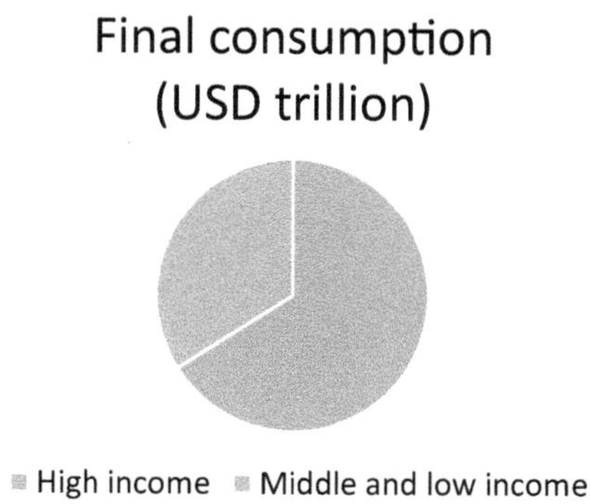

Graph 5.4 Final consumption (high-income countries vs. middle- and low-income countries).

held in the periphery even by capitalists, displaying the gross data of monetary income distribution, poverty and final consumption is a somewhat imperfect but eloquent indicator of that inequality.

We must go further and attempt to prove inequality specifically in terms of production. An initial approach would suggest that foreign direct investment (FDI) could be an indicator for determining if capital has indeed shifted to periphery countries. However, that is not the case. An indicator of money flows for production to or from a location should be limited to: (a) direct capital contributions in productive sector companies, and (b) other forms of control of productive companies under special contractual modes. At the same time, the following must be excluded: (a) purely financial investments, and (b) shares in non-productive entities (for example, holding companies, companies that operate as "cash desks" or management service providers for multinational groups, etc.).

The FDI measurements available, however, do not meet those requirements. Both inward and outward FDI flows and stocks include, respectively, capital contributions received by and made to entities that not only do not have productive activities, but that operate, precisely, as cash desks for multinational groups, holding companies, and the like. This obscuring and partial invalidation of statistics has been recognized even by the statistics working group of the International Monetary Fund (IMF), which can hardly be suspected of having a Marxian bias in objecting to neoclassical statistical data (Borga 2021, 3).

In any case, this distorted way of measuring investment is presumably more effective from the perspective of core countries in terms of both outward and inward flows: outward flows from core countries most likely contain a significant portion of that "false investment", as do inward flows, since presumably many of them are the headquarters of non-productive entities that are part of MNEs. A major evidence of this is provided by OECD statistics, where Luxembourg features as a relevant recipient of FDI from other OECD countries, in contrast to the evolution of that country's production. Let us look at the data for the United States,

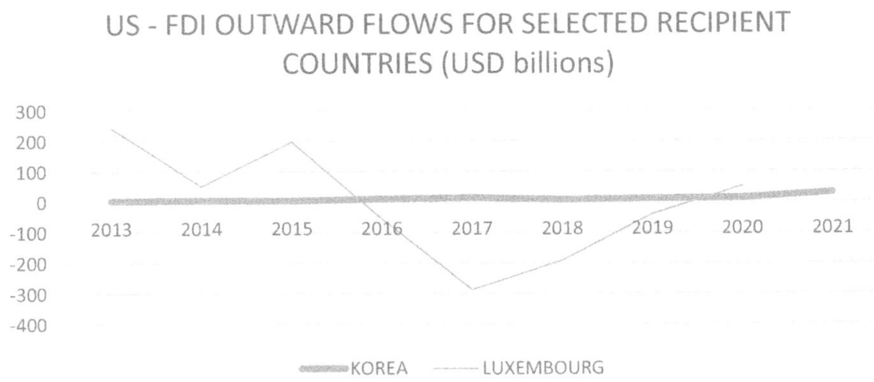

Graph 5.5 US Foreign Direct Investment for selected countries (Luxembourg and South Korea).

Source: Author's own calculation on OCDE FDI Statistics. Available at: https://data.oecd.org/fdi/outward-fdi-stocks-by-partner-country.htm#indicator-chart

comparing net flows (i.e., the difference between FDI outward flows minus FDI returns) of that country relative to Luxembourg and relative to South Korea, which is plausibly the country in which inward flows from the United States are mostly productive in nature (Graph 5.5).

Let us now compare the evolution of GDP for Luxembourg and South Korea in the same period (Graph 5.6).

According to these graphs, South Korea's GDP is over one hundred times greater than that of Luxembourg, but in certain periods, Luxembourg received more than one hundred times more FDI from the United States than South Korea did. Moreover, US FDI in Luxembourg saw dramatic swings, going abruptly from

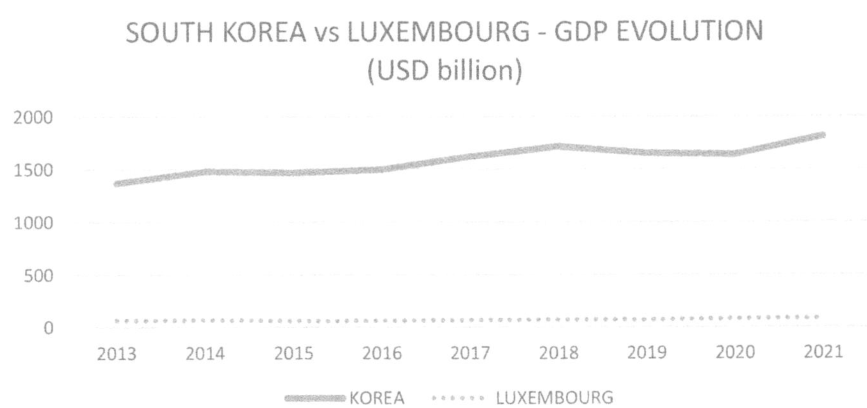

Graph 5.6 Luxembourg and South Korea GDP comparative evolution.

Source: Authors's own calculaions on World Bank. Available at: https://data.worldbank.org/indicator/NY.GDP.MKTP.CD

a significantly positive balance to a significantly negative one from one year to the next before returning to a positive balance. It is thus obvious that, at least with respect to Luxembourg, FDI measurements bear no relation to the transfer of capital from the United States to that country for productive purposes. That is, setting aside its monetary nature and, therefore, its necessarily indirect nature in the empirical validation of Marxian theoretical relations, in general, FDI has a high degree of contamination that prevents us from considering it as an absolute indication of the destination of money as controller of production.

However, for a certain group of cases, FDI data could serve as a relevant indication of the mobility of capital and the shift of production to the periphery. Let us consider, for example, FDI inward flows of middle- and low-income countries, according to data from the World Bank. Again, we must note here that the classification of countries according to "income" is merely an imperfect indication of their location as either core or periphery, which we adopt in the absence of a more accurate indicator.

With that caveat, let us look at the evolution of net inward flows in that group of countries:

We have to assume that, as with all FDI-related information, the data is contaminated by "false investments", that is, by capital contributions to entities that do not perform productive activities, and other similar cases. But since this applies to both inward and outward flows, in broad numbers we can assume that the large difference in favor of inward flows is a strong indication of money flows to low-income countries, which means – in terms of the labor theory of value – that this money is largely converted into capital in those countries, and therefore that production is incorporated into companies controlled from (plausibly) core countries.

Another interesting piece of data is the value added derived from industrial production, as a percentage of GDP. While, again, we know that the available statistics are monetary expressions and not expressions of value in a theoretical sense (so that "value added" is a misleading expression), we can take that value added as a sign of the contribution of the industrial production of said groups of countries, with the same simplistic equivalences (high income = core; middle and low income = periphery) (Graph 5.7).

The World Bank does not have data from before 1997 for high-income countries, but, in the comparable period, it is evident that in monetary terms the percentage of industrial value added in high-income countries is less than the percentage in middle- and low-income countries, and tends to decrease. In middle- and low-income countries, for their part, industrial value added has remained more or less stable for the last four decades or so at around 34–35 percent of GDP. Assuming that industrial activity is more intensive in the use of labor force, especially in the production of final consumption goods, the graph suggests a shift of industrial production in that sector (Marx's Department II) to periphery countries.

Although conducted two decades ago, a study by Jorg Meyer (2004, 11) that analyzed a group of 34 countries from the core and the periphery, also focusing on industrial production, yielded findings that support the hypotheses posited in this chapter. Always expressed in monetary terms, in the period 1980–2004, the share

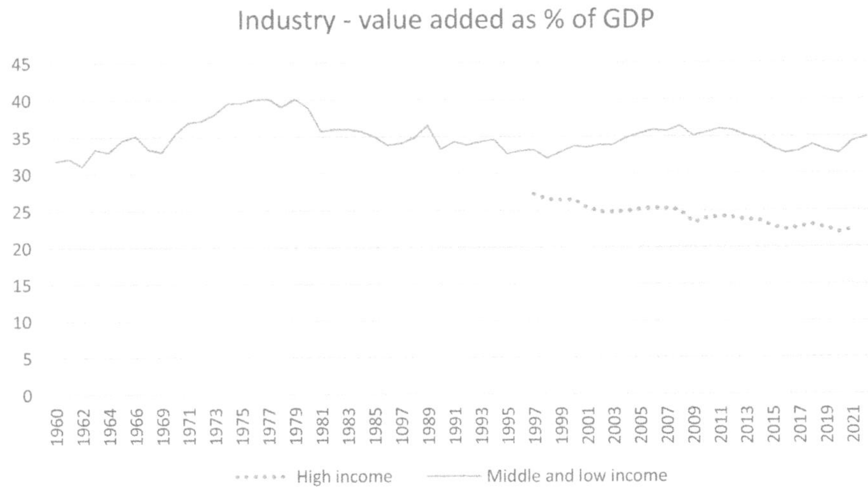

Graph 5.7 Middle- and low-income countries – Net Foreign Direct Investment flows.

Source: Author's own calculations based on data from the World Bank available at https://data.worldbank.org/indicator/NV.IND.TOTL.ZS?locations=XD

of industrial product exports in the total exports of the core countries fell from 90.4 percent to 76 percent in total export prices, and from 90.1 percent to 87.7 percent in "value added" of exports. For that same period, in the selected periphery countries, the percentage of exported industrial goods over total exports went from 8.3 percent to 22.8 percent in total prices and from 8.6 percent to 11.6 percent in "value added" of exports.

If measurements were made in terms of labor value (pondered worked hours) instead of in terms of monetary prices, the percentage could feasibly be even higher in the middle- and low-income countries, given that – as we will see below – in the internal operations of MNEs, the entities located in those countries are arbitrarily assigned lower portions of the global monetary income through transfer pricing mechanisms derived from tax laws. Consequently, everything suggests that the monetary expression of industrial production has a bias in favor of core countries, and that if pondered worked hours were to be considered, a much stronger shift to the periphery would be observed.

Another statistical information that, on the surface, could be considered relevant is the Country-By-Country-Reporting (CbCR) data, required by the OECD under Action 13 of the Base Erosion and Profit Shifting (BEPS) Action Plan (OECD 2015). In application of this OECD recommendation, member states receive global activity reports from MNEs whose management is located in their territories. The information only covers MNEs with an annual income of €750 million or more, but that would not be an obstacle for considering the consolidated data as an indication of the global organization of production. However, there is another, more important problem.

The country-by-country distribution of the income of each MNE is expressed in monetary units, which are ultimately the sum of the monetary prices attributed to each entity in the group. If we interpret these data with the difference between value and price, we will see that the monetary distribution of income between the links of the international value generation chain gives us a distorted view of the weight of the work carried out in the world's periphery to generate the profits of the MNEs. As we saw in the relevant section, the amount of human work is an objective fact, measurable in hours of effort, and it is what ultimately determines the value of the final commodities. The part of the total price of commodities that MNEs attribute internally to each country is determined through an accounting operation, which is done for the most part arbitrarily with the purpose of reporting to taxation authorities, especially when it is done according to transfer pricing rules, which domestic tax laws and relevant international treaties adopt by influence of the OCDE.

Leaving aside the monetary prices reported in the CbCR, we could consider the number of workers employed in each country, a piece of information that MNEs must include in the CbCR. This information, however, also has a serious limitation: the CbCR information does not distinguish between the types of activity included, providing instead global amounts for all of the MNEs in the country, so that the number of workers per country includes both those employed in the productive sector and those employed in the financial sector.

In order for the CbCR information to shed light on my hypotheses of a shift in production from the core to the periphery, in terms of labor value, we must: (a) separate, within said reports, productive MNEs from those in the financial sector; and (b) identify within the group of productive MNEs, the amount of work localized in the core and the amount localized in the periphery, at least in terms of number of workers, assuming that the number of hours worked, and more so the hours of socially necessary labor, are impossible to access at this time. That analysis is not possible either for researchers in general, as neither the OCDE nor its member states have that information so openly available to the public in general.

However, a statistical study along those lines was conducted in Italy regarding the CbCR available to that country's taxation authorities (Santomartino, Bratta, and Acciari 2022). Briefly, the study found that MNE "activities" are concentrated in high-income countries. Naturally, this assertion is based exclusively on the monetary income attributed according to transfer pricing rules, and is therefore distorted in labor-value terms, as it does not take into account the application of labor. Nevertheless, the study provides two important findings: (a) middle-income countries (which we could roughly equate with the periphery) are very relevant in terms of employment, which means that MNEs use a lot of labor in those countries; and (b) in manufacturing and other labor-intensive activities, MNEs have a significant presence in low-income countries (which we can also roughly consider as being in the periphery). These findings are consistent with the hypotheses posited in this chapter: the shift in material production, and specifically the use of labor, to the periphery, and the concentration of money holding in the core.

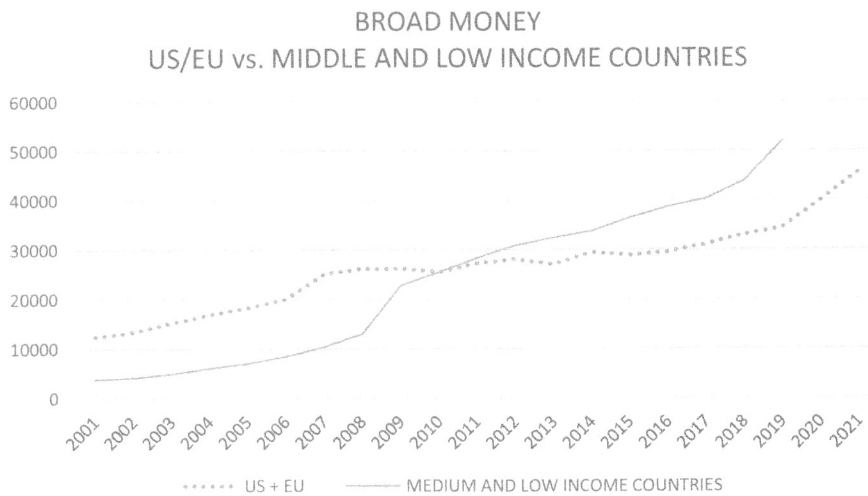

Graph 5.8 Broad Money. US/EU vs. Low- and middle-income countries.

Sources: World Bank, for the United States and middle- and low-income countries, available at: https://data.worldbank.org/indicator/FM.LBL.BMNY.GD.ZS; European Central Bank, for the European Union, available at: https://www.ecb.europa.eu/press/pdf/md/ecb.md2312_annex~3644982b1b.en.pdf

Let us look at the evolution of what in mainstream economics is known as broad money, which is equivalent to the sum of state money circulating in the country, plus local demand deposits and foreign currency deposits, in addition to other financial assets. The comparison shows, on the one hand, the sum of the concept for the United States and the European Union, and, on the other, middle- and low-income countries (as classified by the World Bank), with all the reservations noted (Graph 5.8).

On the surface, it would appear that money holdings have been inverted and the periphery countries (which, with all the caveats indicated, are middle- and low-income countries) have overtaken the United States and Europe. However, that impression is shattered when we realize that in periphery countries a pronounced dollarization of deposits has occurred, a phenomenon identified repeatedly over decades by studies commissioned by the World Bank (Honohan and Shi 2000) and the IMF (Bannister, Gardberg, and Turunen 2018). That is, the money in periphery countries is only partially account money of those states, and a growing portion of it is made up of account money of the United States, thus confirming the dollar conversion into world account money exclusively. But above all, these statistics provide no information regarding the owners of the money, which – as we saw in Chapter 3 – is the most important piece of information for determining who controls production, given that it does not matter where we arbitrarily consider it to be localized. For example, it is an artifice to consider as broad money of periphery countries the deposits or circulating money statistically located in periphery countries but actually owned by MNEs.

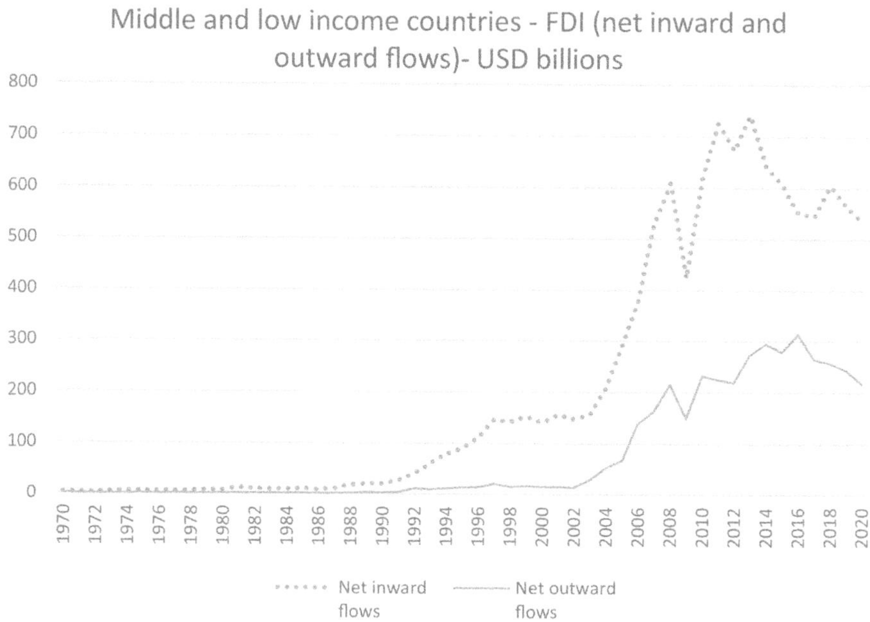

Graph 5.9 Distribution of population. Low- and middle-income countries vs. high-income countries.

Source: Author's own calculations based on World Bank data, available at: https://data.worldbank.org/indicator/BX.KLT.DINV.CD.WD?locations=XO

Incidentally, if we combine the data on broad money with the graph of FDI inward and outward flows of medium and low-income countries (see Graph 5.7 above), which are only one of the components of the balance of payments of countries, it is feasible that a significant part of the dollar deposits in the periphery are – directly or indirectly – owned by residents of core countries (Graph 5.9).

5.6 By way of synthesis

In sum, we can consider the following hypotheses as reasonably well supported:

(a) The global capitalist system has been historically organized in terms of core and periphery regions, which until the mid-twentieth century were determined by unequal terms of trade and today – while such unequal terms persist – are determined by the shift to the periphery of the bulk of production, particularly industrial, extractive, and agricultural production, with the core retaining ownership of great masses of money, and hence, the decision-making power regarding when and where capital is formed, whether to shift it from one place to another, and what is produced and how much is produced, as well as how much labor force to use, and at what price, etc.

(b) MNEs are the leading players in this shifting of production to the periphery, with control maintained in the core countries.

(c) Both the shifting and the control of production are possible through money, the possession of which enables the purchase of capital (both inanimate and human), and its location and relocation as desired.

(d) Marxian economic geography explains that phenomenon as a reaction to the tendency of the profit rate to fall and the need to continue with the process of accumulation of capital, although hypothesis (a) is also accepted by studies conducted under the neoclassical theoretical framework.

Notes

1 The terms core and periphery stem from the dependency approach, a mid-twentieth century non-Marxian explanation of unequal development (Kiljunen 1986, 109ff.).

2 Certain large-sized companies do not fall under this category because, due to their very nature, they are purely national in scope. This is the case of certain companies – often state-owned – that generate energy, supply water, or provide telecommunications services.

References

Bannister, Geoffrey J., Malin Gardberg, and Jarkko Turunen. 2018. *Dollarization and Financial Development.* IMF Working Paper. Washington, DC: International Monetary Fund. https://www.imf.org/en/Publications/WP/Issues/2018/09/11/Dollarization-and-Financial-Development-46164.

Baran, Paul, and Paul Sweezy. 1968. *Monopoly Capital. An Essay on the American Economic and Social Order.* New York: Monthly Review Press.

Borga, Maria. 2021. "Challenges in Measuring FDI: Addressing them in the Update of BPM6." Presentation at a parallel event of the Eleventh Meeting of the Statistical Conference of the Americas of ECLAC. Economic Commission for Latin America and the Caribbean (ECLAC). https://www.cepal.org/sites/default/files/events/files/challenges-measuring-fdi-maria-borga-fmi.pdf.

Fujita Masahisa, Paul Krugman, and Anthony J. Venables. 1999. *The Spatial Economy: Cities, Regions and International Trade.* Cambridge, MA and London: MIT Press.

Harvey, David. 1975. "The Geography of Capitalist Accumulation: A Reconstruction of the Marxian Theory." *Antipode* 7(2): 9–21. https://doi.org/10.1080/08911916.1997.11643946.

Honohan, Patrick, and Anqing Shih. 2000. *Deposit Dollarization and the Financial Sector in Emerging Economies.* Washington, DC: Development Research Group, The World Bank. https://documents1.worldbank.org/curated/es/688721468766211450/123523322_20041117161053/additional/multi0page.pdf.

Kiljunen, Kimmo. 1986. "The International Division of Industrial Labour and the Core-Periphery Concept." *CEPAL Review* 30: 97–115.

Kliman, A. 2012. *The Failure of Capitalist Production.* New York: Pluto Press.

Luxemburg, Rosa. 2003. *The Accumulation of Capital.* London: Routledge.

Marx, Karl. 1959. *Capital. A Critique of Political Economy.* Vol. 3. New York: International Publishers.https://www.marxists.org/archive/marx/works/download/pdf/Capital-Volume-III.pdf.

Meyer, Jörg. 2004. *Industrialization in Developing Countries. Some Evidences from a New Economic Geographic Perspective*. UNCTAD Discussion Paper No. 174. Geneva: United Nations Conference for Trade and Development (UNCTAD). https://unctad.org/system/files/official-document/osgdp20048_en.pdf.

OECD. 2015. Transfer Pricing Documentation and Country-by-Country Reporting. Action 13. Final Report 2015. OECD/G20 Base Erosion and Profit Shifting Plan.

Prebisch, Raúl. 1950. *The Economic Development of Latin America and Its Principal Problems.* Lake Success, New York: United Nations Department of Economic Affairs, Economic Commission for Latin America (ECLA). https://repositorio.cepal.org/bitstream/handle/11362/30088/S4900192_en.pdf.

Quentin, David, and Liam Campling. 2017. "Global Inequality Chains: Integrating Mechanisms of Value Distribution into Analyses of Global Production." *Global Networks* 18 (1): 33–56. https://doi.org/10.1111/glob.12172.

Santomartino, Vera, Barbara Bratta, and Paolo Acciari. 2022. "Analysing MNEs Structure and Activities Using Country-by-Country Reports. Evidence from the Italian Dataset." *Transnational Corporations Journal* 29 (2). 000-000

Sassen, Saskia. 1999. *The Mobility of Labor and Capital.* Cambridge: Cambridge University Press.

Simmons, Beth A. 2003. "The Internationalization of Capital. In *Continuity and Change in Contemporary Capitalism,* edited by Herbert Kitschelt, Peter Lange, Gary Marks, and John D. Stephens, 36–69. New York: Cambridge University Press.

Suwandi, Intan and John Bellamy Foster. 2016. "Multinational Corporations and the Globalization of Monopoly Capital: From the 1960s to the Present." *Monthly Review* 68 (3): 114–131. https://doi.org/10.14452/MR-068-03-2016-07_9.

Vlados, Charis. 2019. "Notes on the Main Analytical Insufficiencies of the Marxist Theoretical Tradition for the Comprehension of the Contemporary Global Economy." *Journal of Economic and Social Thought,* 6 (3): 132–155.

Wright, Erik Olin. 1975. "Alternative Perspectives in Marxist Theory of Accumulation and Crisis." *Critical Sociology* 6 (1): 5–39. https://doi.org/10.1177/089692057500600102.

6 Taxation and space

Hypotheses and theoretical discussion

6.1 The hypotheses

Having set out the theoretical framework in the preceding chapters, we can now say that rather than speaking of "international taxation", it would be more fitting to speak of "taxation and space" in mercantile economies and, in particular, in capitalism. As with all other components of the state, such as its administrative institutions, its conflict resolution system, and its military apparatus, taxation has specific spatial profiles in line with the modality of accumulation of space of the mode of production of which it forms part.

Therefore, the spatial trajectories of the modes of production, and the state forms to which they give rise, also determine what we could more rigorously call taxation from a spatial or geographical perspective.

We know that taxation is inextricably linked to two other social phenomena: money and the state. We also know that all three are associated with mercantile modes of production: money, because it is what enables the emergence of commodities; the state, because it is what creates and regulates money; and taxation, because, along with public spending and public debts, it is one of the concrete regulatory instruments through which the state creates and manages the volume and distribution of money so that it can perform its economic function.

Moreover, as established in previous chapters, money plays a much greater leading role under capitalism than under precapitalist economies. In the first place, because it enables large-scale exchanges, but secondly, and more importantly, because the formation of capital and its incessant accumulation, which are distinctive features of capitalism, are not possible unless money is constantly growing. In addition, profit and the profit rate, which are instrumental in defining the course of capitalism, are purely monetary phenomena.

These premises entail that, in capitalism, public finances are a field that determines, through money, the fundamental conditions for production to continue with the typical features of that mode of production, namely, the labor force as a commodity, the generation of surplus value, incessant accumulation, etc.

In Chapter 5, we also saw that capitalism has special ways of relating to territory ways that have evolved over time, but which have the following common features: (a) expansion, so that capitalism links all of global production in its system, first through plundering and/or exchange, even with regions outside capitalism, and

DOI: 10.4324/9781003458678-6

then by implanting the capitalist mode of production as such in regions that were until then outside that mode; (b) disparity in the conditions of incorporation into the global capitalist system, generating two regions that we have called – roughly speaking – core and periphery; and (c) the use of space and, in particular, of that spatial disparity, as an instrument for maintaining capital accumulation as a growing process and reversing the tendency of the profit rate to fall.

As in every internal process of capitalism, money is always the vehicle for all of these phenomena and processes to take place. Furthermore, the global expansion of capitalism, especially when it also reaches production, entails the progressive emergence of a global money stock. "Global" means that, as the functions of money must be performed throughout the planet, there can only be one (or a few) account moneys in the world: the US dollar and – to a lesser extent – the euro, and also that such money must be completely mobile.

These special properties that money acquires in order to fully respond to the requirements of the global capitalist system mean that the total volume of money and the way in which it is distributed can no longer be left in the hands of national states, and rather demand a supranational and, ultimately, global control. The core-periphery structure is broken down into two chains that run in opposite directions, but which are perfectly consistent: a value chain, whose center of gravity shifts to the periphery (toward which production is directed), and a money chain, whose center of gravity is located in the core countries. While value, being the result of production, derives from the first chain, control is exercised by the money chain, since it is money that turns goods into capital, moves capital from one place to another, appropriates space, etc. It is precisely the concentration of the control of global money in certain places – and not in others – that makes those places core and the rest periphery.

Thus, we can now formulate the general hypothesis for taxation in space: given its money stock-regulating role, tax revenue must be aligned with the money chain and concentrated in the places where money holding is concentrated.

Note that the hypothesis does not exactly refer to the location of money itself, but to the location of the holders of money. This is because money is not a physical object at all; rather, it is a special social relation in the terms described in Chapter 3. The fact that we formally say that there are "deposits" or "financial assets" and such in a given country is an illusion: those "locations" usually refer to the place where the debtor in the relation (the bank that must return the deposit, the person who must settle the forward transaction, etc.) is located, but the location that actually matters is that of the human person that is in the position of power in that relation. Therefore, when I speak of "concentration of money", I am referring to concentration of the persons who control money.

The above hypothesis can be complemented with the following hypothesis: if the concentration of money is spatially unequal, then tax revenue will also be unequal in the same sense as the concentration of money is.

These hypotheses have factual and observational implication. Both must be valid for all modes of production in which money exists, that is, for all mercantile modes of production. In capitalism, in particular, the alignment between taxation and money holding should prove to be much more intense for two reasons: it is the monetary mode of production par excellence most, especially so for today's late capitalism, and its spatial expansion is planetary in scope and creates a profound inequality in terms of participation in production. Therefore, we have that: (a) the greater the spatial inequality in the concentration of money, the more pronounced the spatial inequality of tax revenue will be; and (b) when inequality in the concentration of money is compounded with a greater intensity in the use of money, the spatial inequality in tax revenue will be even more evident.

Pure and unadorned tax revenue is the economic phenomenon itself, because it is with tax revenue – and not with tax laws and treaties – that money is effectively extracted from civil society, with the essential aim of canceling money and potentially generating unequal money endowments among groups of people. However, the tax revenue phenomenon requires several superstructures to prop it up, which is where the state in particular comes into play. We can thus formulate other special hypotheses regarding taxation and space:

(a) The longer the money chain and the higher degree of internationalization of production, the greater the quantity and quality of international legal instruments concerning taxation.
(b) These legal instruments will introduce solutions that favor tax revenue in places where money is concentrated, which, in late capitalism, entails concentrating tax revenue in the core countries.
(c) Similarly, in those cases, the importance of supranational state structures interested in the phenomenon of taxation will be more pronounced, including as drivers of the legal order noted in (a) and (b) above.

As pointed out in Chapter 1, these three hypotheses are of course not posited as pure questions prior to any observation. Rather, the primary verification that they effectively hold true was the driving force for the formulation of the main international taxation hypothesis and, indeed, for this entire research study. However, they must be inserted in an explanatory chain to turn them from simple intuitions or informal observations into consistent pieces in a general theoretical framework.

Before we begin the historical reconstruction of international taxation (in Chapters 7 and 8), it is worth returning briefly to the discussion reproduced in Chapter 2 regarding the relations between the mode of production and the so-called superstructures. As seen in previous chapters when addressing the two special characteristics of the mercantile and capitalist economy – which are taxation and space – it is an epistemological mistake to assert that superstructures are passive phenomena, and it would be more correct to speak of an "overdetermination" (a back and forth between the base and the superstructure). In this case, the relations between the mode of production and space determine, through money, a specific evolution of tax revenue, which must be materialized in certain institutional, legal, and ideological structures. But it is these structures that determine that the necessary and functional phenomenon (the alignment of tax revenue with money concentrations) actually occurs.

The historical reconstruction method thus involves, in most cases, an observation of the superstructures – which is, in turn, indirect and mediated – but not of the material and economic phenomenon of taxation, which is tax revenue. Therefore, legal structures and thinking about taxation indicate orientations that, if aligned with the hypotheses set out above, should have as a correlation spatial shifts in tax revenue parallel to the shifts in money holding.

In Chapter 9, the above hypotheses will be contrasted with two types of evidence. First, I will analyze legal texts (domestic laws and treaties) from a recent historical perspective (the last few decades), in what is also a form of historical reconstruction, but without the mediation of prior texts loaded with meanings given by previous authors (as is the case in Chapters 7 and 8). It instead involves direct observation and systematization of the legal texts themselves. Second, I will use available statistical information with the same limitations that have been pointed out throughout the book, namely, the fact that they are produced under the neoclassical paradigm and, therefore, they are considered indirect evidence of the proposed hypotheses.

6.2 Theoretical discussion

The hypotheses are an extension of the theory of taxation set out in Chapter 4. More specifically, if taxation has a money-stock-regulating role at the national level, it also has it on a global scale, more so at a time in which money can be easily moved to satisfy the expansion of material production to the periphery. The hypotheses also assume, as noted, that both the flow of money as well as its reflux through tax revenue (among other instruments) are state functions, which explains the creation of state structures that are supranational, such as the OECD, but which do not hinder, and rather reinforce, the regulatory power of national states, in particular of the United States.

More generally, the hypotheses assume that tax revenue is a phenomenon that is strictly functional to the capitalist economy, even when it may not coincide with the specific interests of each individual capitalist. While all individual capitalists certainly want to increase their money endowments – and tax revenue distributes them – the capitalist system as a whole could not survive unless tax revenue was permanently canceling masses of money launched into circulation by states and banks.

These hypotheses have a strong component that is critical of international taxation policies designed by the OECD, the G20, and the European Union, but they differ from others that also object to the prevailing global trends in taxation.

The fundamental difference with Laurens van Appeldoorn (2019) lies in the theoretical explanation of the global capitalist system. Van Appeldoorn employs the same informal and intuitive theory of value that, as we will see below, is invoked in the literature on which the OECD grounds its proposals, and which is a somewhat rough version of the neoclassical theory of remuneration of productive factors. According to that theory, value – which under that conception coincides with the monetary prices at which a good or service is sold to an independent third party (that is, without considering the internal operations of an MNE) – is generated in equal measure in intangible assets, material production as such, logistics and transportation, etc., so that the distribution of that "value" between the national entities of an MNE is factually correct, and, therefore, the system of distribution of tax revenue derived from transfer pricing schemes is rational. These schemes are, however, unfair, according to van Appeldoorn, because they take tax revenue away from low-income countries in which MNEs operate, depriving them of resources that they could use to improve the quality of life of their workers. For van Appeldoorn, "exploitation" simply means taking advantage of low wages in poor countries.

Here, I instead adopt a Marxist-based description of the global economic system, whereby value is only generated by the socially necessary labor required to produce a commodity, with tangible and intangible assets being interpreted as previously accumulated labor. The only "value chain", therefore, is that which considers worked hours, and the amount of value must only be measured in worked hours. Monetary prices are merely a rate of exchange for commodities, and there are no transfer pricing rules that are rational and others that are irrational; none of them is better or worse: they are all arbitrary and have no material basis. In other words, the OECD's theory of value is rejected here in full for theoretical reasons, not because it is unfair. Similarly, the taxation system furthered by supranational state structures certainly reproduces the inequality that exists between the core and the periphery, but this is not an isolated injustice; rather, it responds to an intrinsic and inevitable need of the capitalist mode of production: the reason for it lies in the need to control the global money stock by decoupling tax revenue from labor, which is shifted to the periphery to counter the tendency of the profit rate to fall.

As for Quentin and Campling (2017), I agree with them on many points regarding theory. As they also adopt Marx's labor theory of value, global production can be interpreted as a value chain, but the links in that chain consist in human labor applied to production. I also concur with these authors in that the circuit of money flows (which they call the wealth chain) is independent of the global generation of value in terms of labor value, and in that the dominant taxation proposals seek to align tax revenue with the concentration of money, not with the generation of value. Where we differ is in that, given the theory of money and the monetary function of tax revenue adopted by me, I believe that the dominant trends are necessary products of the current state of the global capitalist system. As will become clear at the end of this book, this means that I do not believe these tax revenue trends can be reversed without a radical change in the global structure of capitalist production, which does not seem likely in the near future.

The theoretical analysis of neoclassical international taxation, which I will review in the following chapter, has been characterized by the theoretical framework under which it is developed. If we compare it with the hypotheses set out above and with the theoretical framework developed in Chapters 3, 4, and 5, it confirms that these are not merely conflicting hypotheses; rather, they are rival and incompatible paradigms.

Neoclassical theory applied to international taxation is concerned with identifying whether or not taxation impacts past or new investment decisions. The underlying assumption, more or less explicitly stated, is that capital mobility is a positive thing, but that it does not respond to a deeper process of the economic system. The adoption of tax incentive measures, however, generates a tax competition between states, which, at least for some (such as, for example, the OECD itself), can have detrimental effects (OECD 1998). Under that theoretical framework, (national or supranational) state structures are exogenous to the economic system, and their decisions are arbitrary and not predetermined by the needs of the economic structure, so that taxation is also exogenous, both in its institutional structure and in the materiality of tax revenue. For that reason, neoclassical approaches are not interested in finding out if there is an explanation for the tax policy trends furthered by the supranationality embodied by the OECD, the G20, the European Union, and the like.

Under the theoretical framework adopted here, everything changes. The mobility of money is what causes a shift in production, but not just in any direction: the shift occurs from the core to the periphery. And it is not fortuitous, as it responds to the search for places with lower wages in order to reverse the tendency of the profit rate to fall. Mobility, which is no longer simply mobility of capital but of production as a whole, is not a random phenomenon then, but a consequence of a basic tendency of capitalism. State and legal structures, whether national or supranational, and taxation in particular, do not react to these phenomena in a random way, because they are not exogenous, but totally endogenous and functional to the global capitalist system. Therefore, the tendencies in legal structures and in tax revenue can be explained by other tendencies of the capitalist system. The focus of this research on international taxation is, therefore, on underscoring that connection between taxation and the spatial evolution of capitalism. That is, international taxation is studied as such in the framework of a general theory of capitalism, and not from the perspective of the effects that it has on the behavior of companies.

This does not exclude the possibility of investigating the effects of international taxation on the behavior of MNEs under the theoretical framework adopted here, but this will be done based on different assumptions, and – above all – always assuming that what matters is tax revenue as a material phenomenon, and the fact that it can never abandon its essential function, which is the regulation of the money stock. But it also leads to a critique of rival theories, which is fundamentally an epistemological critique, as the comparison allows us to detect key elements of analysis that are usually omitted. These critiques will be developed in Chapters 7 and 8, in the order in which the different theoretical approaches were generated.

There is also a line of thought – which has a somewhat diffuse theoretical basis – that is highly critical of the avoidance behavior of MNEs and, therefore, views the policies designed by the OECD as something positive, since it considers them part of a set of "fair" solutions, although it often speaks out against the compromise solutions and concessions made by the OECD to MNEs (see, for example, Zucman 2015; Dietsch and Rixen 2016; Picciotto 2013).

In this book, however, taxation is not viewed as something positive in principle, as is the case of the positions that promote "tax justice". Taxation is understood here as a phenomenon that is strictly functional to the capitalist mode of production, and therefore has no intrinsic component of justice, redistribution, or socialization. It is certainly true that MNEs have adopted tax avoidance behaviors and that this has created tension with the tax revenue interests of states. But given that taxation does not challenge the capitalist mode of production, and rather, on the contrary, its role as regulator of the money stock is also functional to MNEs, the tension must necessarily be resolved with compromises, since both the tax revenue interests of states and the MNEs' interest in preserving their money endowments are tendencies necessary for the global capitalist system to function.

This point will be discussed at greater length in Section 8.6.1, but it should be noted here that the hypotheses posited do not interpret the shift in the focus of international taxation from avoiding double taxation to combating the avoidance practices of MNEs as two different trends. Rather, these are seen as expressions of the same function of taxation in the capitalist economy, and as confirmations of the central hypothesis set out in Section 6.1: that tax revenue must be concentrated in the core countries because that is where the money holders are concentrated. The traditional focus of international taxation on the avoidance of double taxation – which, it should be noted, has not been abandoned by mainstream theory nor in the legal and institutional sphere – actually entails privileging tax revenue in core states (as will be seen in the following chapters), which is the material effect of the choice of residence as the main criterion for distributing taxation power. The fight against tax avoidance by MNEs serves the purpose of fulfilling that same function: the avoidance practices of these companies are combated not because they are unfair, but because they endanger the control of the money stock on a global scale. The solution, therefore, is to create institutional and legal instruments that reduce these practices, but always with the same effect: concentrating tax revenue in the core countries.

As we will see in the final chapter, this does not necessarily entail abandoning all national or international taxation policies, but it does tell us that if taxation is by definition functional to the capitalist system, it can only act within the limits that that system allows it to.

References

Dietsch, Peter, and Thomas Rixen, eds. 2016. *Global Tax Governance: What's Wrong with It and How to Fix It*. Colchester: ECPR Press.

OECD. 1998. *Harmful Tax Competition. An Emerging Global Issue*. OECD, Paris.

Picciotto, Sol. 2013. "Can the OECD Mend the International Tax System?" *Tax Notes International* 71 (12): 1105–1115.

Quentin, David, and Liam Campling. 2017. "Global Inequality Chains: Integrating Mechanisms of Value Distribution into Analyses of Global Production." *Global Networks* 18 (1): 33–56. https://doi.org/10.1111/glob.12172.

van Appeldoorn, Laurens. 2019. "Exploitation, International Taxation, and Global Justice." *Review of Social Economy* 77 (2): 163–183. https://doi.org/10.1080/00346764.2018.1525759.

Zucman, Gabriel. 2015. *The Hidden Wealth of Nations: The Scourge of Tax Havens*. Chicago: The University of Chicago Press.

7 Historical reconstruction of taxation and space

7.1 Methodological issues

From the methodological point of view, the complementary hypotheses posited in Section 6.1 regarding taxation (those referring to the legal and state structures of international taxation) will be useful for one of the verification strategies of the central hypotheses, namely, the historical reconstruction strategy already applied in Chapter 4, and which can now be included in the qualitative method that is generally known as colligation. The texts were chosen using the scoping review method (Arksey and Malley 2005). Three clarifications are in order here.

The first is that it is a form of indirect verification of the central hypotheses since, with few rare exceptions, for the Antiquity periods no quantitative information is available that can serve as direct evidence, or even as indirect evidence but closer to the fact that needs to be verified.

The second is that, as noted in Chapter 3, all historical reconstructions derive from the analysis of more or less contemporary texts that repeat previous texts, which, in turn, are based on historical sources that are surely, to a large extent, also texts. In line with Ricœur's observations, discussed in Chapter 2, we must bear in mind always that such a sequence of texts involves one or several mimeses, that is, reconstructions that reflect meanings attributed by their respective authors to past events (in the case of sources) and to the texts that came before those reconstructions (in the case of texts about texts). This means that colligation based on historical reconstruction – even though it might be unavoidable as a method (among other things because that is how history as a science is done) – does not deal with past events but with texts in which other people talk about the past. Therefore, given that, by definition, mimesis is inevitable, the methodological effort that must be made consists in analyzing texts that refer to taxation and space in past eras and applying, wherever possible, strategies for identifying the emplotments (again, using Ricœur's term) of the authors of those texts. Nonetheless, and as we saw in Chapter 4, the accumulation of different texts on the history of international taxation that converge in the same direction will render that body of evidence more convincing by virtue of their volume.

The third clarification is that the inquiry into the international legal and political structures of taxation in search of the biases anticipated in the hypotheses undoubtedly indicates that observation is not neutral, and is rather planned out in the

DOI: 10.4324/9781003458678-7

theoretical framework developed in Chapters 3, 4, and 5. But, as noted in Chapter 2 with the references to Kuhn and Lakatos, this is nothing new, and it is, moreover, a general characteristic of any research.

The historical reconstruction will include an overview not only of the legal and state structures involved in taxation and space, but also of the explanations with descriptive aspirations (sometimes accompanied by regulatory recommendations) that were provided under the mainstream theoretical framework and its predecessors as those structures developed. The reason for this is that explanatory and regulatory discourses – mainly ideological but also non-ideological discourses – illustrate the context in which both superstructures and the material bases of society operate, and, in some cases, they are directly part of the superstructural complex that generates overdetermination. Indeed, as we will see in greater detail in Chapter 11, superstructural discourses are constantly intertwining and informing each other, with ideologies generating political and legal structures, and political and legal structures, in turn, prompting the development of ideologies that legitimize them.

7.2 Taxes and space in precapitalist formations

In primitive communities, each human group occupies a certain area where it hunts, fishes, and gathers, as well as practicing the most elementary forms of agriculture and animal husbandry compatible with original communism. In areas of relative abundance, this appropriation allows for spatial stability, while in other areas with greater variability of resources, the form of production dictates nomadism. There is nothing in this phase that can be considered taxes. In the purest and most archaic forms, given that all production is effectively collective, the simple distribution of tasks does not entail any exchanges, and there is no money and no state.

With the end of primitive communism and the emergence of the division of production and labor, the forms of relationship between production and territory changed, and, in particular, a need to *accumulate space* was created, which entailed not only retaining the space previously devoted to production but also expanding it. This meant that mercantile modes of production appropriated untouched spaces, as well as spaces where the previous modes of production operated. In this sense, however, we must be very careful not to confuse the emergence of certain despotic authorities with the disappearance of primitive communities and the birth of mercantile modes of production (see Section 4.2). A close examination of such cases (ancient Egypt, Incaic Peru, etc.) reveals that there was no system of exchanges, no commodities, and no money, only a more authoritarian organization of communal production. Consequently, there were no taxes, only personal in-kind contributions in the form of work, military services, and the surrendering of part of production to those who vertically organize social life.

When mercantile modes of production finally appear, they do so simultaneously with the state, money, and taxes. The transition to a mercantile mode of production initially involved a group of persons that occupied the same space as the primitive communities, but gradually expanded beyond that space. This territory also represented the spatial dimension of the state, and the spatial dimension of that state's taxation system. In that situation, therefore, there was already a spatial dimension of taxation: it necessarily had to cover all of the territory governed by the state, for only in that way could it ensure that exchanges of goods could be carried out throughout that area and that the amount of money available for that purpose was controlled and properly distributed.

Additionally, traditional historiography depicts the history of the territorial expansion of states as a political phenomenon. In reality, however, that was the external face of the phenomenon: it was actually the modes of production that expanded spatially, according to their needs (for example, obtaining new arable lands or more markets to sell production to), and states, with their military campaigns, their commercial expeditions, their overseas settlements, etc., put themselves at the service of those modes of production to meet their needs.

The territorial expansions of the earliest mercantile modes of production had two relevant visible features: military conquest and occupation and the imposition of the taxation system of the occupiers on the conquered areas. This corresponds to the first phase of the relations between taxation and space: taxation systems and tax revenue advanced insofar as a mode of production – and the state structure supporting it – advanced. Besides their military presence, the tax presence of the occupiers was the most visible sign of territorial domination.

While from the descriptive point of view, this evolution offers little doubt, the emergence of taxation as a specific phenomenon is very different (Valk 2023). Although taxation historians agree that the monetization of the economy marked a profound change, it is commonly believed that there was a continuity between the ancient systems based on personal and in-kind contributions and monetary taxes. As we saw in Chapter 4, there is no such continuity: non-monetary societies with mechanisms for the "extraction" of goods and services are, actually, continuations of primitive communist societies. And as those personal contributions lacked money, they also lacked the distinctive feature of taxation: its money-stock-regulating nature, which it has had from the very moment money appeared.

The next step occurred with the beginning of exchanges between different societies framed in different state structures. Several references can be found in specialized literature to traces of taxation imposed on activities that, while not strictly speaking "international" – as this adjective necessarily alludes to nation-states, which are unquestionably a product of capitalism – do involve a movement of persons or goods from one human community to another. Marilyne Sadowsky (2023) mentions ancient texts that allude to the requirement of special tax treatments for persons coming from other cities in Mesopotamia, as well as provisions pertaining to foreigners in ancient Egypt, and tax provisions in Rome – in both the Republic and the Empire – concerning groups of people classified according to their territory of origin. In the Roman Republic, in particular, the military conquest of new territories entailed Rome's monetary expansion into the conquered areas and, at the same time, the establishment of monetary taxes to be collected for Rome, leaving the administration of tax revenue in the hands of the local communities (Tan 2021).

Rome is a particularly interesting case because it involves a mode of production that had clearly evolved beyond the primitive community and become mercantile, with a state segmented from civil society, the presence of money, and taxes in the proper sense, that is, monetary levies forcefully imposed by the state on an already separate civil society. In terms of the specific subject matter of this book, it is also interesting that Rome expanded across such a broad territory and imposed its taxation system throughout that territory. A significant feature of Roman taxation, from the spatial point of view, was the ostensible distinctions it made based on the recognition of Roman citizenship, or how it granted certain privileged statuses to regions or individuals based on whether they were Roman or foreign. This feature is also present in problems that, in appearance, are the precursors of issues addressed by contemporary taxation, as is the case with the medieval discussions on the imposition of taxes by a city-state or, some time later, by the nascent nation-states, or their embryos, on foreigners.

This information must be viewed within the theoretical framework set out in the preceding chapters so that it can shed light on how it relates to what we call "international taxation" today. Were the phenomena of spatial distribution of Roman taxation the embryos of the functions of our current international taxation? The answer is yes.

In precapitalist economic formations, the most important economic phenomenon in terms of space was the exchange of goods. Moreover, territorial expansions by states meant that more groups of people were incorporated into the respective systems of personal contributions and economic levies, both monetary and non-monetary, and they also often generated voluntary migrations or forced movements of people in the form of slavery, but there were no radical changes in production. Let us consider the case of Roman expansion during both the Republic and the Empire. When a region was conquered, Rome was generally content with collecting taxes and, to a certain extent, enslaving part of the population, with an administrative and military apparatus established in the conquered territory but without the forms of mass production absorption that would later be typical of capitalist expansion (Anderson 1978, 65). This was due to the fact that, with a few exceptions, the territories conquered by Rome were in a stage of development of production similar to Rome's or not too far behind it. Thus, the conquering of territories made exchanges between Roman provinces more fluid and, to some extent, determined the movement of Roman individuals to the conquered territories and the incorporation of new slaves into production, but all in a gradual and non-dramatic way.

The state, therefore, performed its function as money regulator and distributor in a much more limited way than it does today. This was not due to money being privately regulated. On the contrary, and as Wray noted (see Section 3.2), state and money form an inseparable pair, and there can be no money without some form of state control. But, as with exchanges, and therefore with the quantity of money, it was far from being what it would later be with capitalism.

Moreover, while the various societies, and their respective states, were not completely isolated, the connections between them were limited to not very intense exchanges. In terms of space, these characteristics entailed the absence of a true "international taxation" phenomenon. What Sadowsky and other authors identify as such are actually modalities through which states, as they expanded in space, distributed their levies, which were intended to maintain their assets, among the people in those growing spaces. The ancestors of capital were immobile, consisting of non-transportable means of production, and they were almost never expressed in money, so taxes did not need to satisfy very complex requirements in order to accompany the spatial organization of production.

Thus, while the type of production of the Roman Empire was quite different from that of capitalism, Roman taxation and the Roman state played a role similar to that of current taxes and supranationality. Indeed, the fact that Rome had a tax revenue system converging on the central state – even if it left its administration in local hands – reveals that the spatial scope of taxation systems must coincide with the space in which the account money (whether one or several) authorized by that state is used.

Moreover, as noted in Section 4.2, in line with Sitta von Reden (2002), archeological discoveries of coins issued by "rich provinces" of the empire found in territories occupied by "poor provinces" evidence the first attempts at a fiscal (and also monetary) policy. The Roman Empire used the money collected in taxes in the rich provinces to support the military and bureaucratic apparatus of the poor provinces, generating through the tax/public spending complex a veritable territorial distribution of monetary income.

Most importantly, however, while these are not yet international taxation phenomena in the true sense, the archeological findings mentioned by von Reden are the first evidence that supports the central hypothesis posited in Chapter 6: from a territorial perspective, tax revenue tends to be concentrated where the money holders are concentrated. Indeed, that is the conclusion that can be drawn from the much larger existence of coins issued by the richer Roman provinces, where producers and merchants had more money and therefore where the Roman state collected more taxes.

In the feudal mode of production (at least in its European version, which is the one we know best), the fractioning of political domination into small units, and the maintenance of very weak state structures with a great territorial scope, also resulted in the fragmenting of taxation. However, the phenomenon that contributed most decisively to the decline in taxation was the retraction of money, which made taxation's function as a money-regulating instrument less necessary (Anderson 1978, 84). What is more, in places where feudalism was – so to speak – more fully developed, such as in Eastern Europe, the importance of taxation was even weaker (Anderson 1978, 288). This allows for a reinterpretation of the history of the supposed struggles against arbitrariness and toward ensuring that taxes were determined by the representatives of the people who were taxed. Such wish did not arise from the existence of a nobility or bourgeoisie that was suffering excessive tax burdens; rather, it was due to the fact that, because taxes were exceptional and occasional, they were experienced as anomalous situations that were disruptive of normal economic life.

In addition to the decline in taxation as a result of the retraction of money (which is also evidence of the role of taxation as regulator of the money stock), feudalism was an even less expansive mode of production, in terms of space, as compared to previous modes, a characteristic that is reflected in the fact that it lacked the taxation distinctions between citizens, foreigners, and other categories of people typical of the Roman state. Normally, units of political domination did not seek to go beyond their narrow territorial boundaries, and for that reason their taxation concerns were limited to the small portions of territory they controlled. The spatial relations among these political units and the groups of people that produced within them consisted of commercial exchanges, which, moreover, were not large.

It is telling that the "international taxation problems" that Sadowsky identifies as occurring under feudalism had to do with the trading of goods, which were normally in the hands of the city-states that were gradually moving away from feudal production in the strict sense and which contained the seeds of future capitalism: capital, which was emerging; and the bourgeoisie, which was the social class that would own capital. There were, as yet, no concerns over the effect of taxation on money flows because there were no spatially relevant money flows. At most, there were problems connected with the taxation of foreigners who relocated to a different area than where they originated from, which was, undoubtedly, of only marginal importance in the general workings of both the tax system and the mode of production. In short, there was no truly international taxation phenomenon under feudalism because there were no states or nations, and neither was there – as there was in Rome – a spatial expansion of taxation, but rather instead a contraction of taxation.

7.3 The irruption of capitalism: changes in the properties of taxes and the first legal solutions to territorial problems

The transformation of embryonic capital into capitalism determined the emergence of the previously discussed features of this mode of production: the existence of money on a large scale, and, with it, the attributing of certain properties to capital, such as the ease of accumulation, and, also, the conversion of the labor force into a commodity, which, combined with a material base that generated sophisticated means and methods of production, allowed for a growth in production until then unthinkable.

What interests us here is the form of appropriation of space that characterizes capitalism, and its connection with the phenomenon of taxation. While externally this form has changed, there is a feature of this mode of production that is a permanent trait, namely, its compelling and increasing need to appropriate new spaces, which has made it the only global-scale mode of production, as we have seen in previous chapters.

The so-called "first globalization", which occurred with the European conquests of the fifteenth to nineteenth centuries, introduced an initial form of globally expanded taxation, which is often overlooked: the imposition on the European colonies of taxes determined by the metropolises, simultaneously with the incorporation of those colonies into the global capitalist system. An important qualification is in order here: the incorporation of these colonies to the global capitalist system meant in some cases the – more or less perfect – introduction of forms of capitalist production, but in others it was limited to various kinds of plundering (slavery, forced appropriation of local production, etc.) without any capital. Therefore, the implantation of European taxation systems in these colonies was determined by how those colonies were appropriated. Depending on each case, the colonial states reproduced the taxation systems of the metropolis or established *ad hoc* taxation schemes, ranging from no taxation at all to the creation of complete taxation systems for a colony (Selkopf 2021, 68–70). These differences are explained by the close parallelism between taxation and the monetary nature of the economy, associated, in turn, with the degree of maturity of capitalism: the colonies that lacked any form of taxation (for example, some regions of Africa) were simply pillaged territories, while – at the other end of the spectrum – the regions that to a large extent shared the taxation system of their metropolis (for example, the British colonies in North America) were places where money arrived to form capital in the strict sense of the term, and to further a capitalist mode of production.

This confirms our main hypothesis: taxation is present where money exists, given its role as a regulator of money. And, conversely, even when a region is appropriated by a European state with fully developed capitalism, if money does not disembark in that new region and capital is not formed, there is no taxation. In those cases in which capitalism also brings money with it, the intensity and complexity of taxation are directly proportional to the degree of monetization of the colonized society: from cases in which monetization is complete and the colony is almost at the same level of capitalist development as the metropolis, where the former has a taxation system that operates throughout, to cases of precarious implantation of capitalism and scarce monetization, where there are non-systematic taxation structures or very coarse structures. From the point of view of the functions of tax revenue, however, we again see something we observed in the Roman Empire, and which also confirms the hypotheses of Chapter 6: greater intensity of monetization is associated with greater importance of the absorption by the European metropolises of the tax revenue of the colonies. That is an indication that the tax revenue of the metropolis goes as far as the account money of that state. This is compatible with the premise that the spatial projection of taxation systems must go hand in hand with the evolution of the account money whose stock is controlled by the tax revenue of that state.

The embryonic forms of international taxation issues as we know them today emerged in the processes of formation of the European nation-states, in connection with the exchanges of goods between capitalist economies or with the first forms of mobility of money. This gave way to two movements: on the one hand, the irruption of solutions specifically aimed at addressing spatial problems in the legal structures of taxes; and, on the other, the emergence of academic lines of thought, both economic and legal, concerned with "international taxation" problems.

With respect to the former, the direct ancestors of international taxation are the eliminations of the "tax barriers" established by the old fragmentary political units emerging from feudalism, which were necessary for the consolidation of markets and national states. This is a spatial feature typical of capitalism that we have already observed: capitalism not only expands into territories previously outside that mode of production, and moves into the micro-spaces that were not yet under capital relations in territories already incorporated into capitalism, its political units also tend to be larger. In particular, this entails constantly expanding the areas that are subject to unified control with respect to monetary regulation in all its aspects, including the determination of the volume of public spending, the regulation of banking activities and interest rates, and the regulation and collection of taxes. The fragmentation of tax revenue, and of the decisions regarding it, are not compatible with the existence of wide-ranging account moneys, which are, in turn, necessary so that capital and capitalist production are not confined within the narrow boundaries of the old political units that existed under feudalism. The centralization of taxation is thus a necessary step in the initial phase of the relationship between capitalism and space. This phenomenon is not incompatible with tax federalism and other similar forms: political units smaller than national states can be allowed to have tax revenue autonomy, but only to the extent that it is regulated and coordinated by a nation-wide norm (usually the constitution).

The first step in that long path was, therefore, the suppression of the authority that duchies, principalities, regions, etc., had to establish taxes, or, depending on the case, their power to collect and manage them. This process took more or less time depending on the country, but it invariably took place (Kiser 2021, 22–25). Being the country where capitalism developed earliest, England clearly experienced the process of centralization of taxation in the seventeenth century. In Spain, the suppression of local taxation powers occurred gradually, spanning from the consolidation of the national state around Castile to the Bourbon period (Bilbao 1991, 43–46). In France, it was one of the consequences of the Revolution at the end of the eighteenth century. In the United States, the granting of power to establish customs duties to the federal government and the ensuing disappearance of taxes imposed on inter-state trade are the result of the same phenomenon.

Something similar can be observed in the German-speaking region of Central Europe, with the exception of Switzerland (which had its own special political process). The geographical area that would become known as Germany and Austria, with all the reservations that may apply to these terms, entered capitalism without a process of state unification on such a large scale as France, Spain, and the United Kingdom. While the formal demise of the Holy Roman Empire of the German Nation in 1806 is often cited as the turning point in the region's political fragmentation, the truth is that before that date the empire was already divided into a multiplicity of small political entities that had never entirely overcome their feudal fragmentation. While this situation continued well into the nineteenth century, a slow but inexorable process of convergence toward the formation of a national state, in the style of other European countries, occurred during that century as part of the consolidation and maturity of German capitalism.

In the nineteenth century, we can identify several major moments in international taxation. One is the *Zollverein* customs union, which was established through an agreement for the elimination of taxes imposed explicitly on commodity exchanges among many of these "German states" (Jogarajan 2011, 12). During the nineteenth century and the early twentieth century, tax authorities entered into cooperation treaties (between France and Belgium and France and the United Kingdom), and the first truly international treaty for avoiding double taxation was signed, between Germany and the Austro-Hungarian Empire in 1899, between Luxembourg and Prussia and Hesse in 1909 and 1913 (respectively), and between the city of Basel and Prussia in 1910 (Jogarajan 2011, 13ff.). In 1869, Prussia and Saxony signed a Treaty for the Avoidance of Double Taxation that included non-customs duties, and which was later extended in 1870 to the entire Reich, which was by then unified (Hattingh 2017). This process can be likened to the phenomenon of unification of taxation experienced by France after the Revolution, through which the local levy systems were eliminated with the aim of concentrating taxation power in the central government.

It is interesting to note that Germany's processes of national "unification of taxation", and the processes of cooperation in taxation and avoidance of double taxation between national states are, in essence, identical. It is true that in the evolution of capitalism there is, on the one hand, a fracturing of "empires" into national states (as occurred in North, Central, and South America), associated, in many cases, with the formation of local capital. But these political independences can be misleading, as local capitalist structures do not emerge to separate themselves from the global capitalist system; rather, they do so to better integrate themselves into that system. From that perspective, the ruptures in the continuity of the taxation systems of the empires run parallel to the disappearance of taxation particularities in the countries where capitalism was at a higher stage of maturity, as was the case of Germany. And, in every region, sooner or later, taxation quickly began a process, however incipient, of convergence.

These continuous reorganizations of states and taxation systems depended, as they have throughout history, on money. The expansion of capitalism requires the proliferation of "moneys", that is, of account moneys governed by many states, essentially for reasons of convenience and proximity, thus leading to the taxation centralizations already mentioned. But this also entails the multiplication of taxation systems, as each account money must have a mechanism for canceling issued money, at the last stage of the circuit, through tax revenue. However, capitalism is an integrated system: there are not numerous isolated "capitalisms", only one true capitalist system, which goes beyond local markets and states at all times. Thus, once capitalism reaches maturity, the process of coordination of taxation systems begins, alongside the international mobility of money. This is compatible with the hypothesis that the internationalization of taxation actually masks an expansion of the tax revenue of a state beyond its geographical borders when its account money is internationalized: if this happens, only by going beyond borders can a state's tax revenue fulfill its function of controlling the amount of its account money.

Furthermore, and confirming what Marx stated in the "Preface" to *A Contribution to the Critique of Political Economy*, the theoretical constructions and legal structures concerning taxes from a spatial perspective run parallel to the evolution of the relations of the mode of production with space. Consequently, in the following section I will analyze both academic and regulatory proposals, whether intended or actually implemented among states.

7.4 Ricardo and his "theory of comparative costs"

The first articulated theoretical construction regarding international taxation was born, paradoxically, from an explanation that did not explicitly mention taxes: David Ricardo's theory of comparative costs in international trade. Despite only containing an elliptical reference to taxes, already in its initial version, this theory had clear implications for the global distribution of capitalist production (Ricardo 1896, 181ff.) While Ricardo's general argument is widely known, it merits setting out here in order to understand its tax corollary.

Ricardo's starting point, linked to his labor theory of value (a predecessor of Marx's theory of value), is that the profits of capitalists and, therefore, the possibilities of continuing the process of capital accumulation and investment have as variable wages: the lower the wages necessary to produce a good, the higher the profit margin, and, conversely, the higher the wages necessary to produce, the lower the profits.[1] Given that, like all classical economists, Ricardo did not consider the role of demand in the determination of the level of production nor was he thinking of a significant mobility of capital – because that did not materially exist – the consequence of the above is that production naturally tends to be concentrated in those sectors where it can be carried out with lower wages. Assuming an immobility of capital due to non-economic reasons (attachment to the place of origin, difficulties in movement, etc.), the factors that can make a certain place more interesting than another for the production of a good are the other non-economic conditions: climate, land productivity, availability of more advanced production techniques, etc. That is to say that each region or country would tend to produce those goods for which it was necessary to use less labor time and lower wages, and abandon the production of goods that could be imported from other countries where they were produced, in turn, with less labor time and lower wages.

Where do taxes come into this explanation? Incidentally, Ricardo states that this international division of labor and production operates if international commerce is "absolutely free". This basic formula has a theoretical underpinning: the flip side of an absolutely free commerce is a commerce in which there are different degrees of restriction to freedom, which respond – although not exclusively – to the existence of taxes on international sale and purchase of goods. Or, in other words: the corollary of Ricardo's theory is that taxes levied on international commerce hinder the achievement of a natural division of production and labor on a global scale.

In order to better understand this hypothesis, it should be noted that, for Ricardo, the burden of all taxes is shifted onto prices until they ultimately impact final consumption. While Ricardo's hypothesis of an invariable shifting onto prices and an absolute impact on final consumption is, obviously, mistaken, it is the first time that shifting and incidence are identified as phenomena related to taxation. Moreover, although in Ricardo, as in Marx, the distinction between value and monetary price is unclear, by focusing the effect of taxes on prices, Ricardo anticipates the purely monetary nature of tax revenue.

This idea, coupled with the omission of the differences in demand (that is, the naive belief that consumption capacities are the same everywhere), implies that import taxes invariable increase the consumer sales prices of imported goods. Ricardo did not realize that if his hypothesis on tax shifting were correct, the differences in the internal taxation of states could enhance or attenuate the effects of import taxes. Moreover, and as Ricardo did not consider that capital could move easily from country to country, the effects of taxes on the international division of production were proposed only for taxes applied to imports or exports. Despite these omissions, Ricardo's theory is the implicit foundation for taxation policies that, from the twentieth century to date, call for the elimination of taxes on foreign trade, the avoidance of international multiple taxation, and/or the uniformity of taxes among states.

Indeed, Ricardo's theory has a strictly descriptive side: the lack of taxes on international commerce would lead to a productive specialization determined by the other conditions for production in each country. If we add that these conditions are the "natural" conditions for production (something that is only implicit in Ricardo's theory), it is easy to argue that a taxation policy that reduces or eliminates import taxes is desirable, as it fits with that assumption of a "natural state" of production. If we further add that the same effects can be expected from taxes that do not have trade as their taxable event, but which affect prices through shifting (that is, regular income taxes or corporate asset taxes), it may also be inferred that the ideal international taxation structure for achieving a supposedly natural division of production on a global scale is one that tends to avoid double taxation, or better still, one that produces uniform levels of internal taxation. These are, of course, projections or corollaries of Ricardo's theory, not assertions made by him. Nevertheless, these projections are much more consistent and solid than the grounds of the "Bruins Report", which I will discuss further below.

Nonetheless, in this theory we can identify ideological aspects, in the sense described in Chapter 3. The most evident of these is that this theory fails to take into account that countries have different degrees of productive development, both before and after the "specialization of production", and that it overlooks the effects of such specialization. Let us take, for example, a simple case: a country that is at an advanced stage of capitalist development, and therefore has a significant level of accumulated capital and production diversification, and which eliminates all import taxes and enters into a dense web of treaties to avoid double taxation. The capital applied to sectors that, as a result of this process, ceased their activities could be turned into money and channeled to other sectors within the country that are not affected by the process triggered by taxation. In a country with a low level of capital accumulation and limited production diversification, instead, the capital applied to sectors that are forced to cease their activities as a result of a similar process (the elimination of import taxes and the suppression of double taxation) has less chances of finding another sector to turn to once it has been reconverted into money. In other words, with an internationally immobile capital (which is the assumption under which Ricardo works), the "natural division" of labor and production at the international level acts on unequal starting points, and most likely enhances and reinforces them.

This is the most evident ideological aspect of Ricardo's theory, as this effect of exacerbating the differences in the degree of capitalist development can be observed by consistently applying the same theoretical tools used by the author.

Returning now briefly to an epistemological issue, Ricardo's omissions are explained by the degree of development of the capitalist system at the time in which he wrote. His failing to take into account the effect of internal taxes, both on prices and on various types of international money flows (dividends, interests, etc.), is explained by both the incipient and rudimentary nature of income taxes and the limited international mobility of money.

7.5 Alfred Marshall's Memorandum to the House of Commons

At the beginning of the twentieth century, Alfred Marshall presented a *Memorandum on the Fiscal Policy of International Trade* to Britain's House of Commons (Robertson 1910). The content of that report reflects the evolution of capitalism in the century that has elapsed since Ricardo published his work. While still focusing on taxes levied on foreign commerce, and particularly on imports, Marshall's descriptive assumptions differ considerably from those adopted by Ricardo, mainly in the acknowledgment of the existence of monopolies and their influence on tax shifting and incidence.

First, Marshall addresses the international incidence of import taxes, observing that it is a consequence of tax shifting, which is manifested as one or more changes in prices. The second aspect to be highlighted in Marshall's report is the assumption that there are unequal terms of exchange among countries, an inequality that is independent of the taxes that affect goods. The third noteworthy aspect of Marshall's analysis is that the effects of taxation on international trade depend on two critical factors: the degree of monopoly of the producing country with regard to the respective goods and the receiving country's dependence on those goods. From these factors, it follows that a country that can somehow internally manage (dispense with) the provision of a foreign product will be in a position to shift back its import taxes, whereas in a country that is highly dependent on those products, the burden of taxes will inevitably be passed on to local consumers. This also applies to export taxes: a country with a monopoly on production of a good that is highly necessary for another country will be able to impose an export tax and shift it to the buyer country without diminishing the returns of its producers.

Marshall understood that, with the exception of import tariffs that are used to protect nascent industries, in all other cases shifting the tax burden to final consumer prices entailed a reduction in real wages. That is, import tariffs ultimately affect workers. But even when they protect certain industries, Marshall argued, import tariffs still cause a reduction in real wages because, while the industry develops the locally produced goods that are meant to replace the imported goods, the local goods will be sold at prices that are higher than those at which the imported ones would be sold. So the imposition of taxes for protection purposes only makes sense, temporarily, to ensure the consolidation of immature industries.

Marshall's report has several conceptual advances with respect to Ricardo's theory. In the first place, Marshall acknowledges that tax shifting is not a uniform phenomenon and rather depends on the degree of monopoly with respect to a good, thus anticipating by many decades the Kalecki-inspired tax shifting theories. In this sense, Marshall implicitly recognizes the role of demand and, particularly, its lack of uniformity, given that he posits different reactions in the purchase of goods on which export or import taxes have been applied. Marshall did not venture a general theory regarding the global distribution of production, but that is explained by the eminently political and strategic nature of his report.

Indeed, Marshall was not interested in discovering how production of different kinds of goods was arranged or rearranged in the world. He was interested in mapping out a concrete design of import and export taxes for the United Kingdom. In line with that – and here he also differs significantly from Ricardo – for the first time the state's concern with tax revenue appears as a relevant factor for the assessment of an international taxation system, and the development of a purely regulatory proposal of a design for international taxation.

It is important to pause here to make an epistemological observation regarding Marx's idea that knowledge is a consequence of the material base of social life. This historicity of social theory sheds light on the evolution of thinking on international taxation from Ricardo to Marshall: Ricardo did not identify the differences in tax shifting according to the degree of monopoly, because monopolies either did not exist or were still incipient when Ricardo developed his theory, and this had changed by Marshall's time; Ricardo did not address the state's concern with tax revenue because the financial sector was local and there were no large international movements of money, all of which had also changed by the time Marshall wrote his *Memorandum*, which reveals an interest in preserving or increasing the tax revenue of the British state. Given that, at that time, the most significant international mobility of money was still prompted by international exchanges of tangible goods, Marshall's concern was focused on taxes levied on the respective money flows in local terms only.

Indeed, capitalism still had some years of maturing ahead of it before the international mobility of money required global money control measures beyond national state structures.

That is the reason why Marshall deals with the tax revenue of the United Kingdom, in relation to international trade, as something that only happens within that country's borders. This is also reflected in the fact that he views the production of UK companies as a strictly local process since the global expansion of production in the hands of MNEs was, in any case, incipient. It is, in this sense, a unique example, since his conception of international taxation indicates a moment of transition in the global capitalist system and, therefore, in international taxation: international money flows had intensified, which implies that the phenomenon of tax revenue was important as a means for controlling those money flows, but the globalization of production was still not very visible, so that tax revenue with respect to companies operating on a global scale was yet to become a focus of attention.

Note

1 It is important to highlight that for Ricardo a reduction in wages did not entail a loss of welfare for workers, since – again anticipating another Marxian concept, that of "wages" – he measured wages in relation to prices, that is, as the capacity they gave workers to appropriate a portion of production. In these terms, Ricardo's idea of a nominal reduction in wages accompanied by a parallel reduction in prices did not mean a real loss for workers.

References

Anderson, Perry. 1978. *Passages from Antiquity to Feudalism*. New York: Verso.

Arksey, Hillary, and Lisa O'Malley. 2005. "Scoping Studies: Towards a Methodological Framework." *International Journal of Social Research Methodology* 8 (1): 19–32. https://doi.org/10.1080/1364557032000119616.

Bilbao, Luis María. 1991. "Haciendas forales y Hacienda de la Monarquía. El caso vasco (siglos XV-XVIII)." In *Historia de la Hacienda Pública Española (siglos XV-XVIII). Homenaje a Don Felipe Ruiz Martín,* edited by Hacienda Pública Española, 43–58. Madrid: Ministerio de Economía y Hacienda.

Hattingh, Johann. 2017. "On the Origins of Model Tax Conventions: 19th Century German Tax Treaties and Laws Concerned with the Avoidance of Double Taxation." Pre-copyediting version. https://papers.ssrn.com/sol3/papers.cfm?abstract_id=3007067.

Jogarajan, Sunita. 2011. "Prelude to the International Tax Treaty Network: 1815–1914 Early Tax Treaties and the Conditions for Action". *Oxford Journal of Legal Studies* 31 (4): 679–707.

Kiser, E. 2021. Premodern Taxation. In *Handbook of Politics and Taxation*, edited by L. Hakelberg and L. Seelkopf. Cheltenham, UK: Edward Elgar Publishing.

Ricardo, David. 1896. *The Works of David Ricardo.* London: John Murray. https://play.google.com/books/reader?id=V0JVAAAAcAAJ&pg=GBS.PA90&hl=es.

Robertson, J.M. 1910. *Fiscal Policy of International Trade. Being a Summary of the Memorandum by Prof. Alfred Marshall, published as a Parliamentary Paper on 1908.* London: Cassell and Company.

Sadowsky, Marilyne. 2023. "The History of International Tax Law." In *OUP Handbook of International Tax Law*, edited by Florian Haase and Georg Kofler. Oxford: Oxford University Press.

Selkopf, Laura. 2021. "The Colonial Tax State." In *Handbook of Politics and Taxation,* edited by Lukas Hakelberg and, Laura Seelkopf, 64–80. Cheltenham: Edward Elgar Publishing.

Tan, Jame. 2021. "The Fiscality of Foreign Relations in the Roman Republic." In *Ancient Taxation. The Mechanics of Extraction in Comparative Perspective*, edited by Jonathan Valk and Irene Soto Marín, 262–289. New York: New York University Press.

Valk, Jonathan. 2023. "A State of Extraction: Navigating Taxation in Acient Regimes." In *Ancient Taxation: The Mechanics of Extraction in Comparative Perspective*, edited by Valk, Jonathan % Soto Marín, Irene. New York: Institute for The Study of the Ancient World.

von Reden, Sitta. 2002. "Money in the Ancient Economy: A Survey of Recent Research." *Klio* 84 (1): 141–174. https://doi.org/10.1524/klio.2002.84.1.141.

8 Taxation and space

Historical reconstruction (cont.)

8.1 Capitalism after World War I

Following the end of World War I, the idea that multiple taxation of income should be avoided emerged. Even before the Bruins Report – which I will discuss below – a general notion had certainly begun to take shape in mainstream economic thinking, as well as in the economic leadership of core capitalist countries, namely, that an excess or disparate tax burden arising from differences in the treatment of domestic taxes, and not just taxes on foreign commerce, had unwanted economic effects. The normative solutions proposed to address this and their rationale, thus anticipated the broad lines that were to govern both the academic analysis and legal structures of international taxation throughout the twentieth century. This too merits an explanation within the framework of the historical evolution of capitalism.

In the beginning of the twentieth century, the mobility of money – which neither Ricardo nor Marshall, as we saw earlier, had adopted as a premise for their analyses – became apparent. That mobility was not of capital in the Marxian sense, but of money as an organizer of capital. This is linked to the increasingly marked differentiation and influence of the financial sector, to the point that, as Luxemburg very perceptibly noted, it needed to be added as a Department III of the economy, alongside the departments corresponding to the production of capital goods (Department I) and of consumer goods (Department II) identified by Marx (Luxemburg 2003, 65ff.). The maturity of the financial sector allowed for the ownership of money created or located in one place to also be recognized practically anywhere else in the world, through the existence of banks with branches or subsidiaries in various countries, networks of correspondent banks, and acceptance practices for bonds issued by foreign banks (bills of exchange). It should be noted again that money is nothing more than a social relation in which a subject has a purchasing power represented by some kind of symbol, so that the "movement" of money is merely the acknowledgment of that purchasing power in a place other than the place where that social relation originated.

Thus, since the formation of capital requires money, and money can move across the planet, all the necessary conditions were present for anyone with large masses of money to control capital and organize production in several countries at once, or to move production from one country to another.

DOI: 10.4324/9781003458678-8

It is interesting to look specifically at the evolution of the profit rate, which, as observed in Chapter 5, is the factor that sets the course of capitalism, especially in space. As of the late nineteenth century and throughout the first decade of the twentieth century, the profit rate experienced a decline, as Marx had predicted. Beginning in the mid-1910s, and especially after World War I, this tendency was clearly reversed (Duménil and Lévy 2016, 534). Gerard Duménil and Dominique Lévy argue that this reversal is explained by the introduction of new techniques for managing the labor force, namely, Taylorism and Fordism, which did not involve technological innovations, just new forms of labor management (2016, 543ff.). This argument seems irrefutable, but the fact that at the same time – although lagging somewhat behind – concerns regarding international taxation began to emerge, with an unquestionable focus on MNEs, which is in itself an indication that an incipient shift of production to the periphery also contributed to reversing the downward trend in the profit rate. That is, the combined observation of ideological and regulatory movements in the field of international taxation and the evolution of the profit rate confirms not only the hypotheses laid out in Chapter 6 but also those in Chapter 5, which are the basis for the interpretation of the global capitalist system.

As in all stages of economic history, this new dimension of the accumulation of space by the dominant mode of production determined a new phase in the application of taxes. If we limit our analysis to the evolution of capitalism as such, we see that the taxation system, in turn, advanced in line with the spatial conditions of money: as the limits for the use of each account money expanded, so did the state's concern with equally amplifying its monetary control tools, including taxes. It is only natural, then, that income taxes, and especially corporate income taxes, should appear as leading players in the process of international organization of taxation. Indeed, in a context of internationalization of production, this type of tax (which also emerged as a specific form of taxation around that time) is second only to customs duties in the global distribution of money flows. Given that corporate income is the source of both dividend remittances and interest and royalties paid to capital owners located far from the places of production, taxes must also be structured internationally, so that tax revenue may be concentrated in the place to which those flows are directed.

8.2 The Bruins Report to the League of Nations and its theoretical assumptions

In 1923, the League of Nations commissioned a group of economists to draft a descriptive and normative framework for international income taxation (Bruins et al. 1923). This report is very important for the matter at hand because its recommendations are the basis, even to this day, for legal structures aimed at avoiding double taxation, particularly model conventions and treaties, including, for example, the current OECD Model Tax Convention and the huge web of bilateral treaties for double taxation avoidance.

It begins by classifying the effects of taxes on investments as a burden or as an interference or barrier. "Burden" is used to describe the direct effect that establishing or increasing a tax has on a preexisting "investment" (the term "investment" is used loosely in the report, but we can overlook that problem for the time being). Investors are thus said to have an additional tax burden, which will either be absorbed through a reduction in their current returns or result in a reduction of their future returns, through the lowering of the sale price of their investment, should they decide to divest themselves of it. This "capitalization" of the tax determines, according to Bruins et al., that the sale price of the investment (or, shall we say, the assignment of the credit or the sale of the stock) is reduced, as compared to the scenario with no local tax, be it because the buyer anticipates the additional tax cost (in the case of a non-resident), or directly because the tax affects the sale of the assets. As this does not apply to potential local buyers, the conclusion is that the "withdrawal" of foreign investors will cause a shift in capital ownership to local "investors". According to the authors, this will ultimately lead to a drop in potential investment, as the country in question will be limited to the availability of local capital.

The authors also argue that an increased tax burden on "existing investments" will generally raise the interest rate, thus affecting all investment in the strict sense (again, the term "investment" is applied loosely here). The example they give is oblique, because it refers to a foreign lender rather than to a direct investment: this lender will demand a higher interest rate in order to compensate for the effect of the local tax, thus shifting the tax burden onto local debtors. According to the report's authors, this will raise the overall interest rate and, therefore, discourage investments in the debtor's country.

All of this is applicable to non-residents who already have investments in the country. With respect to a new or potential investment, the authors consider that the tax operates as a reason for not making the investment, unless it can yield a return equal to what it would yield anywhere else. In this case, the local tax operates as a barrier for investment. It is only in this second case (new or potential investments) that the authors of the report introduce the assumption that non-resident investors also pay a tax in their country of origin, an assumption which allows them to conclude that the existence of a high tax in a certain country can lead them to choose another country with a lower tax burden. In the case of preexisting investments, the excess burden argument can subsist, strictly speaking, without the introduction of the assumption of a tax in the country of residence of the "investor", although presumably, in the authors' view, the supposed disincentive to investment would be enhanced if there were a tax in the country of residence.

In short, they argue that double taxation results in: (a) limiting the amount of capital available in a country to capital owned by residents, preventing the inflow of foreign capital; and (b) stimulating the sale of existing foreign investments to local capitalists, that is, driving out foreign capital.

8.3 The Bruins Report to the League of Nations: normative aspects

After explaining the negative effects of international double taxation, the report moves into normative territory, with the following implicit question: given the need to avoid double taxation, what rules should be established to achieve that aim? The general premise they adopt is the ability-to-pay principle: the level of taxation imposed on a taxpayer must be determined by that subject's capacity to pay taxes, regardless of the state where those taxes are paid and – this is a significant point – regardless of the tax revenue concerns of the states involved. However, the simple ability to pay is obviously not enough to solve a multiple taxation problem, as the subject is one and the same and, therefore, has the same ability in the two, three, or more countries where the activity that generates the multiple taxation is performed.

For the writers of the report, the problem then is determining which state to connect that subject to for taxation purposes. While they do not pose it as a general statement, all of the arguments they deploy link tax revenue to public spending, which taxpayers benefit from, in one way or another. Thus, the reasons for supporting or rejecting each of the possible solutions depend on an assessment of the extent to which each international taxation rule contributes to the achievement of two regulatory ideals: that everyone must contribute in the same measure in which they benefit from public spending; and that the state must not impose taxes on those who do not benefit from its spending.

The criterion of political allegiance, which would lead to imposing taxes on individuals on the basis of their nationality, is considered outmoded, mainly because of the massive dimensions of both human and capital migrations. The authors quickly discard the criterion of temporary residence, preferring the permanent domicile or residence criterion as more appropriate, given that it means subjects contribute to the public spending of the place where they have their permanent home.

The permanent residence criterion has the advantage of satisfying more fully, in principle, the "parity" between taxes and public spending that the authors of the report consider so important. In this sense, the authors assume that those who spend most of their time in a territory will be the main recipients of the activities of the state governing that territory. However, they do raise certain objections, including that: (a) assets located in the country and owned by non-residents benefit from public spending in the country where the asset is located, and therefore non-residents also benefits from it; (b) imposing a tax on residents even with respect to assets that those residents have outside the country means that – literally – the collecting state obtains "gains at the expense of the neighbor".

They also argue, without really explaining, that the location of wealth criterion is reasonable when determining which state should apply a tax on an economic event. This includes both the state where an asset is located (in the case of property taxes) and the state where the income originates, although they perceptively note that the "origin" of the income – which would later be called "source" – could be multiple (for example, because it involves assets located in one state and activities performed in another) and, therefore, controversial.

In short, the permanent residence or domicile and the location or origin of wealth are considered the only reasonable criteria. According to Bruins et al., both criteria respond to the same principle: the economic allegiance principle. In the report, they go on to posit (with some wavering) four dimensions or forms of economic allegiance: the place where wealth is located (the situation of the assets); the origin of the wealth (the place where the income is generated); the exercising of property rights (but it is not clear how these "rights" are spatially separated from the assets themselves); and the consumption of wealth. The concept of economic allegiance, then, encompasses more than just the origin of wealth, so that it would appear to replace it. This part of the report thus veers abruptly and without explanation with the definition of economic allegiance, as the residence or domicile principle is muted.

To confuse readers further, the authors then separate the origin of wealth, which is one of the various elements of economic allegiance, and oppose it to domicile, which in their explanation had been left behind. It would seem, therefore, that the four criteria mentioned in the previous paragraph are variants of what they had earlier called "location of wealth", and not of economic allegiance, which is instead expressed through the origin of wealth and domicile. This would appear to be the conclusion of the report with respect to economic allegiance, since from this point on origin of wealth and domicile are the criteria used for allocating taxation competence among states.

The authors then proceed to classify "wealth" (a term that, judging from the text, would appear to include both ownership of assets and the income those assets generate) in different categories, opting, in each of them, for one of the two taxation criteria, namely, origin of wealth or domicile. These are the categories that, with variations, persist to this day in the model conventions for avoidance of double taxation and in bilateral treaties themselves, so that it is worth reproducing here in Table 8.1 the categories exactly as the authors presented them:

The way to avoid double taxation would be to uniformly apply the criteria indicated. However, the authors note that there are two limitations to this rule. The first is that, even if such criteria are accepted, they mainly indicate which state has the right to impose a tax, but there may be reasons for the other state (origin or domicile, as the case may be) to want to tax that "wealth". The second is that historically

Table 8.1 Bruins Report – Categories of income.

Category of Wealth	*Preponderant Element*	
	Origin	*Domicile*
I. Land	*x*	
II a. Mines, oil wells, etc.	*x*	
II b. Commercial establishments	*x*	
III a. Agricultural implements, machinery, flocks, and herds	*x*	
III b. Money, jewelry, furniture, etc.		*X*
IV. Vessels	*x* (regist)	
V a. Mortgages	*x* (prop'y)	*x* (income)
V b. Corporate shares		*X*
V c. Corporate bonds		*X*
V d. Public securities		*X*
V e. General credits		*X*
VI. Professional earnings		*X*

Source: Bruins et al. 2023.

states have in fact used dissimilar criteria for imposing taxes on manifestations of wealth, which may or may not coincide with the solutions recommended, and it is not conceivable that those policies would be quickly replaced by the criteria proposed in the report. Therefore, and assuming that the main objective is to avoid double taxation, "methods" to that end need to be established, which means that states will not easily and uniformly adopt the taxation criteria proposed by the authors, or others that may be conceived.

Said methods are, according to the report: (a) the admission by the state of domicile of the tax paid at the origin of the income; (b) an exemption granted to non-residents by the state that imposes the tax when the income is already taxed in the non-residents' state of domicile; or (c) the division of income into portions, attributing to each state the competence to impose taxes on a certain portion.

8.4 Analysis of the Bruins Report

In its theoretical or explanatory section, the Bruins Report introduces a tendency that will later be reflected repeatedly in OECD documents: the positing of hypotheses regarding the effects of international taxation, under an ad hoc theoretical framework vaguely connected with some of the postulates of pre-Marxist classical theory and – to a lesser extent – neoclassical theory, but without a consistent structure, with no bibliographical references that would reflect the use of comprehensive theories of international economy and the role of taxes, and with limited empirical data (although, as we will see, this last characteristic has changed somewhat in the most recent OECD proposals).

These features prefigure what will also be a characteristic of future OECD reports: their ideological nature, in the sense posited in Sections 2.1 and 4.7, as they are discourses functional to the dominant economic structure, which present themselves as explanatory but perform their functionality through biases of various kinds, particularly their reluctance to admit empirically-based criticism. In the case of the Bruins Report, the ideological nature is very pronounced, in the first place, because of the absence of an in-depth explanation of the workings of capitalist economy. When the report was issued, neoclassical theory was already well developed and was undoubtedly accessible to the authors (the works by Marshall, William Stanley Jevons, Leon Walras, etc., would have been known to them, with Marshall having even worked on the subject of the international economic effects of taxes). So it is surprising that they do not use the concept of marginal utility in their analysis of the effects of taxes. Had they consistently used it, it would have led them to different conclusions from those they arrived at, as we will see immediately. The absence of bibliographical references to neoclassical economists such as those mentioned above is, of course, also surprising, especially when one of them (Marshall) had analyzed the economic effects of taxation a few years earlier.

The ideological nature of the document, however, is revealed more strongly by what it fails to say. The first premise that is not stated and is therefore implicitly naturalized by the report is, of course, that the capitalist system as such, and the international structure of capitalism, must be assumed as an unavoidable fact. Similarly, the document also assumes that the incessant and indefinite growth of production is something natural and, consequently, that any taxation policy must contribute to it. As I discussed more thoroughly in Chapter 3, incessant growth (especially when it occurs in a higher degree) is a necessity of capital accumulation, which is a defining feature of capitalism, but not of the economy in general nor of human life. Thus, the ideological nature of the report does not lie in the fact that it presents incessant economic growth as a natural feature (which it is), but in the failure to identify that it is a natural feature of *capitalism*. Moreover, it is ideological, above all, because it ignores many of the consequences of incessant economic growth. The relationship with the non-human world perhaps provides the clearest example of this: the Bruins Report, as almost all documents of that time concerned with economic growth, assumes – by remaining silent in that respect – that all other animals, plants, ecosystems, minerals, and, in short, everything that is not part of the human species, is a kind of enormous raw material that exists solely to be used for human production, regardless of the outcome.

Another omission that is ideological in nature has to do with the "mobility of capital", which is actually – according to the theoretical framework adopted in this book – the abundance of money and the ease with which its holders can move it from one place to another, and organize production on a global scale as they wish. The descriptive parts of the report focus exclusively on the obstacles that taxes represent for that global movement of money, presupposing – but failing to state openly – that such mobility must be stimulated.

The Bruins Report is also ideological in a much deeper sense. Both the omissions and the theoretical errors that were mentioned, and those that will be mentioned below, are functional to the normative nature of the document. It appears to follow a descriptive and explanatory path leading to a normative proposition, but in reality, the profound weakness of its pseudo explanations reveals that they are not explanations at all but specially created discourses to justify a normative proposal that has a life of its own. The normative part of the report has, of course, a descriptive rationale, but one that is omitted: it was necessary to create an international and domestic normative current that would adjust tax revenue in space to the new conditions under which money ownership was exercised in the global capitalist system.

As already mentioned, the Bruins Report has major theoretical weaknesses, which I will address here. In the first place, it should be noted that these are very obvious errors, and most are errors even from the perspective of mainstream economic thought. One very evident one is the proposition that the effect that a new tax (on income or assets, presumably) has on capital leads to higher interest rates. This is valid for a tax that affects interests, but not for one that is imposed on dividends or profits – that is, when it is a direct foreign investment instead of a loan. In the case of direct foreign investment, it could still be argued, of course, that there is a disincentive to investment, but not as a secondary effect (more taxes → higher interest rates → diminished investment), rather as a direct effect. In this sense, the Bruins Report fails to take into account that a tax on income or assets can create differences precisely between financial placements and productive investments. Moreover, it does not provide even the slightest empirical evidence on this point (or any of the others it presents as explanations of the international economy).

In the second place, the Bruins Report fully equates financial placement decisions with productive investment decisions. While in neoclassical thinking this confusion is common, I argue that under a theoretical framework that incorporates post-Keynesian elements it must be rejected completely. The differences between financial placements and productive investments can be identified clearly in particular in Keynes's thinking (Keynes 2022, 71ff.). The first difference is ultimately a result of the *propensity to liquidity*: given that money has lower maintenance "costs" as compared to other assets, and is easily convertible into (literally) anything, it generates the impulse to accumulate it and use it in a liquid way, that is, as money strictly speaking, instead of converting it into another type of asset. Note here, incidentally, the similarity with Marx's concept of money-capital. In this type of decision, the interest rate is indeed critical. In any case, even in the restricted field of financial transactions, the Bruins Report's assumption that tax increases have an immediate impact on interest rates is a gross exaggeration, since – as we will see below – in all of these processes the shifting and incidence of the tax burden must always be taken into account.

Productive investment decisions follow patterns that are completely different. If we consider Kalecki's investment theory (1971, 110ff.), which I personally find to be the most well formulated to date, the flaws can be seen even more clearly. According to Kalecki, investment decisions depend, in short, on two factors: the availability of money and the expectations of future returns. In Marxian terms, we could say that both elements are connected with profits and the profit rate: money availabilities depend on the monetary realization of past production, and they constitute money-capital; and expectations of future returns depend on the profit rate expected by capitalists. Kalecki's originality lies in highlighting the incidence of the different phases of the economic cycle on the expectations of future returns (or the future profit rate): in the upward phases of the cycle, investment grows, and as the cycle "flattens" and begins its decline, investment stagnates and decreases, *always as a function of total demand.*

The hypotheses set out in Chapter 5, with respect to the division of the global capitalist system into a core and a periphery to avoid the tendency of the profit rate to fall, can be seen as an international complement to Kalecki's theory. When MNEs decide to shift all or part of their material production to the periphery to take advantage of the low wages in the periphery so as to obtain more surplus value, thereby increasing profits and the profit rate, they are ultimately operating in the way described by Kalecki.

If we compare the explanations in the Bruins Report with the post-Keynesian theory of investment decisions and the Marxian theory of spatial expansion of production, the report's weakness is patently evident. The Bruins Report assumes that increasing the tax burden on the monetary return of an investment (and here I use this term in the strict sense, not loosely as the report does) invariably leads investors either to desist from the decision to invest or to choose to invest elsewhere.

But it fails to clarify that this, in any case, would happen under *ceteris paribus* conditions. More importantly, however, a decision to invest in one country may be much more attractive in terms of return expectations – even with the increase in tax burden and with or without shifting – than a decision to invest in other countries due, for example, to an expected growth in demand or – and this is especially relevant at the international level – because the same can be produced in that country with extremely low wages.

This last aspect must be underscored, as it continues to hold true today. The ideology regarding international taxation introduced by the Bruins Report ignores labor almost completely. This creates a falsified idea of production in general: if we were to go by this report, and by current OECD documents, it would appear that commodities (both goods and services) spring naturally from money. But, most importantly, this ideology generates a falsified image of global production, because it suggests that the quantity, quality, and cost of the labor force are of no importance in the global organization of production. These silences, by concentrating on the purely monetary aspects of production, and not on the level of value in the proper sense, provide the platform for turning the international tax burden into an absolute determinant in the hindering or enabling of production.

The Bruins Report reveals its enormous weakness even when examined in light of some hypotheses formulated under the neoclassical theory. We can compare it, for example, with the *Cobb–Douglas theorem* (Cobb and Douglas 1928), which posits that production is a function of available capital and labor, if technical conditions remain unchanged. If projected internationally, these hypotheses should predict that capital will tend to move toward countries with the lowest wages in search of greater productivity, provided those countries allow for the establishment of a production technology equivalent to that which existed in the country where production was previously carried out. It may be argued that excess taxation in the source country offsets the effect of the increase in productivity derived from low wages, but the disincentive will only occur, in any case, if the tax fully offsets the higher productivity of labor. If that does not happen, and we accept the investment decision theory derived from the Cobb–Douglas theorem, the conclusions of the Bruins Report are clearly proved wrong, and double taxation fails to have a deterrent effect on investment.

Although, like in much of neoclassical theory, the Cobb–Douglas theorem does not consider demand as a relevant factor for investment, it does bring up an important aspect, namely, the available technology, or, in Marxian terms, the quantity and quality of the means of production. If a certain technology for producing a commodity is affordable only in a few places, it is quite likely that capitalists will decide to invest in those places, even if faced with a greater tax burden there.

Finally, the Bruins Report completely ignores tax shifting and incidence. In fact, the three effects it proposes are: depreciation (the tax burden is absorbed causing a loss of value of the asset); increase in the interest rate (by shifting the tax burden onto interest combined with a diffusion effect); or reversal of the investment decision. In that sense, the Bruins Report is several steps behind both Ricardo and Marshall, who (especially the latter) tried to consistently explore, based on a more general pricing theory, whether the tax burden was shifted or not, and if so, who ultimately bore that burden. Conspicuously absent is any reference to wages and how they are impacted by international taxation, through shifting, an issue that was addressed in particular by Marshall. This silence reflects, more glaringly than other flaws, the ideological nature of the report: it would appear that the authors believe that capitalists are the only members of society, since the only effects they identify have to do exclusively with movements of money, its conversion into capital, and the reverting of money as profits for capitalists.

But when we observe its regulatory proposal, it becomes clear that this is the essential part of the report, and that its (apparently) descriptive and explanatory part is a platform that, far from having been developed neutrally, was conceived exclusively for the purpose of justifying the design of an international taxation system.

With respect to its normative proposal, the Bruins Report introduces several general notions that are entirely debatable. The first of these is the thesis that holds that taxation competence should be determined by the place where taxpayers benefit from public spending. This assumes a descriptive conception of taxation that sees taxes as a kind of price paid for a set of commodities, which are the goods and services provided by the state. Naturally, this thesis is completely disproven if one adopts, as in this book, the conception of taxation as a tool for regulating the money stock. In this perspective, given that no tax is a counterpart of anything, no allegiance or similar rule can be inferred from the existence of taxes.

Moreover, a counterpart conception of the taxation system is also untenable if we consider that there is no link between the beneficiaries of the state's goods and activities and those who – at least in the legal sense – required to pay taxes. Indeed, many people who receive goods and services from the state are not bound to pay taxes, at least not formally, and, conversely, many people who receive little from the state are required to pay taxes. If this way of organizing the public finance system is accepted in the strictly domestic sphere, why then should it be any different in the international sphere, and a correspondence be required between paying taxes and benefiting from state services and goods? Of course, if one accepts a conception of taxation as a general guarantee of "individual rights", in the sense posited by Stephen Holmes and Cass R. Sunstein (1999), there could be no prevalence determined by allegiance, given that – if that were the case – each state would, in turn, guarantee such rights both in the place of residence and anywhere taxpayers carry out their activities or hold assets.

In sum, the regulatory criteria used in the Bruins Report to justify not only its preference for the residence criterion but also the very idea of tax allegiance as a criterion for determining the state that must prevail in imposing a tax are groundless.

Now, then, when we interpret the "residence preference" under the theoretical framework described in Chapters 4 and 5, such preference is explained for reasons that have nothing to do with company allegiance. According to the central hypothesis proposed in Chapter 4, taxes have a money-stock-regulating and distributing role. If that hypothesis is correct, tax revenue must follow the money holders, as posited in Chapter 6. In a capitalism in which MNEs predominate, production is spread across the world, but money holding is not: there is a greater proportion of it in the core countries, from where it organizes production both in those countries of origin and in the periphery. Money needs to circulate extensively and very freely for this to happen, but taxes cannot have the same freedom and dispersion, because if this were to happen, they would fail to perform their function. Establishing the place of residence as the principle for imposing income taxes meant the same as it does today: given that the headquarters of the vast majority of multinational corporations were located in core countries, most of the tax revenue derived from the income of those corporations would be concentrated in those core country states

In this context, if my hypotheses are correct, there should be a concentration of tax revenue in the core countries, where money holders reside, to the detriment of the tax revenue of the periphery. The regulatory recommendations of the Bruins Reports are consistent with the hypothesis posited in Chapter 6: while we do not know the material tax revenue effect that could be expected from the proposal in 1923, the legal structure suggested is along the lines anticipated. That is, we have a further indication that corroborates that hypothesis.

Both in terms of the report's supposedly descriptive parts and in terms of its recommendations, its content calls for an ideological interpretation of the proposal as a whole. Even considering that, at the time of the report, there were plausibly no statistics in this regard, it was easy to intuitively draw the conclusion that the recommendations tended to concentrate the tax revenue in the core countries to the detriment of the periphery. The omission of these facts is ideological, regardless of whether it was done consciously or not (as ideology operates to a large extent at unconscious level): the discourse generated by Bruins and the other members of the drafting committee overlooks two essential facts for discerning a general solution for international taxation, and instead prompts a discussion around a topic that, as we can see, is completely disconnected from both dominant and heterodox theories. More specifically, the selection of this unprecedented criterion for spatially organizing taxation seems to be tailor-made to arrive at the residence solution, as the argument is determined by the conclusion, instead of the other way around.

It is no coincidence that this report was produced by the League of Nations. We know that legal configurations do not occur spontaneously; rather, they emerge from the state. It is therefore necessary for the state superstructure to take on a new dimension and assume new functions. An increasingly stronger supranationality was thus born, with the function, among others, of globally organizing tax revenue – at first tentatively, and later with growing intensity – , while maintaining the preponderance of the core states on the matter. This process should not be seen as a world conspiracy: while many of the people who produce such documents and issue such orders certainly make conscious projections of the results of the actions, as a whole it is a process in which the players perform roles that are already assigned to them by the very social fabric. The normative solutions that emanate from these international structures, and are then implemented by national states, are characterized by the overdetermination described in Chapter 2: they are the consequence of a need for production, but they are not merely passive phenomena;

rather, on the contrary, they generate in turn material and economic phenomena, such as the re-organization of the global distribution of tax revenue.

This is the central significance of the Bruins Report: it is the starting point of a chain of acts of the supranational institution (the League of Nations), which would then be propagated to national states in the form of treaties and domestic laws, the effect of which would be the re-channeling of tax revenue to core countries in a context in which production was starting to slowly shift away from those countries. For that reason, ignoring the tax revenue effects of the Bruins Report's proposal is a clearly ideological feature: the main issue is not relegated to a secondary position; it is directly omitted.

In short, the Bruins Report is the starting point of an international taxation system that was developed over the course of the twentieth century and the current one, in its most significant aspects, namely:

(a) Its departure from the most widely known theoretical frameworks regarding international taxation, including those derived from mainstream economics, and the invocation, instead, of ad hoc hypotheses on the workings of the global economy and the effects of international taxation, with little or no evidence to support them;
(b) The design of normative proposals for the distribution of international taxation competence that are clearly biased in favor of core states;
(c) The focus on avoidance of international multiple taxation, in particular with regard to income, and the division of income into categories (corporate, interest, royalties, etc.) as the basis for the distribution of competence for establishing and collecting taxes.

8.5 From the League of Nations to the OECD

Even before the Bruins Report, the United States had already unilaterally adopted the first measure for the avoidance of international double taxation in the contemporary sense: the granting of a fiscal credit for foreign source income, naturally circumscribed to income taxes.

In 1928, after issuing the Bruins Report and building on it, the League of Nations drafted its first Model Treaty for the Avoidance of Double Taxation. In 1932, the United States and France signed the first treaty for avoidance of double taxation (Avi-Yonah 2015), and the United States and Canada also signed a treaty in 1942 (Vann 2011). While, strangely enough, a historiographic reconstruction of the double taxation avoidance treaties that preceded the OECD model is not an easy task (Vann 2011), we can infer that the general aspects of these treaties are similar to those of the OECD model, as well as of the treaties based on that model and the ensuing domestic legislation on the subject. These aspects include the centrality of income taxes, and in particular corporate income taxes; a focus on avoiding double taxation through the distribution of "taxation rights"; the predominance in that sense of the residence criterion; and the establishment of methods to avoid double taxation, all under an income classification derived from the one contained in the Bruins Report. In other words, the trend of the Bruins Report is strengthened, and that, consequently, provides another confirmation of the hypotheses posited in Chapter 6.

The Bretton Woods Agreement, which is often cited as the foundation stone of the post-World World II economic system, did not explicitly address fiscal issues (neither public spending nor taxation), concentrating instead on purely monetary regulation aspects.

However, in 1961, the OECD was created as a successor to the Organisation for European Economic Cooperation (OEEC), which had been formed in 1948 as an association of many of the countries of Western Europe. The OECD did not have a clear mandate, and precisely for that reason, it rapidly became an international forum for the development of normative proposals on a wide range of issues, including, from very early on, taxation (Woodward 2004). The first model convention on the subject (the "Draft Double Taxation Convention on Income and Capital"), which dates back to 1963, was, in fact, based on the League of Nations model and ultimately followed the recommendations of the Bruins Report. A web of double taxation conventions (DTCs) then emerged, which were naturally fully aligned with the OECD model, with only minor variations.

Over more than three decades, the OECD and its members focused all their efforts on furthering the signing of conventions for the avoidance of double taxation, creating a dense network of these instruments. The specific solutions of the OECD model and the DTCs are described below.

In all of these legal instruments, for example, the residence criterion is applied as the basic rule for distributing income tax revenue, with few substantial variations since the 1923 Bruins Report. This criterion has several expressions, which I will attempt to summarize:

(a) When an individual or an entity carries out a business activity on their own in a territory other than that which corresponds to their state of residence, the money flows (which are normatively called income) obtained from exchanges will be subject to a tax in their country of residence, not in the country from which that money comes. An exception to this is when a subject has a permanent establishment in the territory that is not the territory where they reside, understood as a "fixed place of business", in which case the flows attributed to that establishment are taxable by the state of the territory where it is located. The legal nuances of this definition notwithstanding, the concept ultimately refers to a permanent presence in a state other than the state of residence. However, the definitions of permanent establishment contained in the OECD Model and followed by the UN Model, the DTCs, and domestic laws, have significant cases of permanent structures that do not qualify as such, so that the respective money flows are taxable in the country of residence. A strategy for diverting tax revenue to the core states has consisted, precisely, in adjusting the definitions of permanent establishment in order to reduce the flows attributed to it and, consequently, the taxation power of the states where they are located.
(b) When an individual or an entity operates in another state through a domestic entity, which is controlled through the ownership of its capital (and is known as a "subsidiary", "controlled company", or other similar names), the residence

criterion is translated into the rule that holds that dividends (that is, the flows that the shareholder receives from that entity) are to be taxed in the country of residence of the owner of the entity's capital. The OECD and UN models, and the DTCs and domestic laws as well, allow the states of origin of the flows to apply withholding taxes on the dividends mentioned above, but with quantitative caps that have been gradually reduced over time, as we will see in Chapter 9. In addition to this solution, there is a Global Minimum Tax that, as we will see, entails that, under certain circumstances, the MNE must include an amount subject to an income tax in the country of its parent company.

(c) In the case of money flows that are the result of other activities (for example, interest on loans or deposits, royalties, services, proceeds from the sale of shares, etc.), the method followed is the same as with dividends: a tax applied in the country of the recipient of the flow and – often, but not always – a limited possibility for the country of origin of the flow to impose a withholding tax, which gradually decreases over time.

(d) One group of specific solutions for multinational corporations are transfer pricing rules, which I have already mentioned and will discuss separately. Briefly, these are rules for attributing or assigning to the different entities that make up an MNE portions of the total flows it receives from third parties. Any criterion that internally attributes within an MNE parts of that MNE's flows is necessarily artificial, because the company is always just one company, so that the criteria in this sense are subtle tools for (unequally) distributing the taxable bases, and with them the tax revenue, among states.

(e) Other types of money flows emerging from more specific situations (airline or shipping companies, financial instruments such as derivatives, options and the like, etc.) have required special rules, always along the same lines.

Therefore, there is an invariable pattern, namely, the prevalence of the residence criterion – that is, the taxation of flows in the country of their destination – thus confirming once again the hypotheses posited in Chapter 6.

8.6 The last decades: focus on MNEs and avoidance practices

8.6.1 Brief remarks on domestic taxation systems

Before proceeding any further, in order to understand the tax revenue effects of the guidelines of the OECD, the G20, and the European Union, it is important to briefly summarize the dominant taxation structures adopted (with variations) by states.

Almost all national governments (that is, not considering the taxation structures of smaller political entities, such as states, provinces, regions, etc.) impose: (a) an income tax on the income formally received by individuals as such (not including the business activities performed directly or through a company), which is, therefore, applied to salaries, interest, dividends received from companies, rents, etc.; (b) a corporate tax applied to entities (and sometimes also to individuals who carry out business activities in their own name); (c) payroll taxes or social security contributions, paid by workers in respect of their wages (in which case, they are exactly the same as a wage tax), and sometimes also by employers; and (d) a VAT, with the notable exceptions of the United States and Brazil, which have sales taxes regulated and collected by the individual states and not by the federal authority.

In addition to these taxes, normally applied to the activities of all the subjects that are residents, including local subsidiaries of MNEs, almost every country has a system for withholding taxes, sometimes inserted in one of the general taxes and other times with autonomous legal structures, but which follow a common pattern: they are imposed on money flows paid abroad for various reasons, including dividends, services, interest, proceeds from the sale of corporate stock, etc.

8.6.2 The shift in the focus of attention: avoidance practices of MNEs

As of the late 1990s, and while continuing to pressure for the signing of treaties drafted under its model, the OECD began to take an increasing interest in the design of taxation policies meant to be incorporated into national legislations, beginning with the movement to stop what was referred to as *harmful tax competition.* Even before that, many of the solutions contained in the double taxation avoidance treaties, including those regarding permanent establishment and transfer pricing, had already been massively incorporated into national taxation legislation.

The origin of this problem lies in the natural tension that exists between taxation and private property, a tension that is inherent to the capitalist system given that both types of social relations are completely functional to it (Blanco 2017). All the modes of production that have existed since the destruction of primitive communities have in common the establishment of a special kind of relationship with respect to the means of production, and even to personal effects. That relationship is private property, which entails that only some people can authorize or force – depending on the case – other people to apply their labor force to such means, to carry out production. This includes – in particular in capitalism – money, which is in itself a type of social relation of power. This type of social relation, which is absolutely essential in capitalism along with the existence of money, clashes with taxation, as taxation takes money away from individuals to cancel it without there being any exchange, thereby rupturing the social relation of private property. More importantly, tax revenue as a coercive phenomenon is also strictly functional to capitalism, as explained at length in Chapter 4. That tension has to be resolved, necessarily, at some point that does not entail a significant threat to private property, nor adversely affect tax revenue in such a way that it jeopardizes the money reflux phase. It is in these terms that the tension between states and the new supranationality, and MNEs, regarding avoidance practices must be seen.

As we saw in Chapter 5, the global expansion of MNEs, not just in terms of trade now but in terms of the relocation of production, has a concrete cause: the moving away from the tendency of the profit rate to fall by shifting production to places where monetary wages are lower. This tendency, which has achieved its objective, is translated into greater endowments of liquid money in the hands of MNEs and, correlatively, of the financial sector. The international taxation system arising from the Bruins Report and the League of Nations contained the essential elements for preventing such a reorganization of production from affecting the tax revenue power of the core countries, particularly of the United States, which had, and have, to maintain a tax revenue prevalence due to the exclusive leading role of the US dollar in the global capitalist system. However, the effectiveness of tax collection began to be threatened when many states, largely in the periphery, implemented differential tax relief measures for multinational corporations under various forms – direct exemptions, special deduction systems, tax collection that tolerates the effects of artificial legal forms, etc. – in addition to the legal designs of core states, which incorporated "perforations", as those exemptions and benefits are sometimes called.

This phenomenon (which partially corroborates the hypotheses of some sectors of Open Marxism discussed in Chapter 3) resulted in MNEs stepping up their strategic use of national legal taxation systems to pay less taxes overall. When such practices – which for the sake of convenience we can refer to collectively as tax avoidance or avoidance practices – began to jeopardize the effective performance of tax revenue as a stabilizer of the money stock, thus triggering dysfunctional phenomena in the global capitalist system, supranational state structures acted with increasing force to rebalance everything.

Thus, in 1998, the OECD effectively shifted its attention on the subject of tax avoidance (OECD 1998) with an action plan that targeted harmful tax competition, which was extremely basic compared to the BEPS Plan. The plan focused on identifying states that allowed for zero or low taxation of multinational corporations, either in general or for certain kinds of operations. The actions recommended under the plan were limited to various types of more disadvantageous tax treatments for activities performed with entities located in such states.

This trend entered a new phase with the Base Erosion and Profit Shifting Plan (BEPS Plan), launched in 2013, which constitutes an ambitious project aimed at globally reforming corporate income tax systems. The plan includes several chapters that address multiple aspects of this type of tax (transfer pricing, intangibles, corporate financing, etc.), with some notable features that also characterized the "convention era" that preceded it:

(a) It focuses exclusively on corporate income taxes, with almost no relevance given to personal income and asset taxes.
(b) It is explicitly aimed at MNEs, although many proposals ultimately impact domestic companies.
(c) It remains markedly biased toward concentrating tax revenue in residence states, that is, in core states, which is where MNEs have their headquarters.
(d) Apart from the effect mentioned above, it completely ignores any other tax effects, including income redistribution or environmental protection.
(e) It surrounds itself with very lengthy documents that provide a rationale for the normative proposals, including ad hoc theories detached from the developments proposed by authoritative academic sources, both mainstream and – all the more so – heterodox theories.

I will devote one of the remaining chapters to the interpretation of some actions of the BEPS Plan under the theoretical framework of this book. For now, I would like to highlight that its most salient features, as noted above, also confirm not one, but all of the hypotheses set out in Chapter 6: (a) the new tax designs continue with the bias of shifting tax revenue from the periphery to the core, explainable by the internationalization of the dollar and – to a lesser extent – the euro as account moneys; (b) the plan advances in the creation of supranational structures, responding to the need to globally regulate the money stock; and (c) an ideological discourse is built around the legal and state apparatus that furthers and supports the economic phenomenon (the shifting of tax revenue), thus creating a (distorted) context for the reforms that are promoted, while at the same time legitimizing it, in what is a canonic example of overdetermination (in the terms of Althusser and Resnick and Wolff).

With the BEPS Plan, the OECD took a major step in the construction of this new supranational state form through a multilateral legal instrument called "Framework Agreement" that simultaneously binds many states and empowers the OECD – for the time being – to modify the content of the DTCs without negotiations among states. This marks a substantial and qualitative change in the existence of a truly supranational state structure on the subject of taxation, and it opens the door for it to broadly modify even domestic legislation in the future (since the power to modify treaties involves that possibility, but in a veiled way).

All the actions mentioned above have to do with so-called corporate taxes. In the case of sales or consumption taxes, such as the VAT, the residence rule is replaced with the "destination rule", which means the tax is applied in the country where the good or service is consumed or used. The effect sought and achieved, however, is the same: since consumption is also concentrated in core countries, because there are more money holders there, the destination criterion entails concentrating revenue from this type of taxes in those same countries. With these taxes, avoidance practices are not the issue, as these are not normally directed at the VAT or other sales taxes. The focus with consumption taxes is instead a much more open concern with the re-channeling of tax revenue to countries with higher consumption, which are naturally the core countries.

In all cases, the actions proposed for corporate taxes reinforce the prevalence of the state of residence as a tax revenue beneficiary. Given the continued full application of the residence criterion for determining which state has taxation power, the modifications will entail an increase in the tax revenue of those states. Setting aside the large-scale modifications, such as the global minimum tax or the transfer pricing rules, all the other actions may have a minor effect when taken separately, but their consequences are amplified when their combined effect is considered.

Let us look, for example, at Action 4, which seeks to limit interest deductions for corporate taxpayers, but is clearly aimed at MNEs (OECD 2016). On the one hand, the document proposes establishing a maximum deduction rule for interest in terms of an interest/fixed asset ratio, applied generally. In the case of indebtedness with third parties (that is, with banks), exceeding such ceilings will mean that, economically, the effective rate of the respective tax will be raised. Assuming, as the document itself does, that the debts contracted by MNEs with the financial sector are higher in the "higher taxation" countries, it follows that such an increase in the effective rates will favor those countries, which are plausibly core countries. Regarding the indebtedness with related entities, it is logical to assume – again, as the document does – that the entities that charge such interest are located in "lower taxation" countries, which correspond either to tax havens or periphery countries with incentive regimes. Limiting these deductions will raise effective tax rates (ETRs) both in core countries and in periphery countries where MNEs have actual activities. But we must assume that those intra-group interest flows are, in essence, monetary profit flows that, with some delay, will eventually be available to the parent companies. Eliminating their deduction, therefore, encourages a faster delivery to the parent companies of the flows from actual activities of the MNEs in the periphery in the form of dividends, service payments, or otherwise, thus increasing the effective rate of those parent companies.

8.7 Other supranational actors and supposed dissidences

The incorporation of other actors, in addition to the OECD, into the supranational state forms dealing with taxation matters is significant. Among the new players is, first of all, the G20, which, while lacking a formally established legal base (it has no founding treaty, no bodies, no operating guidelines, etc.), functions as a state superstructure that is just as efficient, or more so, than an international body, at least in taxation matters, as we will see with the global minimum tax. Second is the European Union, which, much like the OECD, not only has authority over its members but also issues orders directed at – and accepted by – other countries in the world, as we will see with the so-called passive income.

Dissenting attempts have been few and all unsuccessful. In 1980, almost two decades after the first OECD draft and following a long discussion process, the United Nations developed its own Model Double Taxation Convention between Developed and Developing Countries, with the aim of better contemplating the interests of developing countries, a concern that was even reflected in the title of the document (UN 2017). However, the success of the OECD Model – and ultimately of the general concept of double taxation and the prevalence of the residence criterion established by the Bruins Report – was so absolute that the UN Model rested on the exact same assumptions and had the same exact structure as the OECD Model and its predecessors, so that it merely expanded somewhat the taxation powers of the countries that are the "source" of the income (which are assumed to be periphery countries), but without affecting the prevalence of residence countries.

With respect to the United States, besides being part of the movements of the supranational state structures, it also made changes in both its domestic legislation and in its fiscal control practices, which went in the exact same direction (PWC n.d.). The following changes, among others, can be identified between 1988 and the mid-1990s: (a) the reform of tax information exchange norms; b) the establishment of special penalties in cases of "valuation errors" in the application of transfer pricing rules, obviously aimed primarily at MNEs; (c) new cost sharing norms, also aimed at MNEs; and (d) the creation, within the Internal Revenue Service (IRS), of the Transfer Pricing Practice, with the specific purpose of controlling international operations between entities of the same MNE. A decade later, in the 2000s, the United States introduced new transfer pricing regulations for services. In 2010, in what could be called the preliminary phase of the BEPS Plan, the United States passed the Foreign Account Tax Compliance Act (FATCA), which establishes reporting obligations for financial institutions with respect to the operations of foreign entities, for tax control purposes. Finally, in 2017, the Global Intangible Low-Taxed Income (GILTI) was created under the Tax Cuts and Jobs Act, which is a tax levied directly on the income obtained by US companies from the use of intangible assets in countries with low taxes (IRS 2017).

In all that time, the only attempts to propose a taxation structure truly different from the OECD Model and its predecessors were made in Latin America with the Andean Pact Model and the LAIA Model, which were strictly in line with the income source criterion as a way to avoid international double taxation (Herrán Ocampo 2000, 68ff.) These models, however, were never applied anywhere, as the member countries of the respective supranational entities ultimately adopted the OECD Model, despite not being members of that organization. In any case, these Latin American models represented a merely superficial break from the diktat of the OECD, the UN, and the tradition that began with the League of Nations and the Bruins Report. These "alternative models", in fact, also assume double taxation as an invariably unwanted phenomenon: while they do not explicitly mention it, the mere fact of designing a model aimed exclusively at avoiding double taxation entails, despite certain nuances, accepting the Bruins Report's hypotheses of "excess burden" and taxes as "barriers" to new investments. And, naturally, these models also share (most likely without realizing it) the obvious theoretical errors of the Bruins Report.

The resounding success of the OECD proposal is moreover corroborated by the involvement of the so-called Group of 24 (G24) in the design process for the BEPS Plan's Pillars I and II solution (which will also be considered below). While this group of states claims to respond to the interests of the societies of the periphery, its participation in the discussion of Pillars I and II of the BEPS Plan was limited to certain observations that did not call into question the essence of the measures proposed by the OECD and the G20.

The conceptual shortcomings of the dissident approaches, and their ensuing failures, reveal the overwhelming power of ideologies: when a discourse and the beliefs that generate it are completely functional to the mode of production, they become so firmly rooted that nobody challenges them because nobody imagines that its claims can be anything other than true.

8.8 The mainstream theoretical approach

Mainstream economic thinking on these issues remains tied to the concepts that were coarsely outlined in the Bruins Report, although often more subtly developed and with attempts to draw on other general theoretical hypotheses. In this sense, Roger Gordon and James Hines (2002) argue that in a "closed economy" (presumably with this term they refer to a country that imposes taxes on imports and/or establishes restrictions to the international movement of money) the incidence of taxes on capital gains affects capital, that is, there is no tax shifting, although they do not provide any reasons for why that is so. In an "open economy", instead, taxes on capital returns would ultimately affect wages. The argument for this conclusion is, in short, that in an open economy competition between local products and foreign products is absolute with respect to "tradable commodities" (i.e., goods and services that can be obtained at similar costs locally or brought in from abroad), so that any increase in income taxes will not be translated into a price increase, given that local producers will not be able to raise prices above what is demanded for the same goods and services that are foreign in origin. Therefore, an increase in a tax on capital returns will allow companies that produce tradable commodities to maintain their profitability by lowering salaries. With non-tradable commodities, on the other hand, an increase in a tax on capital income will have as an effect a rise in the prices of commodities.

If the government wishes to offset those effects, it would have to reduce wage and sales taxes, and such reductions would cancel out the higher tax revenue obtained from the tax on capital returns. From another perspective, Gordon and Hines argue that a tax on the returns of capital that is applied to the production of tradable commodities is, in tax revenue terms, equivalent to a tax on wages and/or the sale of those commodities.

The above concerns the domestic sphere. With respect to the international sphere, since the scenario in which they develop their model is one of an open economy, an increase in the tax on capital gains discourages the "importing of capital" and forces the economy to operate with local capital only, not just for tradable commodities, but also for non-tradable ones. The consequence, from an international point of view, is that it is preferable to have a residence-based income tax system, since in that way capital owners pay the same tax both in their country and in any other country in the world. In their own words, Gordon and Hines posit a total sensitivity of foreign investment decisions to tax increases in the country where the investment is made (2002, 24). That is the basic argument, although the article goes into other considerations.

This proposal is a more refined version of the old rationale of the negative effects of double taxation contained in the Bruins Report, and consequently it has essentially the same flaws. First, it appears to assume that investment decisions depend solely on taxes, and that demand remains completely static, along with the availability of money, which are all obviously not true. As for pricing mechanisms, Gordon and Hines only consider the "tradable" or "non-tradable" nature of commodities, and not the conditions under which the companies that sell them operate, particularly whether they sell them under a monopoly, oligopoly, or competitive scheme, which is absolutely decisive for determining the feasibility of raising prices to react – for example – to a tax increase (Kalecki 1971, 43ff.).

At the international level, the most striking flaw of this approach, as was the case with the Bruins Report, is its total disregard for factors that are crucial when it comes to making investment decisions in a country by capitalists located outside that country. Most notable in this sense is the wage level in the country where the investment is made. On this point, as we saw in Chapter 5, there is abundant literature, from both mainstream and heterodox economics, that shows with empirical data that low wages are decisive factors in the shift of production to the periphery. As this evidence also holds for the hypothetical shift of production from one core country to another (which will be less feasible the more similar the level of wages is), we can conclude that the propensity for production mobility is inversely proportional to the level of wages, given the same available technology. It should be noted, incidentally, that this conclusion reveals a surprising similarity between the Marxist explanation of global capitalism and the Cobb–Douglas theorem applied to the same sphere.

Another factor that could be important for the movement of money and, with it, the production of a good or service is the ease of access to certain natural resources. From this perspective, Ricardo's theory of comparative costs has much greater explanatory power than the hypotheses put forward by Gordon and Hines and by the Bruins Report, for which everything is subordinated to the tax burden. Even more so, and without departing from the dominant theory, Marshall's memorandum also provides a much more realistic explanatory framework, in particular because he analyzes tax shifting and incidence according to the monopolistic or non-monopolistic nature of the activity being taxed.

The empirical studies that Gordon and Hines cite to support their hypothesis on the influence of taxes on investment decisions (2002, 43) have major epistemological weaknesses. For example, in addition to being considerably dated, the study by David Hartman (1981) effectively upholds the argument in favor of the sensitivity of investment to increases in taxes in the host country, but the only empirical data it draws on is the origin of the funds for the expansion of the investments of existing US MNEs (external funds vs. retained earnings). The rest of the argument consists of a string of assumptions. Joel Slemrod (1990), for his part, only examines the effects of tax changes on FDI to the United States, and not from that country (or other core countries) to the periphery, so that his conclusions are completely unrelated to the issue considered here, which is the relationship between tax designs and core-periphery relations.

Gordon and Hines, however, make an interesting observation. Assuming investment decisions can be influenced by tax reductions in the host country, that is only possible to the extent that in the home country the obligation to pay the tax arises when the flow of dividends, interest, service payments, or the like actually occurs. This is indeed the case in the United States, so that if a subsidiary of an MNE receives a benefit with respect to its corporate tax, it would be effective if it were allowed to defer the application of the tax in the United States until the dividends were distributed. This was a central piece in the design of avoidance practices and it is its effect that the Global Minimum Tax seeks to offset.

George Zodrow's arguments (2010) evidence positions that are totally contradictory. On the one hand, he admits that it is impossible to measure the effect of tax reductions on the evolution of FDI and, in general, to measure the influence of taxation on investment decisions, whether they be new investments or expansions of preexisting investments. However, a little further on he claims the exact opposite: that there is reliable empirical evidence that taxation has decisive effects on a country's investment decisions. Nonetheless, when commenting on the results of empirical studies also conducted under a mainstream framework (particularly the study by Altshuler et al. 2001), he notes that the ETR applied in other countries to MNEs with parent companies in the United States can be influenced by avoidance strategies against which those countries have no efficient regulatory or fiscal remedies. Zodrow's observation in this respect will help us interpret some of the evidence gathered by Altshuler et al., which I will return to in Section 9.2.

In light of its use by Zodrow, let us look more closely at the notion of ETR developed within the mainstream approach, which we will also use for our purposes in Chapter 9. ETR is the ratio between the amount actually paid by a company for income tax purposes and its total net income calculated according to acceptable accounting rules. Given that the legal delimitation of the taxable amount almost never coincides completely with acceptable accounting standards, consequently, the tax paid is almost never equal to the application of the statutory rate (SR) on the net accounting income, and the ETR differs from the SR. The discrepancies between the legally defined taxable amount and the net accounting income can be due to diverse reasons: tax exemptions or reductions of various scopes, prohibited or admitted deductions, rules for the territorial assignment of income, etc. In short, the ETR as a concept can be useful for measuring the importance of avoidance practices, so that we will come back to it in Chapter 9, although for purposes and within an explanation completely different from those in mainstream economics.

A work by Michael Devereux and Rachael Griffith (1998) that is often cited as a leading reference on the subject because it developed a model for calculating the importance of taxes on productive investment factors in a country yields results that are of no interest to the study of taxation in core-periphery relations. Indeed, that work concludes that the ETR is a crucial factor in a US multinational corporation ultimately deciding between producing locally or taking its production abroad, but the comparison is between the United Kingdom and France, two core countries. In particular, and predictably, wage levels are not decisive factors in this study, and they should reasonably differ substantially if the comparison were made with periphery countries.

For its part, the study by Altshuler et al. (2001), while employing empirical information that is considerably old, emphatically supports the confirmation of the hypothesis of the "sensitivity" of FDI mobility as a function of ETRs. This study takes into account both core and peripheral countries, but it has two serious limitations: first, it does not consider new FDI from the United States to foreign countries, only the substitution of one country with another country where there is already FDI; and second – and crucially – it does not delve into the importance of wage levels in investment decisions. Therefore, the conclusion that FDI decisions are determined primarily by the ETR of the destination country is, in my opinion, invalidated by that essential omission. Nevertheless, the chronological systematization of the ETRs of several countries yields interesting data (despite being old) for verifying the hypotheses set out in Chapter 6.

It is striking that the Cobb–Douglas theorem, mentioned several times in the previous chapters, has not produced a theory specifically aimed at explaining the mobility of production. As we saw, this "theorem" proposes a very simple hypothesis: that a country's production, and therefore its growth, depends on the existing quantities of capital and labor, as well as on the available technology. A simple corollary of this hypothesis is that, with technical means remaining the same and an absolute mobility of capital (which is actually mobility of money) on a global scale, capital will flow to those places with higher "labor productivity", which, in international terms, means that production will shift to the periphery, where wages are lower. However, there are few, if any, global studies on the international distribution of capitalist production according to such an interpretation, let alone international taxation, which, again, reveals the ideological features of theoretical constructions. For example, it is interesting that Hülya Başeğmez (2021), who specifically addresses the application of the Cobb–Douglas theorem to growth prediction of "developing" countries, fails to include such an analysis in her study.

The set of hypotheses apodictically proposed and supported by weak or no empirical evidence, as well as the omission of elements of analysis, again leads us to the realm of ideology, which will be dealt with in greater detail in the final chapter. Before that, we must first systematize certain concrete evidence provided by texts produced over the course of the historical development described above, adding also statistical evidence.

But the most relevant feature of the mainstream approach that gives it an ideological quality, is its complete silence regarding the effects of the different international taxation systems on the distribution of tax revenue among states. In a projection of the neoclassical ideological imaginary, in which the economy is composed of companies and "households", and the state is not relevant, the tax revenue effects of international taxation policies do not appear to exist. Reality is obviously profoundly different: changes in international taxation cause effects in terms of differential tax revenue gains and losses, which, ultimately, alter the participation of each state both in the essential function of taxation, which is the regulation of the money stock, and also in the possibility that each state has of modifying individual money endowments. This is an ideological bias because a general view of the taxation phenomenon is presented that omits its main effect, which is tax revenue, and its leading actors, which are states.

A comparison of these approaches with the OECD documents that will be discussed shortly will reveal that the latter do address the tax revenue effects of the proposals. Its ideological features, however, are to be found elsewhere, namely, in the unequal way in which those effects are borne by the different states, and particularly the unequal way in which they are borne by the core and the periphery.

References

Altshuler, Rosanne, Harry Grubert, and T. Scott Newlon. 2001. "Has U.S. Investment Abroad Become More Sensitive to Tax Rates?" In *International Taxation and Multinational Activity*, edited by James R. Hines Jr., 9–38. Chicago: University of Chicago Press. http://www.nber.org/books/hine00-1.

Avi-Yonah, Reuben. 2015. "Who Invented the Single Tax Principle? An Essay on the History of US Treaty Policy." *New York Law School Law Review* 59 (2): 305–315.

Başeğmez, Hülya. 2021. "Estimation of the Cobb-Douglas function for Developing Countries." *Journal of Research in Business*: 6 (1): 54–68 DOI: 10.29228/JRB.3

Blanco, A. 2017. "Fraude a la ley y fraude a la ley fiscal: Juegos de estrategias." *Revista de Derecho Público* (Universidad de Chile) 86: 33–56. https://doi.org/10.5354/0719-5249.2017.47243.

Bruins, Gijsbert Weyer Jan, Luigi Einaudi, Edwin Robert Seligman, and Josiah Stamp. 1923. *Report on Double Taxation Submitted to the Financial Committee of the League of Nations*. https://adc.library.usyd.edu.au/view?docId=split/law/xml-main-texts/brulegi-source-bibl-1.xml;chunk.id=item-1;toc.depth=1;toc.id=item-1;database=;collection.

Cobb, Charles W., and Paul Douglass. 1928. "A Theory of Production." *The American Economic Review* 18 (1): 139–165.

Devereux, Michael P., and Rachel Griffith. 1998. "Taxes and the Location of Production: Evidence from a Panel of US Multinationals." *Journal of Public Economics* 68 (3): 335–367.

Duménil, Gerard, and Dominique Lévy. 2016. "Technology and Distribution in Managerial Capitalism: The Chain of Historical Trajectories à la Marx and Countertendential Traverses." *Science and Society* 80 (3): 530–549.

Gordon, Roger H. and James R. Hines, Jr. 2002. *International Taxation*. NBER Working Paper 8854. Cambridge, MA: National Bureau for Economic Research. http://www.nber.org/papers/w8854.

Hartman, David G. 1981. *Tax Policy and Foreign Direct Investment*. NBER Woking Paper No. 689. Cambridge, MA: National Bureau for Economic Research. https://www.nber.org/system/files/working_papers/w0689/w0689.pdf.

Herrán Ocampo, Catalina. 2000. "La doble tributación internacional. Principios y realidades de los Convenios." Undergraduate thesis, Facultad de Ciencias Jurídicas, Pontificia Universidad Javeriana, Bogotá. https://repository.javeriana.edu.co/bitstream/handle/10554/56369/Tesis14.pdf?sequence=1.

Holmes, Stephen, and Cass R. Sunstein. 1999. *The Cost of Rights. Why Liberty Depends on Taxes*. New York: W. W. Norton & Co.

Internal Revenue Service (IRS). 2017. "SOI Tax Stats – International Tax Studies Based Upon Provisions Introduced by the Tax Cuts and Jobs Act (TCJA) of 2017." Internal Revenue Service, United States Government. Accessed July 27, 2024. https://www.irs.gov/statistics/soi-tax-stats-international-tcja-studies.

Kalecki, Michal.1971. *Selected Essays on the Dynamics of Capitalist Economy*. Cambridge: Cambridge University Press.

Keynes, John Maynard. 2022. *General Theory of Interest, Employment and Money*. Global Grey. globalgreyebooks.com/general-theory-of-employment-interest-and-money-ebook.html.

Luxemburg, Rosa. 2003. *The Accumulation of Capital*. London: Routledge.

PwC. n.d. "United States." https://www.pwc.com/gx/en/international-transfer-pricing/assets/united-states.pdf.

Organisation for Economic Co-operation and Development (OECD). 1998. *Harmful Tax Competition: An Emerging Global Issue*. Paris: OECD. https://www.oecd.org/ctp/harmful/1904176.pdf

Organisation for Economic Co-operation and Development (OECD). 2016. *Limiting Base Erosion Involving Interests Deduction and Other Financial Payments. Action 4. 2016*

Update. OECD/G20 Base Erosion and Profit Shifting Plan. https://read.oecd-ilibrary.org/taxation/limiting-base-erosion-involving-interest-deductions-and-other-financial-payments-action-4-2016-update_9789264268333-en#page16.

Slemrod, Joel. 1990. "Tax Effects on Foreign Direct Investment in the United States: Evidence from a Cross-Country Comparison." In *Taxation in the Global Economy*, edited by Assaf Razif and Joel Slemrod, 79–122. Chicago: University of Chicago Press. http://www.nber.org/books/razi90-1.

United Nations. 2017. *Model Double Taxation Convention between Developed and Developing Countries*. New York: Department of Economic Affairs, United Nations. https://www.un.org/esa/ffd/wp-content/uploads/2018/05/MDT_2017.pdf.

Vann, Richard J. (2011). Writing Tax Treaty History. [S.l.]: SSRN. https://ssrn.com/abstract=1788603.

Woodward, Richard. 2004. "The Organisation for Economic Cooperation and Development." *New Political Economy* 9 (1): 113–127. https://doi.org/10.1080/1356346042000190411.

Zodrow, George. 2010. "Capital Mobility and Capital Tax Competition." *National Tax Journal* 63 (4): 865–901.

9 Regulatory and statistical evidence

9.1 Evidence from regulatory texts

In previous chapters, I provided a reconstruction of the history of international taxation through a narrative describing successive model regulations, norms currently in force, and pseudo theories. Such a historical reconstruction, whether in narrative form or mapped chronologically, serves as evidence to support the hypotheses laid out in Chapter 6, since they are the projection onto taxation superstructures of the dynamics of the global capitalist system, as examined in Chapter 5. Those superstructures can cause the material effects that were posited in Chapter 6 as hypotheses pertaining specifically to taxation and derived from that structure of the global capitalist system, namely: the concentration in core countries of the tax revenue obtained from activities carried out by multinational companies – and *a fortiori* of global economic activity – to the detriment of the periphery; the consolidation of new supranational state forms; and the generation of ideologies to support the whole. That sequence of superstructure events provides indirect evidence of these hypotheses. While the events do not indicate the phenomena themselves, they are – by virtue of the concept of overdetermination – the necessary requisite for the material effects to occur.

In Section 9.1, I will graphically represent some easily accessible elements of this historical superstructure process, such as the double taxation conventions (DTCs) and some domestic laws, to then examine statistical evidence of the material effects in Sections 9.2 and 9.3. DTCs are bilateral regulatory texts aimed at distributing taxation power, and therefore tax revenue, with respect to income obtained in the territory of one state by a subject residing in another state. Following the OECD Model and its predecessors, starting with the Bruins Report discussed in Chapter 8, as a rule, DTCs assign that taxation power to the country of residence of the subject obtaining the income. In any DTC between a core state and a periphery state, this means that the subjects (most likely MNEs), identified as "residents" in the core state, who obtain monetary flows from the periphery country for whatever reason (as direct income from a business activity, interest, dividends for shares in a company, etc.), generally pay taxes to the core state and not to the periphery state in which the flow is generated. Nevertheless, both the OECD Model and DTCs allow, within certain limits, for the states of origin of the flows (for our purposes,

DOI: 10.4324/9781003458678-9

the periphery states) to levy taxes on those subjects. Such taxes are usually called "withholding taxes".

If the first hypothesis posited in Chapter 6 holds true, we should be able to identify two phenomena in the texts of the DTCs, combined with domestic legislation. In a historical perspective, we can observe a tendency to reduce the taxation power of the countries of the periphery in the most recent DTCs as compared with the earliest. On the other hand, a static examination reveals that the distribution of taxation power between the core state and the periphery state with respect to flows from the latter to the former is clearly favorable to the core state. Statistical information that gathers and classifies purely regulatory texts naturally has a major shortcoming: its qualitative value is limited, given that it lacks any sort of assessment against its background and actual tax revenue effects. Even so, it provides an indirect picture of the evolution of the behaviors of national states and supranational state structures.

Consider, for example, the case of dividends, which are flows emerging from the net monetary profits of a country's companies (as measured in accounting terms or pursuant to tax rules) and distributed by them to their shareholders. I choose dividends because the differences and changes over time in regulatory texts are easily identifiable, since they are visible as a maximum rate allowed in the country of origin of the flow ("source country"). Indeed, in the case of DTCs, the withholding tax rate on dividends indicates the maximum taxation percentage on the gross amount of dividends that can be applied in the country where the company paying the dividends is located. If the DTC is between a core country and a periphery country, the stipulated withholding tax rate indicates the maximum level of taxation on dividends that the periphery country can impose on dividends paid by local companies (which are most likely part of an MNE) to their shareholders located in the core country. In theory, the same percentage is stipulated (although not in all cases) for dividends originating in a core country and paid to shareholders in the periphery country, but the cases in which this actually occurs are, obviously, very few. Therefore, the graphical comparison of the distribution of legal a periphery country will provide a fairly accurate idea of the percentage of an MNE's dividend flows that is taxed in the periphery country and the percentage that is taxed in the core country.

The following graph shows the historical evolution of the maximum rate of withholding tax stipulated in DTCs in force between the United States and periphery countries (Graph 9.1) (Blanco 2022):

Let us now look at a similar graph for treaties signed between the United Kingdom and periphery countries. The treaties are grouped by periods of five years, reflecting the largest number of treaties in force, and for each period the average withholding tax rates at the source is shown. In the absence of precise indicators of what "core" and "periphery" mean, the countries have once again been selected according to the medium and low-income criterion, with some additions (Chile and Uruguay) that, because of their productive structures, must be considered periphery, and others that are excluded for similar reasons (China and large oil producers, with the exception of Iran) (Graph 9.2).

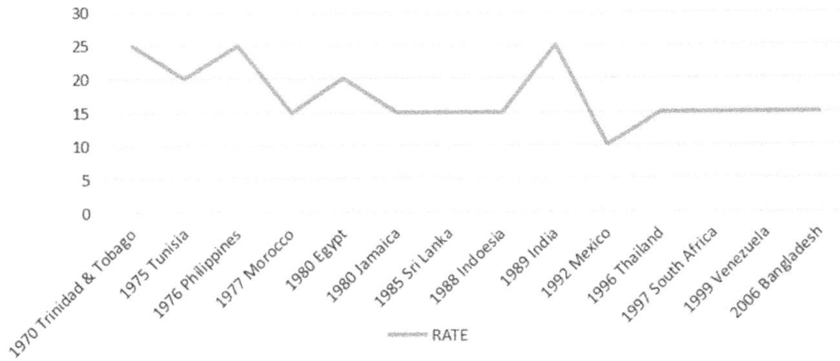

Graph 9.1 US – Maximum withholding rate at source (DTC).

Source: Author's own calculation based on information drawn from the IRS, available at: https://www.irs.gov/businesses/international-businesses/united-states-income-tax-treaties-a-to-z

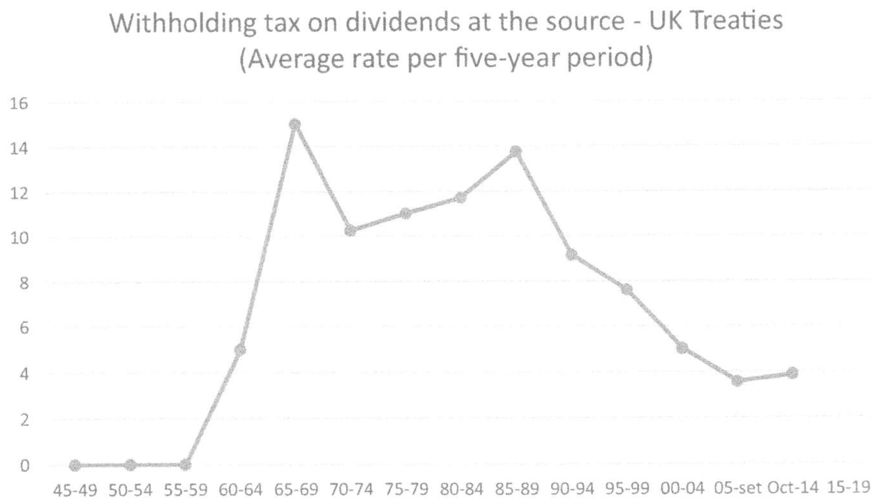

Graph 9.2 UK – Average maximum withholding rate at source (DTC).

Source: Author's own calculations based on information drawn from HM Revenue and Customs, available at: https://www.gov.uk/government/collections/tax-treaties.

Both graphs show a clear drop, especially as of the last decade of the twentieth century, in the maximum withholding tax rate stipulated for the countries of origin of the dividends – that is, a reduction in the taxation power of the periphery countries as compared with the United States and the United Kingdom. A similar tendency can feasibly be identified in treaties between the United States or the United Kingdom and other core countries. But the difference is in the plausible tax revenue effect of one and the other group of treaties. While in a treaty between two core countries its solutions will likely be applied to flows in significant amounts in both directions, in a treaty between a core country and a periphery country the flows from the core country to the periphery country will probably be marginal. Nevertheless, these solutions do entail a diversion of tax revenue between the core countries themselves, since they do not all have the same number of resident multinational companies: the United States, as the country with the largest number of MNEs headquartered in its territory, is certainly the main collector of tax revenue diverted from other countries. That, moreover, is entirely consistent with the money-stock-regulating function of tax revenue, given the complete predominance of the dollar as the world's account money.

The following graphics represent, for a set of periphery countries, the total taxes levied on dividends paid to residents of a set of core countries. Total taxation is divided into two portions: the percentage collected by the periphery country (withholding tax) and the percentage collected by the residence country.[1] The absence of a percentage of withholding tax (for example, in Malaysia and Brazil) for all dividends paid abroad means that dividends are not taxed in the country in which they originate (Graph 9.3).

The graphs show the same trend, but in this case from a static perspective: the treaty networks of which the countries are part entail, from the point of view of the periphery countries, that dividends (which are money flows) from their territories to the core countries are taxed, predominantly in the latter.

Graph 9.3 Author's own calculations on information drawn from Tax Offices.

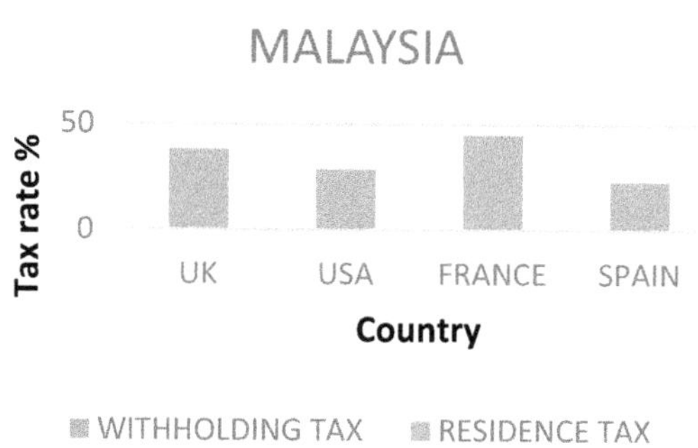

Graph 9.4 Author's own calculations on information drawn from Tax Offices.

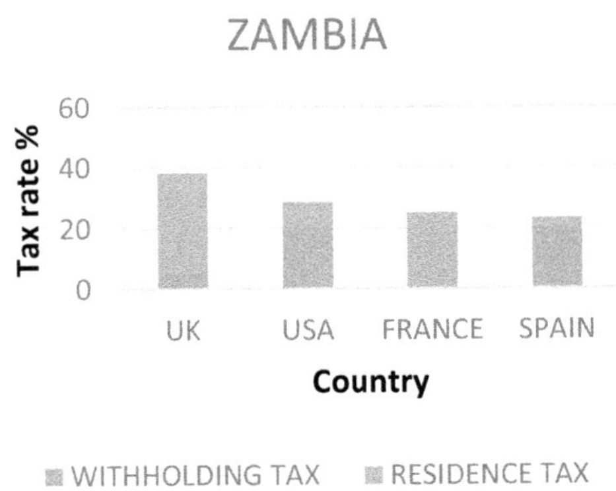

Graph 9.5 Author's own calculations on information drawn from Tax Offices.

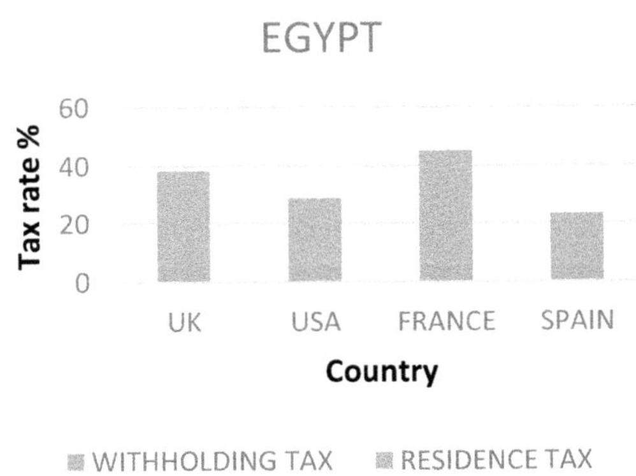

Graph 9.6 Author's own calculations on information drawn from Tax Offices.

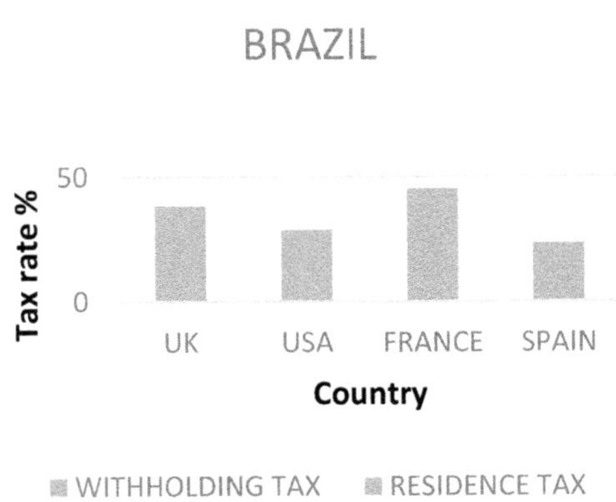

Graph 9.7 Author's own calculations on information drawn from Tax Offices.

Graph 9.8 Author's own calculations on information drawn from Tax Offices.

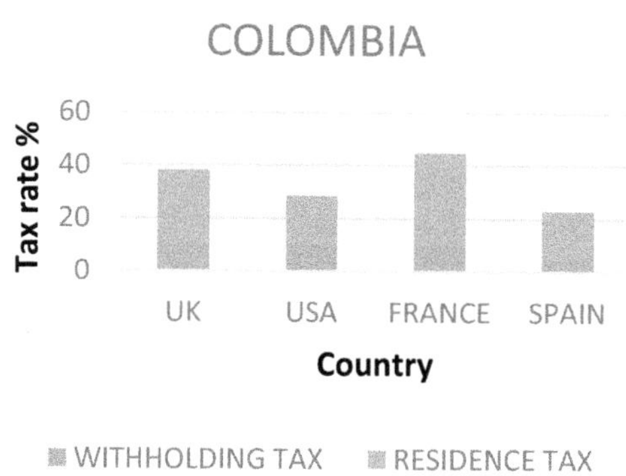

Graph 9.9 Author's own calculations on information drawn from Tax Offices.

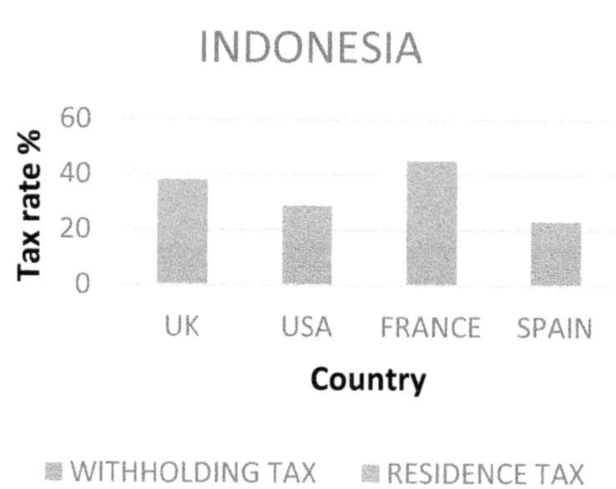

Graph 9.10 Author's own calculations on information drawn from Tax Offices.

A study conducted by Lukas Hakelberg and Thomas Rixen (2020) on the tax rates for dividends stipulated in recent years in the legislations of OECD countries shows that the average statutory rates on dividends, for all OECD countries, went from 20 percent in 2009 to 25 percent in 2017. While this is a generic average for dividends originating in any country in the world, the evident upward trend reveals that in flows between OECD countries and periphery countries a net gain in terms of tax revenue is to be expected for the former, provided that dividend flows remain constant. If flows were to increase, or if the taxable bases were to change (for example, partially or fully affecting undistributed profits), the favorable tax revenue effect for the core countries would be enhanced.

The above notwithstanding, it is interesting that these authors associate the increase in tax rates for dividends with greater international tax cooperation, that is, with the strengthening of controls by taxation authorities as a result of information exchange agreements furthered by the OECD, as noted in Chapter 8.

9.2 Evidence provided by tax revenue and taxable bases

9.2.1 General matters

The most direct evidence for the hypotheses posited in Chapter 6 is provided, first, by tax revenue and second, by taxable bases. A first difficulty encountered in this sense is that the regulatory tendencies described in Chapter 8, which are the manifestation in the superstructures of these hypotheses, have been operating for a century, so measuring their material effects would require detailed statistical data dating back to before the Bruins Report and from there to later periods. This is not possible due to the lack of statistical data for a significant part of the twentieth century. We must also resist the temptation to argue counterfactually (in the sense of "if *x* had not happened, then *y* would have happened"). Indeed, and while counterfactual reasoning is not to be dismissed as a strategy for proposing hypotheses, using it directly for statistical purposes entails modifying actual data with assumptions, which, as they are developed under the same theoretical framework adopted by the researcher, implicitly contain their own self-validation, so that the outcome is unlikely to differ from the hypotheses to be validated (Lewis 2001).

However, the main difficulty in assessing the material effects of these international taxation tendencies furthered by the OECD, the G20, the European Union, and the like is the scarcity of publicly available data with a sufficient degree of accessibility to allow for the identification of tax revenue variations in the core countries that can be related to correlative losses in periphery countries. National states, the OECD, the European Union, and the G20 all display a significant reluctance to give the public access to information on MNEs in general and on their tax revenue from international operations in particular.

An exception is the United States, where publicly available statistical data sheds some light on this matter, although it does not provide direct information on the country's volume of tax revenue from money flows originating abroad, and, consequently, neither does it provide that information for money flows from the periphery. Admittedly, this is the most interesting case because the United States is, without a doubt, the main core country (the core of the core, so to speak), and it is where such changes are likely to have a clearer impact, given that it is where the largest number of MNEs are headquartered. Let us now look at some statistical data on tax revenue and taxable bases with respect to the relations of US MNEs with certain regions of the periphery. The regions chosen are Latin America and Africa, because given the periphery status of all their economies, it may be correctly assumed that the statistical data is less contaminated by countries with a more controversial categorization as core or periphery under the theoretical framework adopted here.

9.2.2 Taxable bases and tax revenue of operations by US MNEs conducted in Latin America

A study from the early twenty-first century (Costa and McGrath 2010), conducted by the IRS itself, clearly shows that in the period 1986–2006 the total volume of foreign-source income obtained by US corporations and taxed in the United States exceeded by far the volume of foreign-source income on which those same companies paid foreign taxes: the former stood at 0.5 trillion dollars at the beginning of the period and rose to 1.3 trillion dollars by the end of the period, while in the same period the latter went from 0.1 trillion dollars to 0.4 trillion dollars. This information is not disaggregated according to region of the world where the United States corporations generated that income, so there is no way of knowing which portion of those amounts corresponds to activities in periphery countries. The above notwithstanding, and assuming that the countries of the periphery follow the same tendency as the rest of the world, we can infer that, also with respect to them, there was a spectacular growth in US taxed foreign-source income originating in such countries.

Based on more recent information that makes it possible to discriminate the income's source region, the following graph shows the relationship (as a ratio) between the profit received by US residents from US-controlled foreign companies located in Latin America and the taxes paid in Latin America. The ratio is shown, on the one hand, only with respect to the withholding tax on payments made by the companies to their parent companies in the United States, and, on the other, as the ratio of profits received in the United States to the sum of the withholding and corporate taxes paid by Latin American-resident companies to the respective states in which they operate. In short, the graphic shows the relationship between profits obtained and taxes paid in Latin America by MNEs headquartered in the United States (Graph 9.11).

Before analyzing the data in the graph in the context of Latin America, we can see that a comparison of the ratios for Latin America and their African counterparts presented below in Section 9.2.3 reveals that taxation levels in the former are markedly lower than those in the latter, with respect both to withholding taxes and to corporate taxes paid by the subsidiaries of US MNEs. A fairly plausible

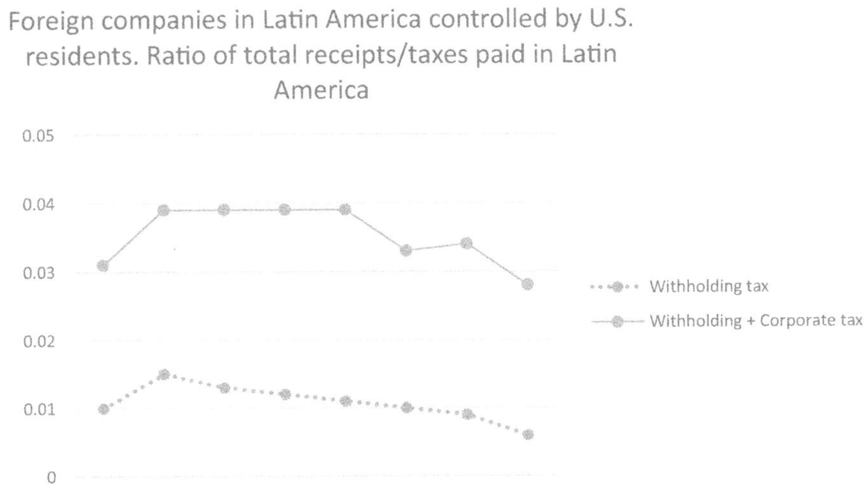

Graph 9.11 US Residents income from Latin America – ratio of income/tax revenue in source country.

Source: Author's own calculation based on data drawn from the IRS, available at: https://www.irs.gov/statistics/soi-tax-stats-corporate-foreign-tax-credit-statistics.

explanation for this may be found in the adoption by many Latin American countries of a tax policy that applies various types of reductions to corporate taxes in favor of MNEs.

Returning now to the graph, a comparison of both lines shows that the ratio of withholding taxes to gross income of MNEs in Latin America declined sharply in the period analyzed, as did the total tax revenue of Latin America obtained from withholding taxes and corporate taxes combined. These data prompt the question of whether the loss by Latin American countries of tax revenue from US MNE subsidiaries entails an increase of tax revenue from those companies by the United States, which is what would actually corroborate the central hypothesis posited in Chapter 6. In this sense, let us look at the ratio of withholding tax paid in Latin America on flows from US resident companies to the gross sums of those flows (Graph 9.12).[2]

The ratio of withholding taxes to money flows from Latin America to the United States remained stable. The explanation for this emerges clearly from the figures shown in the graph below: flows from Latin America to the United States were significantly decoupled from the gross income of MNEs in the region, and that decoupling, in turn, reasonably responds to a behavior of the companies themselves that consists in maintaining monetary profits formally in the hands of subsidiaries in Latin America and reducing payments to their related companies (most likely their parent companies) in the United States. The line representing inflows is expressed in biennial and not annual figures as in the previous graph, in order to make it comparable with the line representing total receipts (Graph 9.13).

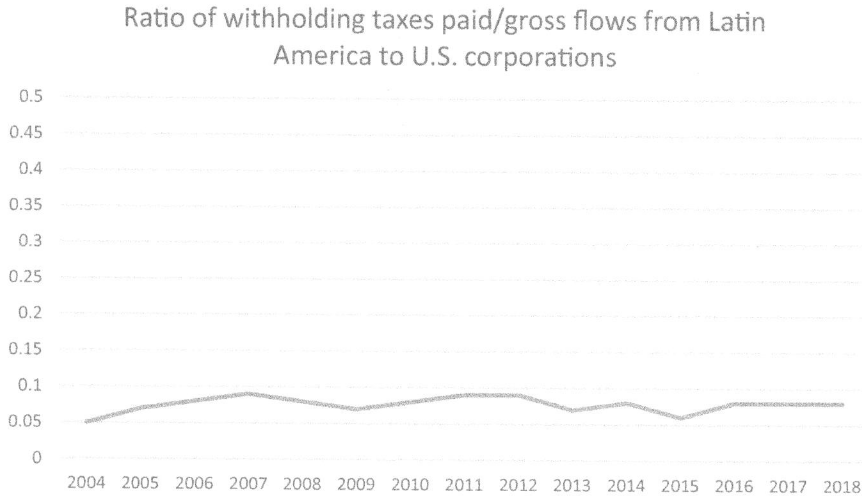

Graph 9.12 US Residents – ratio of money flows/withholding taxes (Latin America).

Source: Author's own calculation based on data drawn from the IRS, available at: https://www.irs.gov/statistics/soi-tax-stats-corporate-foreign-tax-credit-statistics.

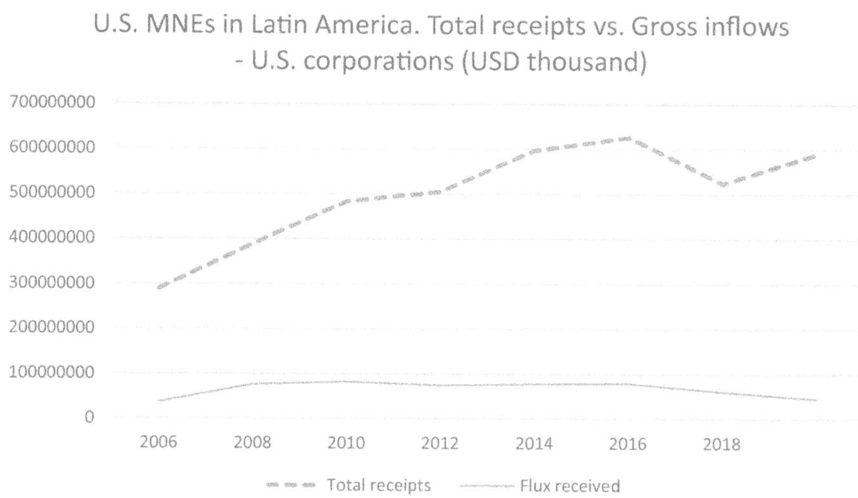

Graph 9.13 US Residents – gross income vs. money flows (Latin America).

Source: Author's own calculation based on data drawn from the IRS, available at: https://www.irs.gov/statistics/soi-tax-stats-corporate-foreign-tax-credit-statistics

This means that at least a substantial part of the tax revenue losses of Latin American countries is due to the behavior of US MNEs, which strategically apply the solution provided by US domestic legislation of taxing profits gained abroad only if they are repatriated.

Is it possible to infer, nonetheless, that in the same period the United States saw an increase in its tax revenue from the monetary income (withheld or repatriated to the United States) of its MNEs in Latin America? There is no publicly available statistical data that can provide a direct answer to that question. A superficial interpretation of the MNEs' behavior would lead us to conclude that an increase did not occur, since the motivation behind that behavior was to reduce their total tax burden. However, another interpretation is plausible. Firstly, and given the enormous growth in the total income of MNEs in the period, the decrease in their total tax burden as a percentage of their income or profits is compatible with the increase in gross tax revenue obtained from them. Based on that, it is possible that, along with the stagnation of revenue in Latin American countries, the United States has increased its revenue even while decreasing the percentage it represents with respect to the income of MNEs originating in Latin America. In particular, such an increase in tax revenue could be associated with two sets of events indicated in Chapter 8.

The period considered coincides, in the first place, with a number of regulatory changes in the United States, which took place over the last decade of the twentieth century and the first decade of the twenty-first, mainly regarding transfer pricing, as noted in Chapter 8. These regulations required an adjustment in the amount paid for various items between related companies, including payments of interest, royalties, and services, for example, made by foreign subsidiaries to their parent companies. Given that these provisions are applied unilaterally by the United States, and not under a DTC, they are very likely to determine increases in the taxable base of the taxes collected in the United States without affecting the amount of withholding taxes or corporate taxes paid in the countries of the subsidiaries.

Significantly, however, in the last sub-period considered (2016–2018), both ratios experienced a sharp decrease. This timeframe coincides with the entry into force of the GILTI tax, which, as we saw in Section 8.6.2, is directly levied in the United States on income earned abroad from intangible assets and which is subject to low or no taxes in the country where it is obtained. As of that moment (2017), the United States undoubtedly increased its direct tax revenue from foreign-controlled corporations.

The increase in gross tax revenue despite the avoidance practices of MNEs has an important confirmation with the second graph that will be presented in Section 9.2.4. It shows that the moments of changes in international tax regulations effectively coincided with upward changes in the gross tax revenue of the US.

9.2.3 Taxable bases and tax revenue of operations by US MNEs in Africa

Let us analyze the same type of statistical data of US MNEs that we considered for Latin America, but now with respect to their operations in Africa. The following graph shows the ratio of withholding taxes on US receipts to the total gross income of African subsidiaries of US MNEs, and the ratio of the sum of withholding and corporate taxes paid by subsidiaries of US MNEs to the gross income of those subsidiaries in the African continent (Graph 9.14).

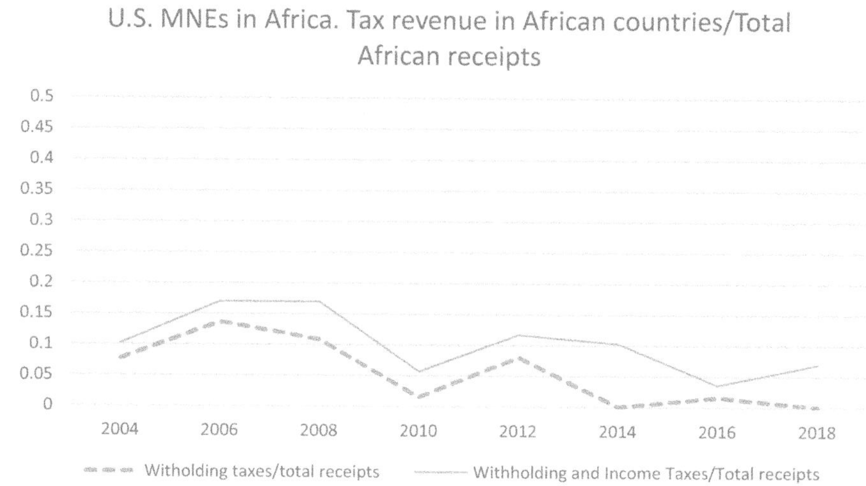

Graph 9.14 US Residents income from Africa – ratio of income/withholding taxes in source country.

Source: Author's own calculation based on data drawn from the IRS, available at: https://www.irs.gov/statistics/soi-tax-stats-corporate-foreign-tax-credit-statistics.

The first notable aspect of this graph is that the ratios are significantly higher than those for Latin America. It was this obvious difference that prompted certain conjectures in Section 9.2.2 regarding the taxation policies of Latin American states.

The second striking element is the scant quantitative difference between total withholding taxes and corporate taxes paid with respect to the subsidiaries of the MNEs in Africa. This situation, which is different from that observed in Section 9.2.2 for Latin America, may be explained by the behavior of the MNEs, which in Africa are less prone than in Latin America to retain profits. If that were indeed the case, the question that arises is why, having the same legal domestic solution available, which enables (or enabled) such avoidance practice, US MNEs chose to apply it in one region of the world more intensely than in another. Scale may be a determining factor in this sense: given that total receipts of US MNEs in Latin America are six or seven times greater than those in Africa, it is much more effective to concentrate avoidance practices in the former than in the latter.

In any case, the evolution of both ratios is basically similar to what we observed in Section 9.2.2 with respect to Latin America, so that the same explanations provided in that case may apply to Africa.

Let us now look separately at the ratio of total withholding taxes to gross inflow from Africa for the same period analyzed with respect to Latin America (Graph 9.15).

The performance of this ratio, considered separately and in detail, has at least some erratic periods, which cannot be easily linked to regulatory changes in the United States and which are not paralleled in the evolution of the indicators for

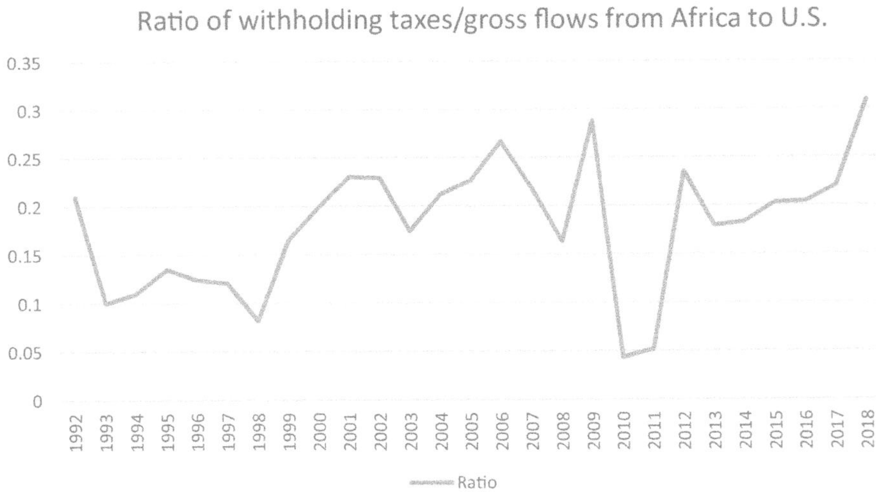

Graph 9.15 US Residents – ratio of money flows/withholding taxes (Africa).

Source: Author's own calculation based on data drawn from the IRS, available at: https://www.irs.gov/statistics/soi-tax-stats-corporate-foreign-tax-credit-statistics.

Latin America, the United States, and the world, described in previous and later sections of this chapter. Neither can the evolution of this ratio be associated with the gross income obtained by US MNEs in Africa, considered in the previous graph. It is very difficult, therefore, to attempt any explanation, given that – as noted in Chapter 2 – the very idea of science is based on the verification of regularities, whether in magnitudes or relationships, so that no conclusions may be drawn nor explanations ventured for a phenomenon that is, at first sight, erratic.

9.2.4 Data connected with the evolution of tax revenue and public spending policies in the United States

In Sections 9.2.2 and 9.2.3, I presented and analyzed data specifically related to the activities of US MNEs, which provide evidence favorable to the hypotheses posited in Chapter 6. However, there is no evidence of the tax revenue effect in the United States, or in core countries in general, that can be associated with the changes in international taxation regulations. The general statistical information on tax revenue should then be at least consistent with the primary evidence provided in Sections 9.2.2 and 9.2.3, and with the regulatory changes discussed in Chapter 8.

Let us look separately and in greater detail at the evolution of the US central government's tax revenue, again excluding social security contributions. This restriction has the advantage of excluding from the statistics the revenue from state-level taxes and the social security contributions, which fall outside the scope of international taxation regulations (Graph 9.16).

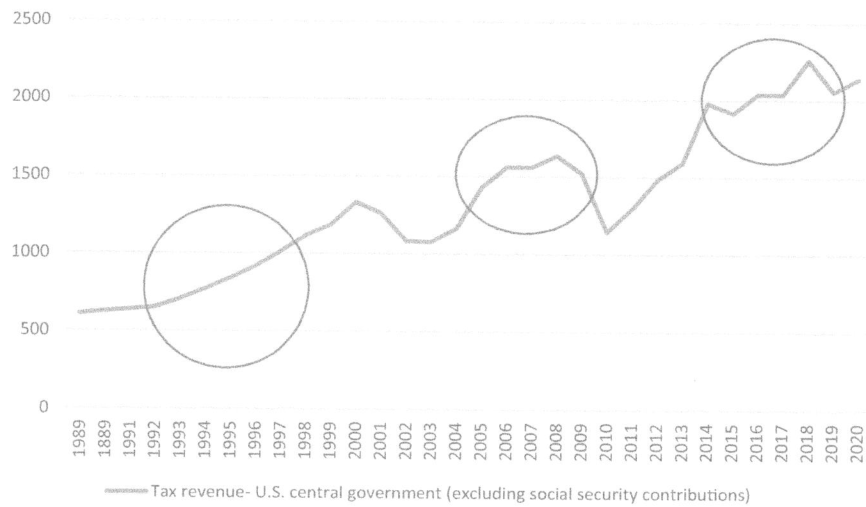

Graph 9.16 US Central government tax revenue – evolution.

Source: Author's own calculations based on data from the World Bank, available at: https://data.worldbank.org/indicator/NY.GDP.MKTP.CD and https://data.worldbank.org/topic/13.

The circled portions of the line coincide, respectively, with three sets of events indicated in Chapter 8 as instances in which US domestic tax regulations (i.e., the superstructures) furthered the shifting of tax revenue from the periphery to the core, namely, in the order in which they occurred: (a) the change in transfer pricing rules in the 1990s; (b) the special regulations that changed transfer pricing criteria for services in the mid-2000s; and (c) the entry into force of the FATCA, the GILTI, the intensification of international taxation cooperation, and the launching of the BEPS Plan. These moments of tax revenue recovery were no doubt influenced by correlative upsurges in the money stock of the United States, primarily through public spending. However, they may have also plausibly responded to the impulse derived from international taxation regulations, given that prior to those upsurges there were tax revenue declines that, because of their timing and/or extension, can only be partially explained by contractions or stagnations in the money stock.

This information, then, is confirmation that reinforces the hypotheses of Chapter 6, since it coincides with both the primary conclusions drawn from the evidence presented in Sections 9.2.2 and 9.2.3 and the last stage of the historical reconstruction in Chapter 8.

9.2.5 Some data connected with tax revenue on a global scale

Other statistical data – much more indirect, but suggestive – can be drawn from the comparison of the tax revenue (as a percentage of GDP) of medium and low-income countries (which, again, can be roughly equated with the periphery) with that of the United States and the European Union. To that effect, the following

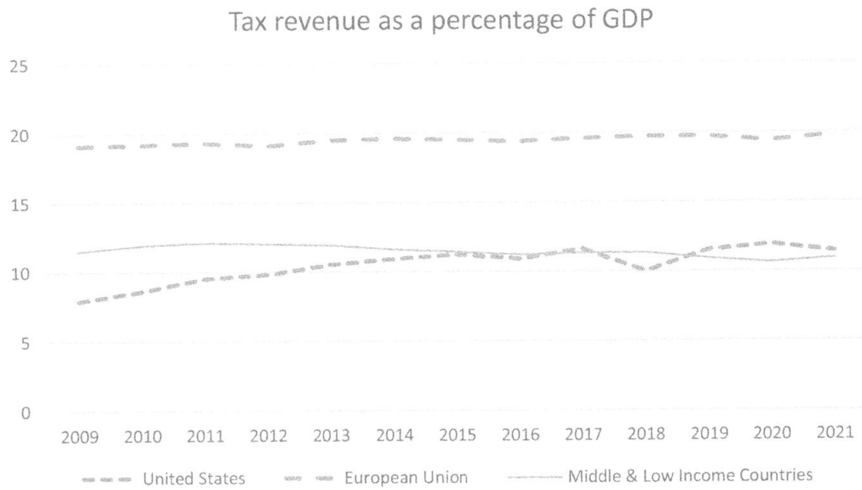

Graph 9.17 Author's own calculations based on information drawn from https://data.worldbank.org/indicator/GC.TAX.TOTL.GD.ZS

graph is based on statistics from the World Bank, which only include taxes collected by the central governments, thus leaving out the taxes of smaller political units (which in the United States include sales taxes) and social security contributions, so that any variations will most likely be related to revenue from income taxes (Graph 9.17).

The graph begins in the year 2009, so as to include the general effect on tax revenue of the crisis of that period. Although GDP as an indicator of production is misleading, its monetary nature means it could be useful for assessing the dimensions of another monetary magnitude, such as tax revenue. The graph shows that while in the European Union and the United States the tax revenue of the central governments remained relatively stable with respect to their GDPs, the same relationship in medium- and low-income countries saw a downward trend. It would clearly be an overstatement to link these trends exclusively, to the international taxation tendencies furthered by the OECD and the new supranationality, but it is not at all unreasonable to suggest that such tendencies have some influence on that evolution. In this sense, as noted, the legal structure of the global taxation system results in core countries (primarily the United States and the countries of the European Union) collecting taxes on flows generated in the periphery, while the reverse does not occur.

Altshuler et al. calculated (2001) the average ETRs, or effective average tax rate (EATRs), which is obtained by comparing effectively paid corporate taxes with net income, apart from the statutory rate, as gathered by Altshuler et al. for companies controlled by US MNEs during the period 1980–1992. That calculation has several limitations. The first and most glaring is that it is based on data from three or four decades ago. The second is that the EATRs are not pondered; that is, they simply measure the net profit/tax ratio without considering the volume of profits earned in each country by US MNEs. In any case, the graph shows that (a) the EATR of periphery countries is almost invariably lower than that of core countries; and (b) there is a downward trend in both groups.

While there may be several causes for these two phenomena, they are all derived from legislative and/or administrative practices aimed at reducing the collection of corporate taxes: tax incentives of various scopes (exemptions, statutory rate reductions, company avoidance practices either tolerated or undetected by tax authorities, etc.). That means that, at that time, there were indeed situations that were leading toward a reduction in tax revenue on a global scale.

This phenomenon corroborates the hypotheses put forward in Chapter 6. Under the theoretical framework set out in Chapter 4, any tax revenue reduction that occurs in parallel to an increase in the money stock is actually or potentially dysfunctional to the mode of production: while, on the one hand, it has the potential to expand demand, therefore favoring capital accumulation, on the other, it always brings with it the risk of inflation as the money reflux phase reaches its limit. When this is projected onto the global capitalist system, the reduction of EATRs, even restricted to a comparatively minor sector of total tax revenue (as it involves only corporate tax and excludes personal income tax and VAT), implicitly contains that potential danger. Therefore, the movements observed in supranational spheres as of the late twentieth century can be interpreted as forms of restructure of the reflux phase through the reorganization of its most stable and relevant component, which is tax revenue.

The graph would therefore be proof of the phase prior to the current one, in which all indicators point to an increase in the tax revenue of the core countries, in both gross and relative terms. Certainly, nobody disputes the fact that the trends in international taxation from the end of the last century until today were caused by the situation reflected in the graphs drawn from Altshuler et al. What is peculiar is that the recovery in tax revenue benefited only the core countries, and not the periphery, which is consistent with the hypothesis of Chapter 6 and not with other hypotheses that challenge them.

9.6 By way of conclusion

Each of the elements presented as evidence in this chapter has its limitations. The graphs illustrating regulatory evolutions are limited because they focus on legal superstructures without considering their material effects. The graphs that group statistical data in Sections 9.2 to 9.5 have limitations in terms of the scope of the quality of the information, as noted in each case.

However, what matters is all the evidence as a whole, which together supports the hypotheses proposed in Chapter 6, with respect to the institutional restructuring of international taxation and, particularly, the redistribution of tax revenue in favor of core countries and to the detriment of periphery countries.

If we add the evidence from the static regulatory analysis in Section 9.1 and the historical reconstruction in Chapters 7 and 8, we can say that the more general hypothesis is convincing: tax revenue tends to align with the location of the money owners, and not with the generation of value. Both the alignment with money and the disparity with value are consistent with the theory of taxation as regulator of the money stock, discussed in Chapter 4, and, above all, with the difference between value as the product of labor, which is situated at the deepest level of the economic phenomenon, and money as the condition for commodity exchanges, which operates at a more superficial and apparent level of social relations.

Notes

1 The set contains countries of Latin America, Asia, and Africa that are signatories of DTCs with a correlative set of OECD countries. The rates considered are those applied to individuals. The rates are the statutory rates and reflect only the tax on dividends *stricto sensu* (i.e., not combined with corporate tax rates on the local company). The assumed shareholders' percentage of capital is 100 percent. Withholding tax rates are, depending on each case, the general rates established by domestic legislation or the maximum stipulated by an applicable double taxation convention. For Colombia, the 10 percent withholding tax rate assumes the dividends derive from benefits taxed by corporate tax at the paying company level. Sources: GOV.UK https://www.gov.uk/government/collections/tax-treaties; IRS: United States Income Treaties A to Z https://www.irs.gov/businesses/international-businesses/united-states-income-tax-treaties-a-to-z; République Française. Impôts.gouv.fr. https://www.impots.gouv.fr/portail/les-conventions-internationales; Government of Spain. Ministry of Finance. Double Taxation Conventions. https://www.hacienda.gob.es/es-ES/Normativa%20y%20doctrina/Normativa/CDI/Paginas/cdi.aspx#:~:text=La%20existencia%20de%20los%20convenios,la%20fiscalidad%20de%20dichas%20inversiones; Deloitte: International Tax, at https://www2.deloitte.com/ ; Harding and Martin (2018). See *References.*

2 Flows include dividends, interest, royalties and other license fees, branch remittances, services fees, and other residual items.

References

Altshuler, Rosanne and Harry Grubert. 2001. "Has U.S. Investment Abroad Become More Sensitive to Tax Rates?" In *International Taxation and Multinational Activity*, edited by James R. Hines Jr., 9–38. Chicago: University of Chicago Press. http://www.nber.org/books/hine00-1.

Blanco, Andrés. 2022. "An Ideological Critique of the OECD Beps Action Plan." *Griffith Law Review* 31 (3): 333–360. http:⁄doir.org// 10.1080.10383441.2022.2096966.

Costa, Melissa, and Nuria E. McGrath. 2010. "Statistics of Income Studies of International Income and Taxes." *Statistics of Income. SOI Bulletin* 30 (1). U.S. Government Printing Office. Accessed 27 July 2024: link.gale.com/apps/doc/A242016557/AONE?u=anon~3c675a0b&sid=googleScholar&xid=21356e63.

Hakelberg, Lukas, and Thomas Rixen. 2020. "Is Neoliberalism Still Spreading? The Impact of International Cooperation in Capital Taxation." *Review of International Political Economy* 28 (5): 1142–1168. https://doi.org/10.1080/09692290.2020.1752769.

Lewis, David M. 2001. *Counterfactuals.* Oxford: Blackwell Publishers.

10 Special international taxation modalities

Transfer pricing, consumption taxes, Pillar I, and the global minimum tax

10.1 Transfer pricing

Transfer pricing rules are a set of legal solutions contained in the OECD Model, in bilateral double taxation conventions, and in almost all domestic corporate tax legislation. They stipulate that costs and income from transactions conducted between legally separate entities belonging to the same international company must be adjusted for tax purposes. This determines all or a substantial part of the taxable base of the corporate tax, as well as the amount of the corporate tax itself. Therefore, for a multinational corporation with units in several countries, the transfer pricing mechanism determines the portions of its total profits to be assigned to each entity of the corporation, and how much tax is to be paid in each country (Blanco 2022a).

I will start by analyzing transfer pricing rules in the framework of the dissociation between value and monetary price and, consequently, between the value chain and the money chain (see Chapters 3 and 5). When an MNE operates throughout the world, it does so under formally separate legal entities, with the exception of branches. This separation is undoubtedly a mystification, as, materially, the MNE is always one and the same company. The exchanges of goods and services between these entities are also mystifications: there is no real change in the ownership of the commodities, nor material transfers of money ownership, given that those so-called exchanges occur within the same company. The only genuine exchanges are those the MNE conducts with third parties. There is, instead, a dispersion of the value chain: the work done in one part of the world generates different amounts of value, based on the human work hours involved and how they are pondered, which are incorporated step by step into the commodities (goods or services) that the MNE produces.

Domestic taxation systems are organized pursuant to legal forms, which is not surprising since taxation systems operate as part of the legal systems that are themselves complete mystifications, so that the rule is that a taxation system must abide by other mystifications created in other parts of its legal system (for example, company laws). Thus, each of these entities must be assigned a monetary "income" and "costs" from the MNE's total operations, so that the respective national state can collect its corporate tax. But the way such income and costs are assigned is necessarily arbitrary. If it is based simply on the prices the MNE wants to set, those

DOI: 10.4324/9781003458678-10

prices will inevitably be set in such a way as to pay the least total taxes. This can be achieved through a number of practices, including, among others, by assigning greater income to entities located in countries with lower statutory rates, or to entities with accumulated losses (see, for example, Bernard et al. 2006). When such avoidance practices became excessive, states – starting, as always, with the United States – were forced to change course in order to, once again, resolve the tension between private property and tax revenue, striking a balance. The artificial division of an MNE into multiple domestic entities was admitted, but legal rules were established at the national level to determine how prices were to be set for transactions – that were formally real but materially nonexistent – between that MNE's entities.

The first observation that emerges from this simple description of transfer pricing is that all systems for the allocation of monetary income and costs are necessarily artificial. Whatever the criterion used, the result will never be a reflection of an authentic circulation of money from one owner to another. Second, this artificiality of the criteria completely contaminates every type of statistical information that includes MNEs. Indeed, all monetary statistics used around the world, even those used in this book, are based on the accounting data of the national entities, which is reported to taxation authorities, government statistics agencies, and other administrations. This is the case with GDP, the balance of payments, value added, etc. But, since it is evident that these companies' accounting records include those of the domestic entities that belong to MNEs and that their monetary income and costs are set arbitrarily according to transfer pricing rules, it follows that all statistics, everywhere in the world, are distorted as a result of those rules. Tax laws that deal with transfer pricing, therefore, do not affect tax revenue alone; they also trigger a succession of mystifications extending far beyond taxation.

Focusing exclusively on tax revenue, transfer pricing rules are a way of distributing taxation power and, therefore, tax revenue among states, whose importance is directly proportional to the weight of the MNEs in the territory of each state. The key, then, is in the criteria used to assign portions of the total profits of a multinational corporation to each company located in each country. Traditional transfer pricing rules establish various methods for determining the "market price", based on the arm's length principle (pursuant to article 9 of the OECD Model Tax Convention on Income and on Capital) (Avi-Yonah 2007, 1–2; OECD 2015). Some of those methods come close to a statistical measurement of the average prices of "comparable transactions", while others are simple rules designed so that the amount of income that is subject to corporate tax is not left to the discretion of corporate management (for example, by adding preset margins to actual costs).

Lately, transfer pricing rules have evolved to adopt a criterion based on multiple factors for distributing the portions of the total profits of multinational corporations among their different affiliates. The change in legal rules (both judicial and statutory) began in the United States with several court decisions, it continued with amendments to the US Tax Code during the 1980s (Avi-Yonah 2007, 10 ff.), and it entered its most recent (but not definitive) phase with the OECD's global proposal, included in the BEPS Action Plan.[1]

The actions that specifically target this issue recommended by the OECD under the BEPS Action Plan are actions 8 through 10. The title of the final report, published in 2015, is in itself suggestive: *Aligning Transfer Pricing Outcomes with Value Creation*. The OECD does not just set out certain criteria for profit allocation within an MNE, rather, as the report's title indicates, the OECD seeks to give the idea that such criteria are based on a supposed social phenomenon – "value creation" – and not on a mere decision adopted by a group of experts gathered for that purpose. It is a specific case of the procedure discussed in Chapter 8. The OECD adds a pseudo theory (a rather crude version of the neoclassical theory of value) to a purely regulatory solution, providing no bibliographical references or empirical evidence whatsoever. Hence its ideological effect: it creates a context for readers so that they will "read" the regulatory suggestion from the perspective of that context, and it legitimates the regulatory proposal (although, as will be shown shortly, it can be critiqued from the point of view of the labor theory of value).

The OECD argues that profits from business activities are associated with risk-taking, that is, with the uncertainty of the outcome and the possibility that such outcome may generate losses. Thus, risk-taking is at the center of the criteria for allocating profits to the different sections of an international corporation: the more risk taken by a member entity, the larger the portion of the multinational corporation's overall profits that is to be allocated to that entity (OECD 2015, 9–12). After some observations regarding the relative importance of the cash box and intangibles, the document goes on to stress the need for a "functional" analysis to determine the comparative importance of the various parts of the business (see, for example, OECD 2015, 20–23). The document lists decision-making, logistics (the packing, grouping, short-distance transporting, etc., of goods), warehousing, and so on, as examples of the parts into which a business is divided.

A feature of the discourse of the BEPS Action Plan that stands out is that it *completely omits the process of physical production of goods as an activity that is relevant for the internal distribution of profits* among the units that make up an international corporation. The activities of any MNE obviously involve more than management, decision-making, or risk-taking. No concrete empirical evidence is needed to prove that when an MNE sells a good or service generated by it, there is a productive process behind that good or service, and that even when an MNE resells goods or services, that activity requires not only managers, decision-makers, etc., but also people who carry out the purchase and sale of the goods or services. In fact, the real core of a business are the strictly productive processes, namely, the extraction or manufacture of the goods they sell. The same is true when the commodities exchanged are services, as those services are ultimately human labor reified or objectified (transformed into objects), and resold by the company that buys the worker's time and labor. Similarly, when a company delivers goods to third parties for their use, this involves, at the very least, certain people who prepare and maintain those goods.

A method whereby profits are allocated, for tax purposes, to the places where business decisions are made (particularly strategic and financial decisions), while disregarding material production processes, would result in a comparative increase in the taxable bases in core capitalist countries and a reduction in the taxable bases in peripheral countries.

The two parallel "chains" in international capitalism described by Quentin and Campling, could serve to illustrate the above effect. The "value chain" – formed by the productive units, where the main labor force is applied to produce commodities – is not relevant for tax purposes. The "money chain", instead, is the only one considered by transfer pricing rules. More precisely, transfer pricing rules build a money chain that is not even real in monetary terms, given that money, insofar as it is a social relation, can only be spatially located where its owner is.

Two additional examples will illustrate the artificiality of the rules. These rules assign greater importance to "intangibles", that is, elements whose "ownership" (or rather, the attribution of "ownership by an entity") entails the need to assign a portion of the MNE's monetary income to the respective entity. But "intangibles" or "intellectual property" are a product of labor: like factory workers, "intellectual workers" produce. In their case, they carry out a mental process to produce, for example, an image, a software program, a design for an accounting structure, etc. Converting those products of human labor into "intangible assets" entails, first, alienating them from their producers to put them in the hands of capital, and second, using such intellectual products as "rights" to appropriate the value generated in other production processes under the form of "royalties" (Resnick and Wolff 1987, 132–133; Vercellone 2007; Marx 2015, 616, 625). So, intangibles do not exist as objects, and what is in fact a reification of human labor certainly cannot be considered a spatial location.

The traditional methods for assigning income and costs are always unrelated to the generation of value, because they are determined by market prices, that is, by the monetary exchange rates of the commodities and not by the pondered work hours incorporated into them. The new methods outlined in the BEPS Action Plan, however, are completely blind to value, as they do not even take into account the production process. Essentially, the emphasis placed on decision-making and the localization of risk-taking brings this method closer to the general rule observed in previous chapters: the concentration of tax revenue in the core countries, and the decreasing relative importance of tax revenue in the periphery, as a result of the redistribution of taxation power.

Let us consider a simple example of two comparative criteria for assigning profits among different parts of an MNE (Blanco 2022a). This MNE's main characteristics are: (i) a global income of US$1,000 stemming from sales of manufactured goods; and (ii) a management center, with ownership of a trademark, and 500 worked hours in a year, located in a core country (A); and two manufacturing factories, with 2,000 worked hours in a year each, in two periphery countries (B and C). Assuming corporate income taxes with similar structures in all three countries: a taxable base equal to the gross income minus all costs, and a 20 percent rate. Costs incurred with third parties are not taken into account, so that the costs considered include only the income assigned to Country A, under the items "management" and "use of trademark fees".

Now, let us assume the following three criteria for distributing global income: (a) the traditional criterion based on the arm's length principle; (b) a method based on worked hours pondered depending on whether they are directly productive or indirectly productive, multiplied by a 1.5 factor for directly productive hours and by 1 for indirectly productive hours (a variant of the proposal stated below in Chapter 13); and (c) a third method aligned with the OECD recommendations, attributing a substantial portion of income to decision-making processes and intangibles (say 40 percent), and the rest to other activities. The corporate taxes to be paid would be as follows:

(a) Arm's length criterion

Country A: Arm's length management and intangible use fees: 400
Gross income: 400
Tax: 400 x 0.2 = **80**

Country B: Arm's length sales income: 500
Gross income: 500
Net income: 500 – 200 = 300
Tax: 300 x 0.2 = **60**

Country C: Arm's length sales income: 500
Gross income: 500
Net income: 500 – 200 = 300
Tax: 300 x 0.2 = **60**

(b) Worked hours criterion

Pondered hours by country and total
Country A: 1,000 x 1 = 1,000
Country B: 2,000 x 1.5 = 3,000
Country C: 2,000 x 1.5 = 3,000
Total: 7,000

Corporate taxes

Country A
Gross income: 142.85
Tax: 142.85 x 0.2=**28.57**

Country B
Gross income: = 428.51
Net income: 428.51 – 71,425 = 357.85
Tax: 357.85 x 0.2 = **71,417**

Country C
Gross income: = 428.51
Net income: 428.51 – 71,425 = 357.85
Tax: 357.85 x 0.2 = **71,417**

(c) Decision-making and intangibles Criterion
Income assigned according to "relevance"

Country A:
Gross income: 1,000 x 0.4 = 400
Tax: 400 x 0.2 = **80**

Country B
Gross income: 1,000 x 0.25 = 250
Net income: 250 – 200 = 50
Tax: 50 x 0.2 = **10**

Country C
Gross income: 1,000 x 0.25 = 250
Net income: 250 – 200 = 50
Tax: 50 x 0.2 = **10**

10.2 Destination criterion: from indirect taxes to corporate taxation

10.2.1 Some historical background: the origin of the destination criterion

So-called indirect taxes are those whose taxable event is, legally speaking, a transaction in which goods or services are exchanged for money. These include the VAT, specific taxes levied on certain goods and services, and traditional import or export tariffs, among others. They are called "indirect" (and sometimes "consumption" taxes) due to the naive assumption that the economic burden derived from them is invariably shifted and impacts final consumer prices, in contrast to the (equally naive) belief that income or asset taxes are not shifted. Although today it is widely accepted (under any theoretical framework) that all taxes can be shifted, regardless of their legal structure, I will use these terms for the sake of clarity.

Briefly stated, the destination criterion means that in international trade transactions these taxes are applied only once, by the state that receives the commodity (good or service), and, at the same time, that the commodity is not taxed by the country of origin of that commodity. This criterion's underlying objective, which can be observed intuitively, is to avoid double taxation, as is the case with respect to corporate taxes. I will therefore try to identify the origin of this criterion.

For Ricardo, as we saw in Chapter 7, the economic burden of any tax is shifted (Ricardo 1896: 87ff.). If we extrapolate this idea to his theory of comparative costs in the global economy, we quickly arrive at the need to avoid double taxation in international exchange transactions, or perhaps even eliminate all taxes thereon. Indeed, Ricardo's elliptical allusion to an international trade free of any obstacles, as a premise for achieving a natural division of labor internationally, can easily be interpreted as an invitation to eliminate international indirect taxes, or, at least, to minimize their effects.

The mainstream literature developed in the twentieth century that deals with the effects and design of indirect taxes often assumes the need for the absence of double taxation as an unquestionable premise requiring no justification, and, furthermore, that such taxes need to be "neutral", that is, that they should not distort the natural international division of labor, a corollary of Ricardo's old theory. This is the case with Clara K. Sullivan in her classic VAT study, in which, after simply stating that taxes *should* adopt an inter-jurisdictional principle, she quickly moves on to discuss whether the most suitable criterion is the destination criterion or the origin criterion, without questioning why adopting a uniform criterion is necessary at all (Sullivan 1965, 30). This author then focuses on justifying the destination principle by virtue of the ability of consumers to pay, assuming, again, a uniform shifting of the burden onto consumer prices. Similarly, the origin criterion (i.e., the uniform taxation of exports of goods and services) is rejected by Sullivan because of its supposedly distorting effects (31–33).

The comparison between Sullivan's analysis and Marshall's, discussed in Chapter 7, is striking. While they both agree on the assumption that import taxes are shifted, Marshall's analysis is infinitely more nuanced as he identifies wages as what is truly impacted by these taxes, in contrast to "the community" mentioned by Sullivan as a homogeneous whole in which there are no social classes. Sullivan's ignorance of the effect of international monopolies on shifting is also significant, and it results in her failing to realize that setting a tax on the exporting of goods with an inelastic demand abroad will not mean (as long as that situation lasts) any harm for local producers and will moreover entail a tax revenue advantage for the respective state, as Marshall noted. This comparison is particularly relevant because it is the origin of a phenomenon identical to the one we observed with respect to income taxes: the uncritical proposal of an effect and a tax design rule, while ignoring alternative effects that would rationally lead to a different conclusion, which, once again, indicates an ideology presented as a theory.

In the 1960s, as the newly formed European Economic Community (EEC) started going down the path of "tax harmonization", the Report of the Tax and Financial Committee (known as the Neumark Report, after its chair, Fritz Neumark) also understood that the application of an indirect tax in the destination country did not alter the competition between states, provided that goods or services were completely free of an explicit or implicit tax burden in the country of origin (EEC 1963, 146). This recommendation was implemented with the Second EEC Directive, which is the first legislative design of the VAT, and it was replicated in domestic legislation throughout the world, not just in Europe, with a virtually identical mechanism: uniform application of the import tariff, no tax applied on exports, and the granting of a credit or refund to exporters for the VAT applied to their purchases (EEC 1967).

10.2.2 The criterion today: the OECD proposal for the VAT and the application of a corporate tax (Pillar I)

All domestic VAT legislations, as well as European Community regulations, remain to this day aligned with the destination criterion in the terms expressed above: taxation of imports and non-taxation of exports, with refunds or credits granted to exporters for the VAT applied on their purchases.

Invoking the need to redesign domestic VATs in the context of the "digitalization of the economy", the OECD drafted a new proposal that is in no way novel; rather, it simply takes up solutions that the European Union had already implemented in the first half of the 1990s (OECD 2017). Digitalization or no digitalization, international exchanges of physical commodities certainly have no peculiarities with respect to the destination criterion: once the good enters the country or the region in question, the VAT will be uniformly applied on a monetary amount (generally the price), in accordance with that criterion. With respect to commodities that are pure labor, whether as an act or consolidated to give the appearance of an asset (these are what are considered intangible goods), the OECD's proposal is exactly the same as what was already in force in the European Union and in many other countries, namely, the application of the VAT in the country of residence of the person purchasing that activity, with the addition of the legal category of "taxpayer reversal" (categorizing the receiver of the activity as a taxpayer in the legal sense of the term). That is, it proposes generalizing, without exceptions, the destination criterion.

At the start of the twenty-first century, however, the idea that corporate taxes could, or even should, be applied at the destination of the commodities, especially in transactions conducted by MNEs began to take shape (see, among others, Avi-Yonah 2000, 1670–1673; Devereux and de la Feria 2014). It is not a complex idea: instead of the traditional residence criterion, and its complementary source criterion, the proposal is that MNEs be subject to corporate tax in the place where the goods they produce are consumed, and/or in the place of origin of the cash-flow from third-parties purchasing their goods. In short, this entails erasing the structural differences between the VAT and the corporate tax designing the latter (at least for MNEs) similarly to the former.

The proposal was formally accepted and it is being implemented by the OECD through the so-called Pillar I (OECD 2021a; OECD 2021b; Blanco 2022b, 14–15). While the proposed Pillar I and Pillar II were initially intended for the so-called digital economy, as of the decisive intervention of the United States in the G20, and of the G20 in the OECD in 2021, these pillars became the starting point for a radical reform of the global system of corporate taxation. Today Pillar I is proposed for all MNEs with income above 750 million euros, with their global income divided, for income tax purposes, into two amounts: Amount A and Amount B. While Amount B will be distributed, in principle, according to traditional criteria (probably combined with the transfer pricing rules discussed above), Amount A will be assigned to the countries of final consumption of the commodities. There are other details, more or less relevant in terms of the legal design, but what matters is that it is the first organized and systematic attempt to redirect corporate income taxation toward a scheme similar to that of the VAT. But what is most important is the assessment of the tax revenue effects of this proposal and, in particular, its comparison with the hypotheses posited in Chapter 6.

10.2.3 The tax revenue effects of the destination criterion on the VAT and corporate taxes

Intuitively, when describing the scope of taxation at the destination for any type of tax, one tends to think that the international distribution of the resulting tax revenue will likely favor the countries with higher consumption. That, in my opinion, is effectively the case; therefore, here too we will observe a shift in tax revenue toward the core countries. Nevertheless, let us look at OECD estimates.

A study conducted in the OECD to determine the effects of Pillars I and II estimates that Pillar I will entail greater tax revenue for medium- and low-income countries (or periphery countries, in the terms used here) and less tax revenue for high-income countries (generally, core countries, according to our categorization), while suggesting that Pillar II will have a concentrated tax revenue effect on high-income (core) countries, with lower tax revenue for medium- and low-income (periphery) countries (OECD 2020). The study then makes quantitative estimates based on these assumptions. However, it has gross methodological errors and omissions, which invalidate it completely.

For example, with respect to the effects of Pillar I, the participation of each country in Amount A (which, as we saw above, is the portion of the income of MNEs that will be distributed among final consumption countries), it estimates that it will be divided in proportion to the local sales made in each country by MNE entities in that country, minus the exports of those entities. This is an inadmissible error: the draft Pillar I rules developed by the OECD itself refer only to final consumption as a determining element of the portion of Amount A assigned to each country, so that subtracting exports to estimate the tax revenue effect in that country is methodologically untenable. The only case in which it would make sense to completely remove MNE exports would be if the total income generated by such transactions were to go to Amount A. But that is by definition impossible because Amount A is only a portion of the global income of an MNE under that scheme, so that it can never fully absorb the income attributable to a country under exports. This decidedly erroneous assumption thus results in estimates that bear no relation to the real effect expected from Pillar I.

Furthermore, and as the report itself acknowledges, the estimation of the country-by-country effects of Pillar I completely disregards sales (of both tangible and intangible goods) in a country where the MNE has no local entities, which most likely represent a considerable percentage of that company's sales. The conclusions of this OECD study regarding Pillar I must therefore be dismissed completely.

Let us attempt an estimation based on different assumptions. We do not currently know exactly what percentage of the income of MNEs covered by Pillar I will effectively fall under Pillar I. Therefore, for now we can treat that amount, which we will call A, as a completely random variable. However, we do know that it will entail both a tax revenue loss for certain countries and a tax revenue gain for them and for other countries. Amount A expressed as a loss is represented by L, and by G when expressed as a gain, with indexes added by group of countries. Grossly simplified, index c is added for OECD countries and index p for medium- and low-income countries as they appear in world statistics, which, in the absence of more precise indicators, are assumed to be equivalent to periphery countries.

To estimate the values of tax revenue losses in core countries and peripheral countries), we would need concrete information with respect to the total taxes paid by MNEs in each region. As that information is not available, we must choose another statistical indicator. For industry (including construction), there is easily accessible data from the World Bank regarding value added, disaggregated by OECD countries and medium- and low-income countries. These values are, of course, arbitrary and distorted, even in monetary terms, as a result of the transfer pricing rules discussed in Section 10.1, based on which the accounting records of MNEs are constructed, with these in turn informing statistics. But, since this is the only information available, we can compare the value added of the two regions as amounts in trillions of US dollars and percentages with respect to the sum of both regions' values. According to the percentages of value added in industry reported by the World Bank,[2] the percentages that correspond to each region, with respect to the sum of the values of both regions, are as follows:

OECD countries: 49.2 percent
Middle- and low-income countries: 50.8 percent

Assuming that tax revenue from industrial MNEs included in Pillar I is distributed in the world according to value added (which is very reasonable considering that these values are constructed pursuant to tax accounting practices, influenced by transfer pricing rules), we should have that, whatever the value of A, the tax revenue losses resulting from the application of Pillar I in industrial activities are as follows:

$L_c = \text{A x } 0.492$
$L_p = \text{A x } 0.508$

With regards to gains derived from the redistribution of A, it is reasonable to assume that they will be distributed simply according to the volume of final consumption, provided industrial goods behave similarly to overall final consumption. Based on World Bank data on final consumption,[3] the percentages corresponding to the regions considered, with respect to the sum of final consumption expenditure of both regions, are as follows:

OECD countries: 69 percent
Middle- and low-income countries: 31 percent
Therefore, gains as percentages of A in both regions would be:
$G_c = \text{A x } 0.69$
$G_p = \text{A x } 0.31$

Here it would be very easy to estimate the net tax revenue effect, *NR* (gains minus losses), for each group of countries with respect to A, simply by subtracting tax revenue losses from tax revenue gains, given that, due to the resulting ratios, , and vice versa, , we would have that:

$NR_c = \text{G}$
$\text{NR}_p = \text{L}$

In conclusion, given the above assumptions, which are all fairly realistic, it is to be expected (in contrast entirely to what the OECD forecasts) that Pillar I will result in a net tax revenue gain for OECD states and a net tax revenue loss for periphery countries. This thus provides another corroboration of the hypotheses in Chapter 6, but with a difference with respect to the other elements already considered, namely, that the effects in this case can be empirically identified more clearly.

Moreover, both the proposal's supporting documents and the study on its potential effects completely ignore the tax shifting and tax incidence of the resulting taxation structure (Blanco 2022b). If the tax shifting and incidence hypotheses set forth in this book are correct, and, therefore, tax shifting is a function of the degree of monopoly and tax incidence, for all corporate taxes, affects workers, surely then the MNEs that would be subject to a new income tax regime are already transferring all of their tax burden and causing its incidence on wages. Therefore, it is more than reasonable to argue that, whether or not Pillar I and the change in VAT application to the destination criterion entail greater tax revenue, there will be no variation whatsoever in the final effect, which will be the incidence of money withdrawal on wages, even if the countries whose workers are affected by the incidence vary as a result of tax revenue redistribution. Nevertheless, the relative effects of tax incidence are not the same: in countries with higher relative wages (that is, where wages have greater purchasing power for goods and services), the substantial effect will be less, and, conversely, in countries where wages are lower, the substantial effect will be greater. Moreover, tax incidence can also be territorially uneven, as there are no studies under heterodox theoretical frameworks that can indicate, in the context of a tax revenue increase that nominally affects an MNE, whether tax shifting will occur uniformly toward all territories or preferentially toward some of them. In other words, the incidence on wages may not run parallel to the increase in tax revenue.

In Marxian terms, the analysis of the previous paragraph can illustrate the influence of tax revenue on surplus value. Indeed, and as we observed in Chapter 4, when tax revenue affects wages (which is the rule), surplus value increases as the workers' capacity to appropriate commodities decreases, or – in the best of cases – remains unchanged. Therefore, and while a potential increase in total tax revenue as a result of Pillar I would entail an increase in surplus value by affecting wages, determining whether that increase would be more considerable if the monetary wages in the country in which the incidence occurs are lower (as we saw in the previous paragraph) will require additional studies.

10.3 The global minimum tax

10.3.1 Description of the initiative

Action 1 of the BEPS Action Plan also includes Pillar II. Initially conceived as a set of tax measures intended for the digital economy, over the course of the year 2021 the G20 and the OECD, driven by the United States, significantly redirected their recommendations. Under the influence of the United States, Pillar II became the vehicle for implementing a proposed minimum corporate tax on MNEs. The first OECD documents dealing with this new line of action claimed it was aimed at establishing a "floor on tax competition on corporate income tax" and, among other issues, accommodating the various interests involved, "including those of small economies and developing jurisdictions" (OECD 2021b, 4–5). In later documents issued on the subject, the proposal was adjusted, both in terms of content and in the agenda for its adoption by states.

The current Pillar II entails, in essence, that states where an MNE has its headquarters (strictly speaking, what in the texts is called the "ultimate parent entity") can apply a complementary tax on profits derived from certain foreign jurisdictions, when a third country imposes a corporate tax on an entity owned by that MNE at a tax rate below 15 percent (OECD 2021d). The tax applied by the country where the headquarters are located is set under the Income Inclusion Rule (IIR). For those cases in which the headquarters country chooses not to implement the IIR, the initiative establishes that countries who have adopted it shall apply an Under Taxed Payment Rule (UTPR) tax, which is a complementary tax that also affects income subject to rates under 15 percent, but that such tax will not be levied in the state where the MNE is headquartered, it will instead be distributed among all the states in which the MNE operates, to the extent that they have adhered to the system.

States in which the local income of the MNE is subject to a rate that is effectively lower than 15 percent will be able to establish a *qualified domestic top.up tax*, which is a specific tax on income that will be applied, in general, in the country of the ultimate parent entity, outside the scope of application of the global minimum tax. That is, the country with "relative low taxation" is allowed to reverse it, so as not to lose tax revenue (Noked 2022).

10.3.2 The mainstream rationale and literature on the global minimum tax

The urgency to quickly approve these measures resulted in an abbreviated rationale, in comparison with previous reports on Action 1 of the BEPS Action Plan, and thus the "descriptions" and "explanations" were reduced to a few paragraphs in the brochure issued in July 2021 (OECD 2021d). With respect to Pillar II, these texts briefly argue that states only impose taxes on local source income, assuming foreign source income is taxed abroad – a situation that affects developing countries the most. This assertion means that, according to the OECD, proposals under the current Pillar II will benefit "developing countries", that is, periphery states as defined here.

These claims, especially the second, are clearly false. The OECD itself has estimated that 28 percent of global GDP corresponds to MNEs, while foreign production (i.e., the portion of production generated by foreign-controlled companies worldwide) is overwhelmingly concentrated by MNEs whose headquarters are located in OECD countries (93 percent), and more specifically in a handful of high-income countries (the United States, the United Kingdom, France, Germany, Japan, the Netherlands, and Switzerland) (OECD 2018). Therefore, it is undeniable that the sole beneficiaries of the minimum global corporate tax will be the states where MNEs are headquartered, and not the periphery countries.

Regarding the analysis of this measure by mainstream economics, I will mention only a few works. Niels Johannesen (2022), for example, analyzes the global minimum tax based on a "model" with welfare as a variable and three groups of actors: governments, firms, and households. Governments (or states) are divided into two groups: non-havens, which are those whose corporate income tax rate is at least 15 percent, but which Johannesen assumes – it is not clear why – to be 25 percent; and havens, which are those with tax rates of 15 percent or less. The effects of the proposal on non-havens would be, according to this model, a loss of welfare for firm owners and an increase in general welfare through the increase in public spending that would result in an increase in tax revenue. According to this author, if the welfare of capitalists had "zero social value", the net effect on welfare would be clearly positive, while otherwise the effect would be uncertain, although it would tend to be positive. He does not conduct the same analysis for non-havens, but assumes that they would all tend to raise their tax rates to at least 15 percent, and that it is possible that the effect on welfare would be positive, insofar as the increase in tax revenue would lead to an increase in public spending.

This article's reasoning presents all the epistemological shortcomings of the neoclassical theory. First, it uses "welfare" as a variable without defining what it is, although from the article it would appear that he equates it with consumption. Leaving aside the arbitrariness of reducing welfare to consumption, this variable is also pondered according to another factor ("social value"), which is apparently quantifiable (as the reference to "zero social value" would indicate), but no clue is given as to what that factor is composed of and how it is measured. Also, the social actors in the model are completely unrealistic: "firms" and "households" are presented as homogeneous blocks, within which there are no different-sized companies nor a division into MNEs and domestic companies, and no distinctions are made between capitalists and workers, women and men, low and high income, etc. The assumptions regarding states are completely arbitrary as well: to begin with, there is no evidence that higher tax revenue will translate automatically into increased public spending; rather, we can assume that states will adopt policies inspired in the same mainstream economics that Johannesen participates in, and which tend toward budget constraint. This form of reasoning, which tries to appropriate the concept of "model" from the hard sciences, but instead of constructing models as simplified versions of reality, bases them on unrealistic or directly false assumptions, is epistemologically unacceptable (Blanco 2017, 53–54), and consequently so are its conclusions.

Michael Devereux (2023) proposes an analysis as a trade-off of state policies between tax competition and tax coordination. According to this author, tax competition consists in the granting by a state of tax incentives that are higher than those of other states, with the aim of increasing the welfare of its inhabitants through investment. This assertion is based on the fact that, according to Devereux, investment decisions are determined by capital costs and the ETR (the effective tax rate understood as the actual percentage of deduction on income that a tax represents). States also have an interest in maintaining or raising ETRs in order to obtain resources for public spending.

Tax coordination is one solution for this trade-off, because if all states tend, for example, to unify ETRs, there will be no incentives to shift activities or profits from one country to another. The IIR of Pillar II goes in that direction. As for any states that might be tempted to abandon the agreement and return to a tax competition scenario, that possibility is precluded by the introduction of the UTPR, which ensures the minimum global tax even if the headquarters state does not join the system.

While several of Devereux's assumptions are not acceptable within the theoretical framework adopted here, some of his conclusions are in line with what I will discuss below. First, Devereux's statement that the United States is the great winner in Pillar II in terms of tax revenue, insofar as it is the country with the largest number of MNE headquarters and has characteristics unrelated to taxation that make it highly unlikely that those headquarters will leave the country. This conclusion is correct even without the UTPR, but much more so with it. Also consistent with the theoretical framework adopted here is his assertion – albeit made in passing – that the burden of the global minimum tax will surely be shifted and will ultimately affect workers, although Devereux suggests it for small open economies and here it is posited for the whole world.

10.3.3 Interpretation of the global minimum tax under the theoretical framework adopted

As the global minimum tax included in Pillar II of the BEPS Plan is a tax policy measure, we must start with the concept of state adopted in Chapter 3. While mainstream economics understands that states make all their decisions independently, motivated by goals such as the "welfare" of the population in general or of sectors of the population, the Marxian theory of the state adopted in this book posits something completely different: states, as part of the superstructures, adopt decisions that must be functional to the capitalist mode of production. That functionality should not be understood as a passive reflection of economic relations. On the contrary, the state's actions are a form of overdetermination, according to which the state, with its policies, plays a decisive role, through its legal systems that impose social behaviors, in determining the direction the mode of production must take at a given moment in order to fulfill its fundamental properties.

Taxation decisions are thus translated, above all, in tax revenue, that is, in the withdrawal of circulating money to cancel it. This vital effect of taxation – whose constant disregard by mainstream economics is remarkable and has ideological connotations – is subject to a tension, as discussed in Chapter 8: on the one hand, tax revenue is essential as the ultimate means for controlling the money stock; but on the other, it has to adjust to the countertendencies that make it possible to reverse the tendency of the profit rate to fall and continue the process of accumulation of capital.

That tension is what explains the fluctuations between tax incentives or tax cuts and anti-avoidance measures, such as the global minimum tax. It is not a "competition between states" that is replaced by a policy of confrontation with MNEs or "tax coordination". For some time, states must cooperate with the reestablishment of the profit rate, for which the available money in the hands of the MNEs must grow and move freely around the world to be concentrated in the places where lower wages increase their global surplus value. But when there is a risk that the money stock will grow excessively, tax revenue must be strengthened. But not the tax revenue of any state, only that of the core states, and especially the United States, whose account money is used around the world to the exclusion of others.

In this sense, it is interesting that in mainstream economics the most notable and unquestionable effect of the global minimum tax is not mentioned, namely, the increase in global tax revenue. The second effect, which is the concentration of that increase in the hands of core states, could be inferred semi-intuitively from a simple fact, as the vast majority of MNEs have their headquarters in core countries, and the global minimum tax entails in theory an increase in tax revenue for the countries of those headquarters.

A more rigorous empirical analysis would require access to tax revenue information pertaining specifically to MNEs potentially affected by the global minimum tax, both in the countries where their headquarters are located and in the various countries in which they operate, as well as the actual amount of their income. That information is not available to the general public, so that it is only possible to estimate the actual effect of Pillar II if one or more states open their respective databases. To date, the most important study with those characteristics, because of its scope, is the study conducted by Mona Barake et al. (2021), based on direct information obtained from European tax authorities. The conclusions of that study are categorical: there will be an increase in tax revenue worldwide as a result of the global minimum tax, but it will be concentrated overwhelmingly in the core countries, and in particular in the United States. In short, the hypotheses posited in Chapter 6 are again confirmed.

Finally, it is relevant to note that the global minimum tax will surely be shifted through prices and will ultimately affect wages, which is to say, workers. If we accept that tax shifting is a consequence of the degree of monopoly of companies, which is, in turn, a consequence of company size, it is almost certain that MNEs will shift all (or almost all) the additional tax burden through prices. In the theoretical framework adopted here, this effect is a manifestation of the hypothesis originally posited by Eric Olin Wright, namely, that taxation, through tax shifting, is a socialized form of reduction of monetary wages and, ultimately, of the part of production that workers appropriate, with the ensuing effect of increasing the profit rate (in the monetary sphere) and surplus value (in the sphere of value). This conclusion, which is shared even by Devereux (albeit partially), shows that the notions that the global minimum tax, whatever its structure, will entail something "equitable" (for example, Picciotto et al. 2021) are illusory. Leaving aside that this tax has a monetary function, regardless of what the ETR of the MNEs is, the burden will fall, as it almost always does, on the workers.

Notes

1 Base Erosion and Profit Shifting Action Plan.
2 Available at: https://data.worldbank.org/indicator/NV.IND.TOTL.ZS
3 Available at: https://data.worldbank.org/indicator/NE.CON.TOTL.CD

References

Avi-Yonah, Reuven S. 2000. “Globalization, Tax Competition, and the Fiscal Crisis of the Welfare State.” *Harvard Law Review* 113 (7): 1573–676.

Avi-Yonah, Reuven S. 2007. “The Rise and Fall of Arm’s Length: A Study in the Evolution of U.S. International Taxation.” *Law & Economics Working Papers Archive: 2003–2009* 73. https://repository.law.umich.edu/law_econ_archive/art73/.

Barake, Mona, Theresa Neef, Chouc, Paul-Emmanuel, and Gabril Zucman. 2021. “Revenue Effects of the Global Minimum Tax: Country-by-Country Estimates.” EUTAX Observatory. https://shs.hal.science/halshs-04103899/document

Bernard, Andrew, James, Bradford and Schott, Peter. 2006. *Transfer Pricing by US-based Multinational Firms.* National Bureau for Economic Research. Working Paper 12493.

Blanco, Andrés. 2017. “Reflections on Neoclassical Theory and the Philosophy of Science.” *Journal of Australian Political Economy* 80: 43–64.

Blanco, Andrés. 2022a. “International Taxation and the Global Structure of Capitalism: The Influence of the OECD in the Design of the International Tax System.” *Review of Radical Political Economics* 51 (2): 218–238. https://doi.org/10.1177/04866134211055871.

Blanco, Andrés. 2022b. “An Ideological Critique of the OECD BEPS Action Plan.” *Griffith Law Review* 31 (3): 333–360. https://doi.org/10.1080/10383441.2022.2096966.

Devereux, Michael P. 2023. “International Tax Competition and Coordination with a Global Minimum Tax.” *National Tax Journal* 76 (1): 145–166.

Devereux, Michael P., and Rita de la Feria, R. 2014. “Designing and Implementing a Destination-Based Corporate Tax.” Oxford University Centre for Business Taxation Working Paper 14/07, University of Oxford. https://core.ac.uk/download/pdf/288287693.pdf.

European Economic Community (EEC). 1963. *The EEC Reports on Tax Harmonization.* Amsterdam: International Bureau for Fiscal Documentation.

European Economic Community (EEC). 1967. *Second Council Directive 67/228* f 11 *April 1967 on the Harmonisation of Legislation of Member States Concerning Turnover Taxes – Structure and Procedures for Application of the Common System of Value Added Tax.* https://eur-lex.europa.eu/legal-content/EN/TXT/PDF/?uri=CELEX:31967L0228.

Johannesen, Niels. 2022. “The Global Minimum Tax.” *Journal of Public Economics* 212. https://doi.org/10.1016/j.jpubeco.2022.104709.

Marx, Karl. (1973) 2015. *Grundrisse. Foundations of the Critique of Political Economy (Rough Draft).* Translated by Martin Nicolaus. Penguin Books in Association with New Left Review. https://www.marxists.org/archive/marx/works/download/pdf/grundrisse.pdf.

Noked, Noam. 2022. “Designing Domestic Minimum Taxes in Response to the Global Minimum Tax.” *Intertax* 50 (10): 678–688.

Organisation for Economic Co-operation and Development (OECD). 2015. *Transfer Pricing Documentation and Country-by-Country Reporting. Action 13, Final Report*, OECD/G20 Base Erosion and Profit Shifting Plan. Paris: OECD Publishing. https://read.oecd-ilibrary.org/taxation/transfer-pricing-documentation-and-country-by-country-reporting-action-13-2015-final-report_9789264241480-en#page4.

Organisation for Economic Co-operation and Development (OECD). 2017. *International VAT/GST Guidelines.* Paris: OECD Publishing. http://dx.doi.org/10.1787/9789264271401-en

Organisation for Economic Co-operation and Development (OECD). 2018. *Multinational Enterprises in the Global Economy: Heavily Debated But Hardly Measured*. Paris: OECD Publishing. https://www.oecd.org/industry/ind/MNEs-in-the-global-economy-policy-note.pdf.

Organisation for Economic Co-operation and Development (OECD). 2020. *Tax Challenges Arising from Digitalisation – Economic Impact Assessment: Inclusive Framework on BEPS*. OECD/G20 Base Erosion and Profit Shifting Project. Paris: OECD Publishing. https://doi.org/10.1787/0e3cc2d4-en. https://www.oecd.org/en/publications/tax-challenges-arising-from-digitalisation-economic-impact-assessment_0e3cc2d4-en.html

Organisation for Economic Co-operation and Development (OECD). 2021a *OECD/G20 Base Erosion and Profit Shifting Project. Statement on a Two-Pillar Solution to Address the Tax Challenges Arising from the Digitalisation of the Economy*. Paris: OECD Publishing. https://www.oecd.org/tax/beps/statement-on-a-two-pillar-solution-to-address-the-tax-challenges-arising-from-the-digitalisation-of-the-economy-july-2021.pdf.

Organisation for Economic Co-operation and Development (OECD). 2021b. *OECD Secretary-General Tax Report to G20 Finance Ministers and Central Bank Governors – July 2021*. Paris: OECD Publishing. www.oecd.org/tax/oecd-secretary-general-tax-report-g20-finance-ministers-july-2021.pdf.

Organisation for Economic Co-operation and Development (OECD). 2021d. *Addressing the Tax Challenges Arising from the Digitalisation of the Economy*. Paris: OECD Publishing. https://www.oecd.org/tax/beps/brochure-addressing-the-tax-challenges-arising-from-the-digitalisation-of-the-economy-july-2021.pdf.

Picciotto, Sol, et al. 2021. "For a Better GLOBE: A Minimum Effective Tax Rate for Multinationals." *Tax Notes International* 101. https://papers.ssrn.com/sol3/papers.cfm?abstract_id=3798887.

Resnick, Stephen, and Richard Wolff. 1987. *Knowledge and Class*. Chicago: University of Chicago Press.

Ricardo, David. 1896. *The Works of David Ricardo,* London: John Murray. https://play.google.com/books/reader?id=V0JVAAAAcAAJ&pg=GBS.PA90&hl=es

Sullivan, Clara K. 1965. *The Tax on Value Added*. New York: Columbia University Press.

Vercellone, Carlo. 2007. "From Formal Subsumption to General Intellect: Elements for a Marxist Reading of the Thesis of Cognitive Capitalism." *Historical Materialism* 15 (1): 13–36.

11 The superstructures of international taxation

State, legal, and ideological structures

11.1 General framework for understanding the superstructures of international taxation

I have used the term superstructures to denote all those social relations that are not at the core of production and circulation but are determined by them, and which, at the same time, reproduce and change production and circulation relations. This is obviously a rough definition, and the term itself has even been questioned because it suggests a distancing from economic production as such. But I have yet to find a good substitute.

If there is one conclusion that can be drawn regarding superstructures – and particularly the state, legal systems, and ideology – from what has been discussed in previous chapters, it is that the concept of overdetermination (its variants notwithstanding) accurately identifies how superstructures operate on economic relations. Taxation is a phenomenon that is completely functional to mercantile economies, and most especially to capitalism, due to its role as money regulator, both in terms of the total value of money and its distribution. The strictly material phenomenon of taxation is tax revenue, with other adjacent phenomena – both immediate and mediate – stemming from it: monetary prices are maintained or contracted; investment and consumption expand or contract; surplus value is maintained or contracted, depending on whether wages retain or reduce their purchasing power; and so on. But the starting point of tax revenue is a set of superstructural formations: taxation originates in state structures (traditionally national, but currently moving toward supranationality), takes shape as legal rules, and surrounds itself with ideological discourses that generate a context of beliefs favorable to the established course.

Thus, the material phenomena are truly impossible without the action of the superstructures. It is the superstructures themselves that create certain social relations, both direct and indirect, which, once generated, fit perfectly into the workings of the capitalist economy. In contrast to what happens with ordinary relations of production and circulation, such as the exchanging of commodities, the purchasing of labor force, the extraction of surplus value, the accumulation of capital, etc., in the field of taxation nothing is left to the discretion of civil society individuals. This observation certainly debunks – if there were still any doubts – all the absurd

DOI: 10.4324/9781003458678-11

and extreme claims regarding the lack of connection and the uselessness of the state with respect to the normal functioning of capitalism.

But this origin in the superstructure should not lead to the mistaken notion that the actions of superstructures are deliberate and arise from decisions freely adopted by those who are in charge of state structures. On the contrary, the sequence of events indicates that movements in international taxation follow behind the evolution of global production. First, production expands globally outside the core countries, reconfiguring the periphery, which is transformed from an area that merely produces raw materials and buys finished goods to a region where the same multinational corporations that operate in core countries carry out their activities and where many more links in the chain of production are located. The existence of a supranational state (or states) is then (and not before) reinforced, as we will see in Section 11.2, and it expands its role as creator of international taxation rules, above and against national states, and always in the same direction, namely, tending toward the concentration of tax revenue in the core countries. These institutional changes are accompanied (not preceded) by the generation of a constellation of ideological discourses aimed at surrounding and strengthening the political and legal framework, also after (and not prior to) the occurrence of the described economic processes of expansion of production.

The fact that international taxation adjusts itself to the new modality of the global capitalist system once that modality is already consolidated proves that superstructures are functional to economic relations and follow the course set by these. While overdetermination does mean that superstructures also trigger economic phenomena (such as taxation, in this case), these are complementary to the structure of production: they consolidate it and help reproduce it, but they do not cause it. The OECD, the G7, the European Union, and other similar bodies generate a taxation core and periphery shaped according to each country's volume of tax revenue and its autonomy, but the core and the periphery as areas of the capitalist system are generated by capital, not by the transnational state, nor by the legal system it creates, nor by the ideology with which it is protected.

In the following paragraphs, I will examine the different modalities of the superstructures that have established the new international taxation system and preserve it, but which cannot be considered as operating independently from each other. The most evident is the interweaving of the supranational state with the legal system characterized by specific features, so that the latter cannot exist without the former. But the ideological discourses that accompany the process also emerge from the same center: while, as is normally the case, there are academic centers of ideological production, the OECD itself (and to a lesser extent the European Union) has an ideological mill.

Moreover, the implementation of the superstructures is certainly not the result of a conspiracy of sorts or of premeditated actions taken by all the social actors involved. While ideology, as a system of beliefs, and regulatory systems, as explicit coercive practices, are generators of the behaviors necessary for the reproduction of the mode of production (which is exactly what overdetermination is), at the origin of the generation of behaviors functional to the economic system are, precisely, economic relations themselves. These exert a type of power without the mediation of the superstructures, which has been called mute compulsion (Mau 2023, 3–5): the simple fact of living within the web of social relations of production and circulation makes each person act in a certain way necessary for the mode of production to continue forward and to potentially change course if necessary. That is how the new global taxation system began to take shape and was later furthered: those who were required to act did so in the expected manner, without there being any need for coercion other than their insertion in the mode of production.

11.2 Supranational state structures

As observed, international taxation has been the result of the actions of inter-state bodies, from the League of Nations at its incipient stage in the first half of the twentieth century to the current OECD (and to a lesser extent the European Union, the United Nations, the G7, and the G20). These bodies increasingly absorbed authorities and powers that had previously been in the hands of nation-states: starting with the timid adoption of models as simple references for action, followed by the conversion (with the OECD) of those models into mandatory rules to be adopted by its members, then with a third moment consisting in the design of taxation policies in the form of recommendations to be applied domestically, and finally arriving at the current stage. Today, the OECD's transformation into not only designer but also decision-maker in the fullest sense of the term – first of Pillars I and II and then probably of the rest of the corporate tax and VAT design, and perhaps ultimately of all the taxation systems of the world – is visible as a distinguishing feature of tax-related superstructures. Indeed, the disarticulation of national states as the essential units of the global taxation order is evident. The construction of the global taxation system does not stem from the national level to the global level; rather, supranational institutions (no longer merely international, as we will see shortly) construct a single taxation system that is neither national nor international, but global. This requires a theoretical explanation.

First, this is where theories that conceive the state as an autonomous phenomenon within the complex of social life, as is the case with conceptions derived from Weber – or rather certain non-holistic interpretations of Weber – or with Niklas Luhmann, reveal their explanatory shortcomings. Indeed, today it is very evident to any keen observer that the new profile of world economic production is aligned with the new characteristics of state institutionality: as the former expands and becomes unified, the latter is also unified and strengthened, surpassing the classical national states, to form an institutionality that is particularly focused on economic issues above all others. It is natural, then, from the theoretical point of view, to see a rebirth in the explanatory capacity of Marxism with respect to the relations between institutions and economic life (Robinson 2001, 163).

In this sense, we have observed that certain Marxist currents of thought stress state fragmentation as a functionality of capitalism: when states compete to grant benefits to capital, they further capital mobility and ensure the continuation of the process of increasingly greater capital accumulation. That is the interpretation of

Open Marxism, discussed in Chapter 3. From a different perspective, other lines of analysis (for example, Rosenberg 2010) have argued that the multiplicity of states is the result of the uneven and, at the same time, combined development of the various economies, at least since the transition from primitive communism and the emergence of the social division of labor. Uneven because of the different natural conditions each human group had to face to take that step in production, and combined because of the necessary connection that had to exist at all times between the different social units.

Both approaches are compelling because of their respective explanatory power with respect to certain special features of the sphere of the state. For the purposes of our specific area of study, Open Marxism provides a relatively satisfactory explanation for international tax competition that, in turn, led to the avoidance practices of MNEs. Justin Rosenberg's analysis, for its part, is a good explanation for the persistence of nation-states as historical tax revenue units, and the early need for coordination among them in an "international" instance essential for the capitalist system as a whole to function. But those explanations need to be superseded by one that explains the supranational political institutionality embodied today by the OECD, the European Union, the G7, and the like.

In developing such an explanation, the methodological path taken by Marx for the economy can be useful for the state: after identifying the broad features of the state in general, we can be in a position to explain the specific features of each historical state in particular (von Braunmühl 1978). Let us return then to the role played by state taxation in general: this function is invariably associated with money, or more precisely, money requires at all times state structures that support and organize it: it is the state that establishes account money, regulates the distribution of money endowments among classes and among territories, ensures the transmission of money, and – finally – ensures the closing of the monetary circuit through tax revenue. This last position, and the ensuing and necessary proximity of tax revenue to the location of money holders, is the essential feature of the taxation state. The different modalities assumed by taxation, on any territorial scale, are simply modalities of this fundamental property.

The explanation of the different phases of taxation in space, seen from the perspective of state organization, and in particular the emergence of supranational structures with taxation power, thus reveals a special case of the general phenomenon of capitalist supranationality, as developed by Robinson (2001, especially 169ff.). Following the Robinson's theory, up to a certain point, taxation was able to simply unfold at a domestic scale, requiring only an instance that was merely international. This occurred approximately from the nineteenth century to the end of the twentieth century: each nation-state retained its national taxation power to the extent that in each domestic economy, more or less separated from the rest due to the particularities of its own development, it also maintained its own account money with a significant degree of autonomy with respect to the rest of the world's account moneys. During that period, there was a properly "international" instance, above national taxation powers, for coordination and connection purposes, where certain rules for the distribution of taxation power were set. That distribution was certainly unequal and tended to align tax revenue with the location of the money holders, through, for example, the residence criterion, the unequal allocation of taxation power over the distribution of dividends and the payment of interest, etc. But, such restrictions notwithstanding, nation-states ultimately retained in essence their taxation power. It is in this context that tax competition, as explained by Open Marxism, occurred. The main aim was to ensure the restoration of the profit rate and resume the process of capital accumulation, so that states used their taxation power to selectively reduce tax revenue from MNES.

Between the end of the twentieth century and the beginning of the twenty-first, the relationship between the capitalist system and space took on a new form. Once the new scheme of global production was consolidated and the dollar (and to a lesser extent the euro) was globalized as the world's account money, the need to reinstate the natural function of tax revenue arose, namely, the closing of the monetary circuit through the recurrent cancellation of money stocks. This could no longer be left in the hands of national states and, in particular, in the hands of periphery states. The only way to redirect tax revenue so that it could perform its special function was through the surrendering of taxation power by national states to supranational state formations, such as, for example, the OECD, the G7, the G20, and the European Union. This does not entail the death of national states as tax revenue collectors, at least not for the time being; rather, it is a redistribution of tax revenue power in favor of the states that have direct authority over the world's large money holders, namely, those who run the MNEs.

Perhaps in the not-so-distant future tax revenue, as the final material instance, will also be in the hands of this fragmentary, but very effective, "transnational state", in Robinson's words. But the functionality has in essence already been achieved: a structure was created, which, in turn, established a global taxation system that satisfies the needs of the global capitalist system. And it has done so with respect to the social relations that require such transnational power in order to operate – relations that we generically call "money".

A peculiar feature of this supranational state is the emergence, within it, of structures with no formal foundations, but which are absolutely effective: the G7 and the G20. These "groups" lack founding treaties or explicit texts that regulate their activities, but that informality has no implications in terms of their function as centers for the exercising of political power in general and with respect to international taxation matters in particular. What is more, these groups are not merely at the same level as the formal groups, such as the OECD and the European Union; they are above them. The BEPS Plan and the global minimum tax are the more prominent cases: they emerged as G20 initiatives, which were then taken up by the OECD to be thoroughly implemented and put into effect, but with a design that had already been broadly outlined.

11.3 The legal superstructures of international taxation

While the legal aspects of international taxation are not the focus of this book, it is impossible to reflect on international taxation without taking the legal structures that organize it into account. Assuming, as noted at the beginning of this chapter, that the material phenomena of international taxation (tax revenue as a tool for monetary control and the shifting of tax revenue from the periphery to the core of the capitalist system) are driven by the superstructures, we must inevitably refer to the legal phenomenon, since that is the direct operational superstructure that triggers overdetermination, at least in the advanced forms of capitalism.

First, the inclusion of law within the superstructures by Marx and Marxism (see, for example, Marx and Engels 1998, 92ff.) has been criticized from non-Marxist perspectives for an alleged reductionism or mechanical determinism of legal structures by economic relations. However, this type of criticism can easily be refuted with the adoption of the concept of overdetermination: as with all superstructures, law is not an epiphenomenon of the relations of production and distribution; rather, it constitutes a specific set of social relations that is functional to the economic structure, but far from being a passive reflection of that structure, it actively cooperates in its configuration and reconfiguration. Counter-critiques from within Marxian theory are usually not limited to highlighting the fact that ordinary reductionism or determinism is prompted by biased readings of Marx or Marxian authors. They also tend to advocate legal activism, that is, the need to work within the legal system, with a Marxian basis, to favor the disadvantaged groups that the capitalist system generates (Christodoulidis and Goldoni 2019). I will expand on the possibility of using superstructures in a counter-functional way in the final chapter. But here I will consider legal superstructures in general and in particular from one point of view only.

In this sense, and as with supranationality and the concept of state, I begin with the premise that international law is not an isolated category of analysis, but a concrete manifestation of a general category of superstructure, namely, law. Therefore, we cannot understand law as constructed by the new international taxation system without first understanding law in general.

The Marxian general theory of law tends to focus on two aspects: the ideological nature of law (Pashukanis 2003, 73; Miaille 1977), and the fact that it is a product of class struggle. While these characteristics are not mutually exclusive and, in my opinion, they are correct, they do have some significant shortcomings. First, they are not based on a comprehensive description of the legal phenomenon as a starting point for its insertion in the general framework of the Marxian theory of society. Second, they fail to capture an essential feature of law, which is its normative nature in the strict sense of the term: its function issuing orders and determining behaviors directly (and not in a veiled or oblique way, as is the case with ideology), a function it, moreover, performs very efficiently.

Let us begin by characterizing law as a praxis, understood in the sense of Marx's description of labor as a human product. What characterizes it is the fact that the action is not carried out automatically; rather, it is based on a planning, however elementary, of what is going to be done. Praxis thus involves action preceded by reflection, by a mental process that defines the action before it is carried out (Marx 1995–1996, 126–127).

If we extrapolate that idea to social life as a whole, we have that praxis is a social activity composed of two elements or phases: a discourse that operates as a guide for action; and that action itself, which is carried out according to that discourse. This very broad definition covers the performance of any activity that requires technical aptitude, be it of a productive, cultural, political, or other nature, and it also encompasses law.

The discourse that guides legal actions is formed by a variety of materials: constitutional, legislative, regulatory, and other such texts; legal scholarship, which is constantly organizing those texts and proposing model solutions to concrete issues based on "interpretations" of the texts, or according to other statements it itself generates (principles, aphorisms, etc.); the foundations of decisions adopted on individual cases (court rulings, administrative acts), which also include arguments intended for use by others to guide their acts of authority. The guiding discourse of legal praxis also includes a set of ideologies: apparent descriptions of reality that establish beliefs about it that are functional to the mode of production. These ideologies are sometimes present in the legal discourse itself, as is the case with legal scholarship, or are formally external to it, informing it or legitimizing it, as we will see in the following section regarding the documents produced by the OECD as rationale for its proposals. Actions include the acts of authority – such as constitutions, laws, treaties, and court rulings – that order indeterminate groups, or one or more specific individuals, to act in a certain way. There are also specific actions directed by the guiding discourse: every time a person or group of persons behaves in their private life according to what the legal discourse indicates, they are fulfilling the praxis through those actions.

The overlapping and mutual informing of these two elements of praxis is easy to see: the actions guided by the discourse not only determine behaviors; they also generate, in turn, discourses, and discourses, once they are established and disseminated throughout general knowledge, generate actions. Moreover, both elements of praxis have a prescriptive effect: this is more obvious in acts of authority because they employ a directly prescriptive language aimed at the public, but guiding discourses are also prescriptive since they determine the behavior of the persons who perform the acts of authority (legislators, judges, public officials).

Legal praxis results in a direct normative effect, largely without the need for coercion as an imminent consequence: law spontaneously determines behaviors through the public nature of discourses and acts of authority, which, because they are surrounded by the symbolic mantle of the state (whether national or supranational), trigger obedient behaviors. In these cases of spontaneous compliance, violence against anyone who fails to comply is manifested as a social belief that such noncompliance entails some form of penalty. Moreover, when there are actual or potential deviations from the model of behavior established by legal praxis, those deviations become "legal conflicts" that the legal system resolves through concrete acts of authority that are the prelude to direct coercion (primarily, court rulings).

Both the content and the form of discourses and acts of authority have as their sole essential feature their functionality to the mode of production, whether openly and directly (for example, the explicit protection of the right to property, or taxation laws that require the cancellation of money), or as elements that on their own do not have a direct functionality in the immediate sense but which do so as part of broader sets of elements that do have a direct functionality as such. Therefore, no content or formal requirement for any legal structure is eternal. Let us see, then, how this theoretical framework helps us understand the legal system of international taxation.

The general functionality of international taxation is, as we saw, to concentrate tax revenue in the core countries in order to ensure that it performs its role as regulator of the money stock. That need leads to the existence of a supranational state, which, in turn, generates a legal system for international taxation composed of discourses and acts of authority that determine the concentration of tax revenue in the core countries, as required by the mode of production.

As for acts of authority in international tax law, international bodies, such as the League of Nations, the United Nations, and – most especially – the OECD, have traditionally produced a unique act of authority to impose the necessary direction of tax revenue, namely, "model" regulations, both in the form of treaties (for example, the OECD or UN model double taxation conventions) and in the form of domestic legislation (for example, the model rules recently drafted by the OECD for the implementation of the global minimum tax). These models are not issued in the form legal experts usually characterize as acts of authority: they are not presented externally to society as normative texts, but as draft normative texts. But they are, without a doubt, acts of authority, and they have regulatory effects: they emanate from a body with socially recognized authority (the OECD, the European Union, etc.), and they are also accompanied by coercion, in the form of a threat of penalties from these supranational bodies (see below). This is a first case in which a type of act of authority does not fit the traditional canons: these models are not laws, but they are nonetheless part of the actions that compose the legal praxis of international taxation.

Besides being acts of authority, the texts themselves of the models are guiding discourses: their solutions can be easily used as grounds for a ruling, or for a domestic law, under the term "comparative law", or as a product of a conceptual analysis that is considered intellectually authoritative because of the expertise or its authors, or the prestige of the body from which it emanates (the OECD).

Another special form of legal praxis in international taxation is the recommendations issued by the OECD, for example, in the form of "guidelines", such as the one on transfer pricing. The OECD Tax Model Commentary also falls under this category. Finally, the BEPS Plan took the production of these texts to the extreme, issuing several of them for each of the actions that constitute thematic areas under the plan (Blanco 2022). These texts lack the style typical of an act of authority (they do not openly use prescriptive language, they are not organized as a succession of articles, etc.). Rather, they are written in a narrative style, in part similar to that of legal scholarship and in part similar to a micro-economic analysis text for the general public. Their content is aimed at determining, indistinctly, the content of domestic laws, traditional legal scholarship, and court rulings. The guiding discourse aspect of such texts is, therefore, more pronounced than in the models, but that does not entail that they are not acts of authority, again because they are coated with the symbolism of the supranational state embodied by the OECD. Moreover, as we will see in the following chapter, these texts have ideological features, thus ratifying what was pointed out above at the beginning of this chapter: superstructures in general, but especially those that determine international taxation, operate intertwined with each other, in a continuous process of action, interaction, and mutual feedback.

A major step in this process are the proposals generated under the Inclusive Framework of the G20 and the OECD, mentioned in the previous section. This structure, created in 2016, has been a constant source of models and documents that expand and reshape the content of the BEPS Plan, with more and more increasingly specific and detailed proposals for amendments to domestic legislation and international treaties, or even (as is the case with Pillar I) for a hypothetical multilateral instrument (MLI), such as the MLI that will be discussed below. Briefly, the Inclusive Framework is a supranational structure that operates as an extension of sorts of the G20 and the OECD, with the specific purpose of serving as an international taxation design with a completely vertical operation, given that its Steering Group is formed by 24 states that unilaterally draft proposals, leaving a very limited margin for further discussion. The above notwithstanding, the role of this Steering Group is, as we also saw in the previous section, largely illusory, since the Inclusive Framework actually operates much more vertically: these structures are merely transmission belts for the G20 and, in particular, for the United States, as was patently clear with the implementation of the global minimum tax.

The effectiveness of these documents as guiding discourses, taking over the role of traditional legal scholarship, is very visible in the actions of national courts that rule on tax matters since they often invoke these OECD texts as grounds for their decisions, as is the case, for example, in the United Kingdom (UK Upper Tribunal, Tax and Chancery Chamber 2019).

International taxation and the OECD have, however, played a leading role in the emergence of completely novel acts of authority, namely, multilateral treaties that are unilaterally designed and widely adopted, producing immediate effects on other legal instruments. The first such treaty was the MLI, drafted in 2016 and which has gradually been ratified by more than one hundred states (OECD 2016). This text did not result from multilateral negotiations, but was instead drafted by a group of "technical experts" who, moreover, were part of the G20 and not the OECD. Once completed, states from around the world, not just OECD members, were asked to ratify it, naturally without any possibility of introducing changes. The MLI consists of a number of amendments and additions intended for incorporation into bilateral treaties for the avoidance of double taxation. After a state ratifies it, those amendments and additions are automatically incorporated into all the treaties in force between that state and all the other states that have also ratified the MLI.

Resuming our theoretical reflection, we have that, in the first place, the characterization of the legal phenomenon as praxis is confirmed, given that there is a discourse and a set of actions of a regulatory nature, mutually generating each other in a continuous process.

In the second place, and this is what matters for the specific subject of this book, that praxis is clearly conducted in a sense that is functional to the global capitalist system. That effect is obscured by the legal texts themselves. At the immediate level, and as is usually the case with any legal text, they are presented as a given, neutral, and devoid of any political meaning (Perrone and Schneiderman 2019, 449ff.). At most, anyone attempting to understand this complex web of legal solutions, models, treaties, recommendations, etc., through a simple reading of its texts, will possibly accept the self-declared aim of these documents, which is to create a global taxation system that abolishes the tax avoidance practices of MNEs.

However, if we examine this complex web under the theoretical framework set out in Chapters 3 and 4, everything changes. At its most basic level, a "taxation system" is reduced to its concrete and direct material effect, namely, tax revenue, which constantly eliminates circulating money, through the state, with the functional purpose of controlling the money stock. The "international taxation system" is exactly the same, except oriented toward concentrating tax revenue in the places where the money holders are concentrated. Tax revenue, as a material phenomenon, depends on the superstructures that determine behaviors in the sense that is needed, which, internationally, entails the emergence and operation of a supranational state and legal system, so as to be able to impose a tax revenue structure on a global scale. Therefore, just as national state structures are superseded and overrun by supranationality, traditional taxing rights are superseded and overrun by these new modalities, which were previously unknown, but emerge and are implemented with the greatest of ease, replacing categories and concepts previously believed to be definitive (Perrone and Schneiderman 2019, 447).

At this point, it is clear that, at least in the field of social life, it is economic relations that condition the superstructures, even if these then reshape economic relations. Throughout the process of global establishment of capitalism, taxation followed the same course: concentrating tax revenue where the tendency of money concentrated. Legal forms changed according to the specific moment in time, with treaties giving way to model treaties and treaties, then recommendations, multilateral treaties, and so on.

Even more important is the radical change in terms of the legal system's pretensions of legitimacy. The legal complex developed by the OECD and the G20 based on the BEPS Plan completely disregards any mechanism of democratic legitimacy, at both the international and the local level: the design of the international taxation system is openly in the hands of a handful of states that issue a diktat for the rest of the world, with no negotiations or discussions whatsoever, and national parliaments approve the product of such diktat without any meaningful debate (Fung 2017).

11.4 The ideology surrounding international taxation

Marxism contributed the concept of ideology to epistemology and social theory, not as a mere set of ideas or beliefs but as a discourse that is socially functional through the proposition or defense of certain states of affairs in social life, or in a sector thereof (Blanco 2022, 3ff.). Thus posited, the concept of ideology is both enormously rich and greatly indeterminate (Eagleton 1991, 1–31). I will try to summarize the leading features of ideological discourses and then analyze in that perspective several discourses that are part of the superstructures of international taxation.

The first important feature of ideology is its generation of public beliefs (that is, beliefs that are disseminated among and held by many people in a society) regarding how all or part of society works, beliefs that are invariably favorable to the mode of production. Simply stated, in a capitalist society, ideology tells us that this type of society is, in whole or in part, good and that it is better than others. This can occur in a purely conservationist sense, when ideology perpetuates the state of affairs in a given moment, or in a dynamic sense, when ideology supports a change that has occurred or is occurring *within capitalist society and in a direction required by the mode of production.* Ideological discourses are not necessarily or actually false, although they often are. However, the function of ideology requires that it be reluctant to critique, especially empirically based critique, so that, by definition, ideology is the opposite of science, understood as a discourse and a practice that subjects itself to permanent critique and correction based on experience (Blanco 2022, 5).

Specifically, ideology generates beliefs at the following levels (van Dijk 2006, 119–122): (a) it proposes a general descriptive (or rather pseudo-descriptive) framework for all the social phenomena within which a concrete event will be situated; (b) it delimits a particular type of event by positing it as the only valid factual unit that can describe what is observed; and (c) it legitimizes that context and that event by attributing to it qualities that are positive or beneficial for people.

Situating ideology in the category of superstructures means that its functionality involves, as with the state and law, overdetermination, that is, the prompting and consolidating of behaviors that will ensure the reproduction of the mode of production, through both conservation and change, when change is required. The overdetermination that ideology causes is, however, more subtle than that of law: while law synthetically and concretely expresses in general (through laws) or in particular (through court rulings) what the necessary behavior is, ideology operates through less concise statements. Sometimes, it does so in a complex way (for example, when it is presented as a theory), other times it does so in a simple and vague way (for example, when it is conveyed through mass media). But, precisely for that reason, ideology penetrates deeper than any other superstructure: it does not operate as a discursive agent that is external to its subjects; rather, it modifies their cognitive structures to filter absolutely everything those subjects perceive.

Regarding the world of international taxation, let us consider an analysis of the Bruins Report in light of the components suggested by Teun van Dijk. First, this report proposes a general framework: for example, production as a consequence exclusively of capital, and capital as something self-created, not derived from the accumulation of prior work. It also posits a world in which the decisions for capital placements are determined almost exclusively by greater or lower tax costs, regardless, for example, of the wage level or the demand for what is produced. It then posits a series of events: "amortization" of the tax burden (that is, the reduction of its future sales price), the decision not to invest as a result of the accumulation of tax burdens in two or more countries, etc. The Bruins Report is heavily ideological because it does not provide any evidence whatsoever – not even fragmentary or biased evidence – for its claims. Eighty years after the report, Gordon and Hines proposed, as we saw earlier, a substantially similar explanation for international taxation. In both cases, the legitimizing effect does not occur with respect to that context and that event; it occurs with respect to the regulatory event proposed, that is, the situation in which there is no double taxation and in which capital owners only pay taxes on their returns in their country of residence. This last scenario is the one posited as "good", "desirable", etc.

These ideological discourses, and others with similar content, correspond to a stage of the global capitalist system that continued until the end of the twentieth century. During that period, given that production needed to shift rapidly and massively to the periphery, it was necessary to reduce the pressure exerted by tax revenue on the monetary stock. Consequently, the essence of these ideologies, which naturally permeate legal instruments such as the OECD and UN models, is to contain tax revenue while at the same time maintaining it under the control of the core countries.

As the shifting of production to the periphery became relatively consolidated in the twenty-first century, the relationship between tax revenue and global money changed: the former had to be strengthened to prevent the uncontrolled growth of the money stock due to the arbitrary management of money by MNEs. So the meaning of ideology also changed, in the same way the state and law did.

The supporting documents for the different actions of the BEPS Plan are the most eloquent example of this change (Blanco 2022, 8ff.). To cite one case, the documents produced by the OECD to accompany the new transfer pricing proposals posit a theory of value as vast as it is lacking in theoretical support, even from mainstream theories. It is a totally ad hoc conception aimed directly at justifying the regulatory solution previously conceived by its authors, namely, the distribution of tax revenue according to elements that do not include production in the strict sense (such as, for example, manufacture, in the case of material goods), and focusing exclusively on management activities, decision-making, and even storage. The omission of production as a constituent element of value renders these documents clearly ideological, as whoever reads them and believes their content will have to assume that the commodities (both goods and services) of MNEs emerge from nothing, or are mere natural products. Thus set out, the theory of value of the OECD seems absurd, and it really is, but that is where the strength of ideology lies: if necessary, the ideological mills will produce a discourse that is not only uncritical but also ostensibly false, as long as it fulfills the function it is meant to fulfill.

The ideological discourses that surround the G20 and the OECD and underpin Pillar I and the global minimum tax posit an empirically true event, which is the existence of avoidance practices by MNEs, but they carefully omit the absolutely unequal distribution of the resulting increased tax revenue between core and periphery states. In these discourses the legitimizing role of ideology is much more pronounced: both in the documents of the OECD and in related literature (for example, Picciotto 2013), the BEPS Plan in general is presented as an alternative aimed at achieving taxation fairness, and as a genuine tool for increasing the tax burden actually borne by MNEs.

There is, moreover, a permanent interaction and communication between ideology and the rest of the superstructures. On the one hand, the supranational state has not limited itself to being a center of production for regulatory models, as was the case in the past; it is also a center of production of ideology. Thus, the ideological content of legal discourses notwithstanding, today the regulatory models and acts of authority emanating from the OECD (such as the Inclusive Framework) are directly connected to vast ideological bodies created specifically for them. So the course of international taxation in the sense of redirecting tax revenue toward the core states is the product of a much more highly developed and robust form of overdetermination, one resulting from the combination of institutionality, law, and ideological production in a single center.

One example is enough to show the effectiveness of ideology. When the initial Pillar I proposal was submitted for public discussion, the G24, which is an organization formed by periphery states, presented a proposal that challenged the form in which Amount A (which is the part of tax revenue of the largest MNEs that will be subject to taxation in the country of consumption), is distributed (G24 2019). But the proposal failed to question the essence of taxation based on consumption, although a simple analysis of the composition of final consumption by country reveals that the system as a whole will shift tax revenue from the periphery to the core.

References

Blanco, A. 2022. "An Ideological Critique of the OECD BEPS Action Plan." *Griffith Law Review* 31 (3) 333–360. https://doi.org/10.1080/10383441.2022.2096966.

Christodoulidis, Emilios A., Ruth Dukes, and Marco Goldoni, M. 2019. *Research Handbook of Critical Theory of Law*. Cheltenham: Edward Elgar Publishing.

Christodoulidis, Emilios A., and Marco Goldoni. 2019. "Marxism and the Political Economy of Law." https://ssrn.com/abstract=3273870.

Eagleton, Terry. 1991. *Ideology. An Introduction*. London: Verso.

Fung, S. 2017. "The Questionable Legitimacy of the OECD/G20 BEPS Project." *Erasmus Law Review* 2. https://doi.org/10.5553/ELR.000085.

Intergovernmental Group of Twenty-Four (G-24). 2019. "Proposal for Addressing Tax Challenges Arising from Digitalisation." Working Group on Tax Policy and International Tax Cooperation. https://www.g24.org/wp-content/uploads/2019/03/G-proposal_for_Taxation_of_Digital_Economy_Jan17_Special_Session_2.pdf.

Marx, Karl, and Friedrich Engels. 1998. *The German Ideology*. Amherst, NY: Prometheus Books.

Marx, Karl. 1995–1996. *Capital. A Critique of Political Economy*. Vol. 1. Moscow: Progress Publishers. https://www.marxists.org/archive/marx/works/download/pdf/Capital-Volume-I.pdf.

Mau, Søren. 2023. *Mute Compulsion: A Marxist Theory of the Economic Power of Capital*. London: Verso.

Miaille, Michel. 1977. *Une introduction critique au droit*. Paris: François Maspero.

Organisation for Economic Co-operation and Development (OECD). 2016. *Limiting Base Erosion Involving Interests Deduction and Other Financial Payments. Action 4. 2016 Update*. OECD/G20 Base Erosion and Profit Shifting Plan. Paris: OECD Publishing.

https://read.oecd-ilibrary.org/taxation/limiting-base-erosion-involving-interest-deductions-and-other-financial-payments-action-4-2016-update_9789264268333-en#page16.

Pashukanis, Evgeny B. 2003. *General Theory of Law and Marxism.* New Brunswick, NJ: Transaction Publishers.

Perrone, Nicolás M., and David Schneiderman. 2019. "International Economic Law's Wreckage: Depoliticization, Inequality, Precarity." In *Research Handbook on Critical Legal Theory*, edited by Emilios Christodoulidis, Ruth Dukes, and Marco Goldoni, 446–472. Cheltenham: Edward Elgar Publishing.

Picciotto, Sol. 2013. "Can the OECD Mend the International Tax System. *Tax Notes International* 71 (12): 1105–1115.

Robinson, William I. 2001. "Social Theory and Globalization. The Rise of the Transnational State." *Theory and Society* 30: 157–200.

Rosenberg, Justin. 2010. "Basic Problems in the Theory of Uneven and Combined Development. Part II: Unevenness and Political Multiplicity." *Cambridge Review of International Affairs* 23 (1): 165–189. https://doi.org/10.1080/09557570903524270.

UK Upper Tribunal (Tax and Chancery Chamber). 2019. "Irish Bank Resolution Corporation Limited (in Special Liquidation) and Irish Nationwide Building Society v The Commissioners for HM Revenue and Customs: [2019] UKUT 0277 (TCC)." https://www.gov.uk/tax-andchancery-tribunal-decisions/irish-bank-resolution-corporation-ltd-in-special-liquidation-andirish-ationwide-building-society-v-the-commissioners-for-hm-revenue-and-customs-2019-ukut-0277-tcc.

van Dijk, Teun. 2006. "Ideology and Discourse Analysis." *Journal of Political Ideologies* 11 (2): 115–140. https://doi.org/10.1080/13569310600687908; www.discourses.org/OldArticles/Ideology%20and%20Discourse%20Analysis.pdf.

von Braunmühl, Claudia. 1978. "On the Analysis of the Bourgeois Nation State within the World Market Context." In *State and Capital. A Marxist Debate*, edited by John Holloway and Sol Picciotto, 160–177. London: Edward Arnold.

12 International taxation, public debt, and public spending

The relationship between international taxation and the other components of public finances – public debt and public spending – merits a reflection.

Regarding public debt, mainstream (Barro 1979) and certain Marxist approaches (Bin 2015) posit a direct relationship between the increase in public debt and the increase in tax revenue. According to these approaches, high indebtedness puts pressure on states, in the short or medium term, to increase their tax revenue in order to make interest and principal repayments on their public debt. This conception is based on the budget constraint premise: the state can only spend, for any purpose (including public debt repayment), exactly as much money as it obtains from civil society. In its Marxist version, there is a major additional element in the association between public debt and tax revenue: assuming that the impact of tax revenue falls primarily on wages, the public debt/taxes complex is interpreted as a way for capitalists to extract more surplus value from workers. Indeed, in this version, the flows that are extracted from wages through the incidence of taxation end up as interest repayments in the hands of capitalists, who are the holders of public debt.

The theoretical framework adopted in this book suggests, instead, a different relationship between public debt and tax revenue. Given that public spending does not, in any of its variants, depend on tax revenue, interest and principal repayments on public debt are not dependent on tax revenue either. While public debt may have other functions from the point of view of the private sector (for example, making excess money created in the financial sector profitable), its issuance has a role similar to that of tax revenue in the monetary circuit, as we saw in Chapter 4, namely, withdrawing masses of money from circulation and thus regulating the money stock. For that reason, public debt interest payments and the amortization of the principal would, in principle, have the same effects as any form of public spending, with the major provision that public debt holders (who are primarily in the financial sector) would most likely not use that money for investment or consumption because they are not part of the productive sector of the capitalist economy. That does not mean that public debt is not a way of extracting more surplus value from workers, given that if a state adopts the budget constraint rule, it will surely cut public spending meant for workers (subsidies, pensions, public services, etc.) in order to prioritize debt repayment, thus reducing the workers' capacity to appropriate a part of production. The difference lies in that the increase in surplus

DOI: 10.4324/9781003458678-12

value, which can also occur through the incidence of taxation, is due more to the budget constraint.

While this is not the place for an in-depth examination of these conceptions, it is necessary to connect them with international taxation. If the first hypothesis were correct, the growth in the gross volume of public debt and the interest paid to its holders should lead to a *pro tanto* increase in tax revenue. If, instead, the second hypothesis (the one adopted in this book) were correct, tax revenue would not necessarily be dependent on public debt, even if, insofar as they are both elements of the money reflux phase, there is some kind of relationship between the two. However, this second hypothesis is not incompatible with a concomitant evolution between tax revenue and public debt, given that they are both in the monetary reflux phase.

With respect to the international sphere, the first hypothesis would be consistent with an increase in public debt in the core countries and a concentration of global tax revenue in those countries, and with a less pronounced increase in public debt in the periphery countries associated with an also slower evolution, or stagnation, of their tax revenue. If, instead, the second hypothesis were correct, core and periphery countries would not necessarily have different patterns in the evolution of their public debt, so that the comparative loss of tax revenue in the periphery countries (illustrated in the graph that compares tax revenue with GDP in Section 10.2) would not have as a counterpart a slowing down of public debt growth.

The following graph shows the evolution of the gross volume of public debt, GDP, and tax revenue for OECD countries in the last decades. For data consistency purposes, only central government public debt and tax revenue are included (Graph 12.1).

The graph does not corroborate the hypothesis of a correlation between public debt and tax revenue. While public debt and tax revenue both grew, the former did so at a much faster rate than the latter. This is reflected in the great disparity throughout the twenty-first century between the lines that represent one and the other. While the tax revenue data is general, with the portion that corresponds to monetary earnings from activities in the periphery not disaggregated, this has no bearing on the conclusion, given the absence of an overall correlation.

For their part, “developing countries” (which can roughly be equated with the periphery) experienced, according to UNCTAD data (2024), a much higher rate of growth in their public debt than “developed countries” (which can roughly be equated with the core). This is not compatible with the international corollary of the first hypothesis, according to which we should observe a concentration of debt and tax revenue in the core countries.

While no data is available on the total volume of public debt interest and principal repayments, there is information available on public debt interest repayments in the United States. The following graph provides an annual comparison of that indicator with tax revenue (Graph 12.2).

A concomitant variation between the two variables can be intuitively observed, but as noted above, that observation is compatible with both the hypothesis of a

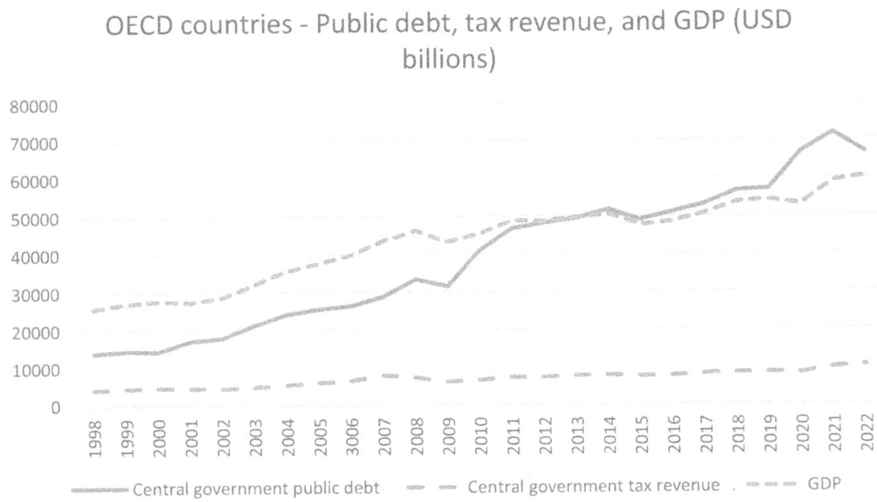

Graph 12.1 OECD Countries – Public debt, tax revenue and GDP.

Sources: For the evolution of public debt, author's own calculations based on data from the Federal Reserve Bank of St. Louis, available at: https://fred.stlouisfed.org/series/GCDODTOTLGDZSOED. For tax revenue, author's own calculations based on data from the World Bank, available at: https://data.worldbank.org/indicator/GC.TAX.TOTL.GD.ZS. For GDP, World Bank data, available at: https://data.worldbank.org/indicator/NY.GDP.MKTP.CD.

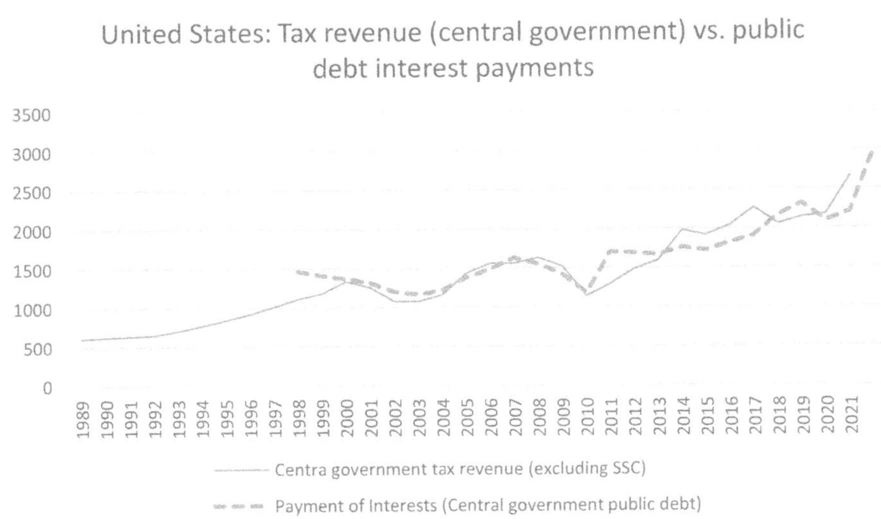

Graph 12.2 US – Public debt repayment and tax revenue.

Source: For interest payments, Federal Reserve Bank of St. Louis. Available at: https://fred.stlouisfed.org/series/A091RC1Q027SBEA. For tax revenue of the US central government, author's own calculations based on data from the World Bank, available at: https://data.worldbank.org/indicator/GC.TAX.TOTL.GD.ZS.

dependent relationship between tax revenue and debt repayment, as well as with the shared function of the money stock reflux. However, the graph does not include debt principal repayments, so if these were added, and assuming that their volume grows in the same proportion as the gross volume of the total debt, we would very likely observe an also increasing divergence between total payments of the public debt and tax revenue.

Moreover, both graphs have the disadvantage that the data on tax revenue does not discriminate the portion that corresponds to foreign income and domestic operations, so that, in any case, we would not be able to draw any specific conclusions regarding the relationship between the tax revenue of core countries from the operations of multinational enterprises (MNEs)in the periphery and their respective public debts.

In short, while international taxation tendencies do not appear to be explained by the concentration of public debt in core countries, and neither does tax revenue appear to be dependent on public debt, the relationship between the two merits a deeper analysis that greatly exceeds the scope of this book.

With respect to the relationship between international taxation and public spending, the hypotheses posited in Chapter 6 can rival a hypothesis that could be derived from mainstream economics and, in particular, from the idea of budget constraint, one proposing that international taxation tendencies respond to the need for increasing funds to sustain the also increasing public spending in core countries.

The problem with this hypothesis is that the theory of money and taxation set out in Chapters 3 and 4 also proposes a relationship between public spending and tax revenue, but in the opposite direction to the mainstream explanation. This is evident in the line graphs and in the regressions in Chapter 4, which simply compare US public spending and tax revenue: the correlation exists, and, in isolation, it is compatible with both this book's hypothesis and the mainstream hypothesis. However, I have already provided strong evidence that tax revenue, at least in the United States, does not determine public spending (see the first graph in Section 9.2.4): while US public spending and tax revenue both grow, the former does so at a much faster rate than the latter, so that there is no doubt that tax revenue is not the determinant of public spending.

On the other hand, the general mainstream hypothesis regarding the dependence of public spending on tax revenue, in the medium or long term, should have a statistical reflection in a long-term (or medium-term) parity between both variables. However, the concomitance between the two is also compatible with the hypothesis considered in Chapter 4, since tax revenue, as an essential part of the money reflux phase, can experience the effects of the increase or decrease in public spending. This includes both domestic and international tax revenue (Graph 12.3).

The result is more than obvious: if the deficit is, by definition, the difference between public spending and tax revenue, then the smaller the distance between the two, the more the former will decrease, and the greater the distance, the more the latter will decrease. Therefore, and even though increases in tax revenue from the activities of MNEs abroad may have the effect of reducing the fiscal deficit (as is the case with any increase in tax revenue), this does not imply a causal relationship

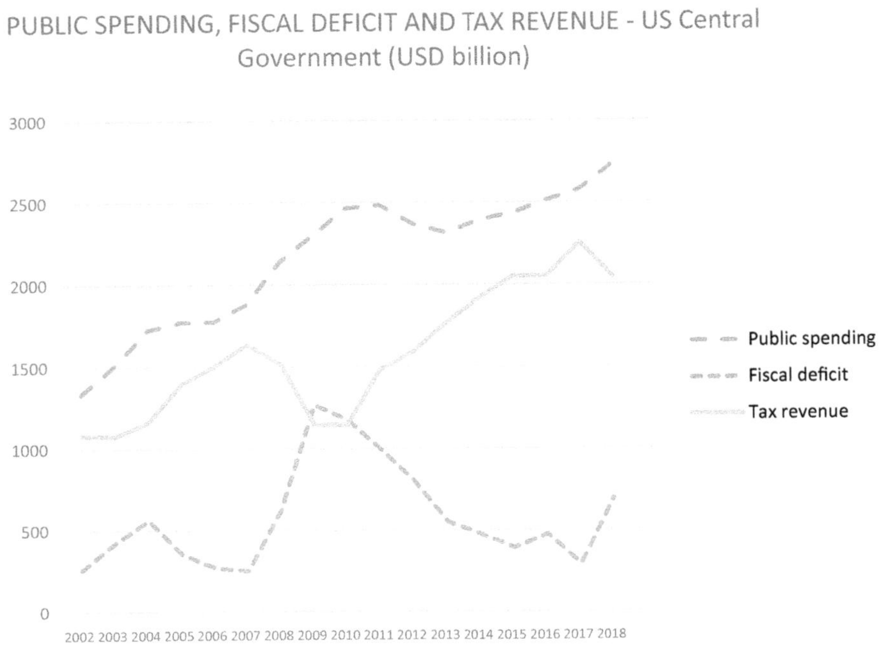

Graph 12.3 US Central Government – Public spending, fiscal deficit and tax revenue.

Source: Author's own calculation based on World Bank data, available at: https://data.worldbank.org/indicator/GC.TAX.TOTL.GD.ZS and https://data.worldbank.org/indicator/NY.GDP.MKTP.CD

between a greater deficit and a push to divert revenue to core countries. This is, in any case, a corollary of the general theory of taxes that was observed in Chapter 4, in which several pieces of evidence were provided to support that the direction of the determination is from public spending (and other money sources) to tax revenue.

References

Barro, Robert J. 1979. "On the Determination of the Public Debt." *Journal of Political Economy* 87 (5): 940–971.

Bin, Daniel. 2015. "Fiscal Superstructure and the Deepening of Labour Exploitation." *Capital & Class* 39 (2): 221–241. https://doi.org/10.1177/0309816815581774.

13 Is another global taxation structure possible?

Any observer will agree that there has been a common pattern throughout the history of international taxation, from its "prehistory" in the nineteenth century to the Base Erosion and Profit Shifting Plan (BEPS) today. I believe I have provided significant evidence to support the assertion that this common pattern is the central hypothesis I posited in Chapter 6, namely, the concentration of tax revenue in the states where the big money owners are located, so that taxation can fulfill its function as regulator of the money stock. Even if that hypothesis – so clearly anchored in a theoretical framework – is not accepted, I believe there are, nonetheless, some aspects that are so evident as to be indisputable: the bias in favor of core countries to the detriment of the periphery in tax revenue matters, and the complete centrality of the corporate income tax and, to a lesser extent, indirect taxes (both custom tariffs and the VAT), with little or no interest in taxing personal income and assets. This immediately prompts the question of whether it is possible to escape that tendency.

Abstractly speaking, the answer to that question is yes. Some economists who work on theoretical issues within mainstream economics have shown an interest in addressing income and wealth inequality and have suggested, among other things, bringing back progressive personal income and wealth taxes as instruments for combating that inequality (Blanco 2022). Their permanence within mainstream economics entails that they must adjust the neoclassical theoretical framework to the end pursued, proposing, in particular, a modified version of efficiency. In contrast with neoclassical orthodoxy, in which total efficiency is exactly equivalent to Pareto optimality and the absence of the state in the market, neoclassical dissidence argues in favor of combating inequality by positing its inefficiency, as inequality curbs investment and growth, for example, and generates social discontent that ultimately turns against the capitalist system itself. It follows, then, that increasing progressive and personal income and wealth taxes can no longer be considered inefficient, as it instead generates efficiency by reducing inequality. It should be noted in passing that this deviation in mainstream thinking confirms its epistemological breakdown: the concept of efficiency explains everything, which means it explains nothing at all.

Let us start by considering the proposals by Thomas Piketty, Gabriel Zucman, and some related researchers. These authors' analysis relies, first, on statistical information that quite overwhelmingly shows that the accumulation of capital has

DOI: 10.4324/9781003458678-13

represented an increasing proportion of income, thus denoting what can be termed "excess of accumulation". For Piketty and Zucman, it should be clarified, "capital" and "capital accumulation" mean something different from what is understood by those terms under Marxism, with their definition being much closer to the neoclassical conception, at the theoretical level. For these authors, capital is the total monetary value of production not consumed in perishable goods, so that it includes very diverse things, such as investment in equipment, buildings (whether used in production or not), and hoarded money. Capital accumulation is simply the increase of these items.

In any case, these authors note that accumulation thus understood has been accompanied by a widening inequality in the ownership of capital, explained not only by different individual efforts but also by inheritance rights (Piketty and Zucman 2014). Deepening inequality and its "inefficiency" (always speaking in neoclassical terms) lead them to radically revise the traditional idea of "zero taxation" as the "optimal solution" regarding taxes applied to capital. They then propose a progressive taxation on capital (both benefits and assets), as well as an inheritance tax with steep rates for higher levels of wealth, in order to mitigate the inequality in wealth ownership (Piketty and Saez 2013; Piketty and Zucman 2014, 1261).

The obvious difference with the Marxian analysis applied in this book notwithstanding, the data collected undoubtedly reveals the growth of both money-capital and physical capital (in addition to the growth of personal wealth not considered "capital" from a Marxian viewpoint). However, and as emerges from the title of an article on the subject by these authors, the process of excessive growth and unequal distribution of wealth (or capital) is observed and critiqued exclusively within core capitalist countries, never from an international perspective. None of these works address the concentration of capital ownership – and consequently the power to decide and the benefits obtained – in core countries and the displacement of material production (and, in Marxian terms, the generation of value) toward the capitalist periphery. If feasible, what Piketty and others propose would only entail a redistribution of wealth within the core capitalist world, but it would not produce a distribution of money holding (i.e., control over the capitalist system as a whole) in favor of the periphery (see Bértola 2017).

Moreover, what these authors propose focuses on the redistribution of income among individuals. This is undoubtedly a legitimate goal (although, as we will see shortly, one that is hardly achievable through taxation), but it does not address the issue of the distribution of tax revenue among states, which is the great problem of international taxation. Indeed, and working on the assumption that money owners are overwhelmingly concentrated in the core countries (which is one of the theoretical pillars that explain the current global taxation system), the proposed international tax on the highest income earners far from reversing the unequal distribution of money on a global scale would aggravate it, given that tax revenue from those income earners is in the hands of their countries of residence.

We must begin by assuming that taxation, as a monetary phenomenon, can only exist in an economy in which there is money, and, in particular, in a capitalist economy. This means that if at some point humanity evolves into a different kind of social structure, there would be no point in discussing taxation because it would have ceased to exist. But it also means that the profound regularities of the capitalist economy cannot be abolished with just any tax policy. One of Marxism's fundamental contributions is precisely that social life and, in particular, the economy are not random phenomena and are rather subject to certain objective tendencies that are imposed on the will of individuals. That would be a first type of limitation to any tax policy different from the current one.

Therefore, and in the first place, no tax policy can free taxation from its essential function as a regulator of the money stock. This is true both for global taxation reforms aimed at redistributing income and for proposals (such as those set out below) of new international taxation schemes. Regarding tax policies aimed at income redistribution, given that income inequality in the capitalist economy is, moreover, an effect of the division of society into classes, as such it is unsolvable within this mode of production. This is not to say that the degree of concentration of income by capitalists is irrelevant. History shows that a general improvement in the lives of workers within the capitalist system is possible, and also that taxation can certainly play a role in that sense. However, the fact that the natural function of taxation is the control of the monetary stock, compounded with the necessary division of society into classes under capitalism, leads to the conclusion that taxation as an instrument of income distribution is, at best, uncertain and weak.

Regarding the problem of the global distribution of tax revenue, we should bear in mind that the properties of the current taxation system are determined by a new structure of world production. It thus follows that it is difficult to imagine a radical change in global taxation structures without there first being a change in the global structure of capitalist production, which is the cause of the current taxation system.

These limitations for active policies within capitalism were identified clearly by Kalecki (1971, 138–145) with respect to measures tending toward full employment, but they are completely applicable to the field of taxation. While there is scope for policies favorable to workers, for example, or the global periphery, it is highly probable that at some point those policies will not be able to go any further due to the structural needs of the mode of production, which override all other motives or drives.

An example of these limitations is the marginal role that the United Nations has had in this process. The possibility that the UN will assume the role that the OECD has today in the taxation supranationality seems unlikely, not only because of the overwhelming preponderance of the OECD and the G20, but also because of the scarce willingness that the United Nations has shown in assuming that role. For example, in 2023 the UN Secretary General issued a report with a timid critique of Pillars I and II proposed under the BEPS Plan of the G20 and the OECD, which includes only a small mention of the concerns of developing countries with respect to the benefit/cost ratio of implementing those solutions, and no mention at all of the unequal distribution of tax revenue that such measures would cause (UN 2023). The UN's counter-proposal, moreover, is centered on strengthening international taxation cooperation mechanisms, mainly with respect to information exchange, but without venturing a proposal that is structurally different from what the G20 and the OECD propose.

Having considered these limitations, we can nonetheless hypothesize a different international taxation model that goes in the opposite direction of the existing (and tacit) model, namely, allowing periphery countries to independently design their taxes and fiscal policies in general. The main features of such an alternative model are outlined below.

First, from the institutional viewpoint, the OECD's role as designer of international taxation policies must be reassigned to a different international body, where all countries are members of equal standing (for example, a UN agency). The OECD's commitment to the current tendencies in international taxation makes a change in those policies impossible within that organization, as long as the OECD does not abandon its prevailing position on the matter.

Second, the transfer pricing mechanism as a system of distribution of the total income of MNEs should be replaced by a different mechanism that is not based on the arm's length principle or on the new criterion currently proposed by the OECD. This proposal is discussed further below because it involves specific problems.

Third, in the case of income derived from digitalized business activities, the preference for income taxation should not be the country of consumption, as was recently recommended by the OECD (2020). Instead, states should be free to establish their own specific rules, depending on their production structures and other needs, and limited only by the non-acceptance of the absence of taxation.

Fourth, the limits in tax on dividends (and other "passive income", such as royalties) should be suppressed, and each country should regain its power to assess dividends paid abroad in the manner decided by its national parliament. That measure would restore to periphery states the capacity to establish policies on money flows abroad and payment balance.

Fifth, limits on the taxing of other passive income, such as royalties and interest, should also be eliminated, with the same objective. Furthermore, the criterion for determining the "source" of royalties and interest cannot be the residence of the payer entity or the origin of the funds for repayment. To the extent the debtor of the loan or other forms of financial debt is an MNE, interest and royalties would be apportioned, for tax purposes, in accordance with the total working hours incurred in each country by the entities owned by such MNE. The rationale of such a criterion is that, under the concept of surplus, royalties and interest are ways of surplus appropriation, and surplus generated in an MNE could be considered a unit on its chain of production.

Sixth, a new progressive tax on individual wealth, as proposed by Piketty et al., would improve the global structure of taxation provided its collection is international, and its revenue is distributed (for example, through an international body) among a set of low-income countries with the sole purpose of establishing a basic income. The evidence of the benefits of a basic income, especially in reducing poverty, is robust enough for it to be proposed for every low-income country. Besides, the simplicity of its calculation (a fixed sum per country inhabitant) provides an also simple method for determining each national portion of the revenue, with greater transparency.

The rejection of the transfer pricing mechanism based on the arm's length principle, and its correlative allocation of income and tax revenue according to monetary price assumptions, must be complemented with an alternative method for apportioning the whole income of international production among states. I consider such a possibility below, starting with some proposals made by Quentin on the subject (2017, 14–19).

Quentin proposes at least three interesting concepts for designing an alternative model of international corporate taxation: (a) aligning taxation with the value chain (i.e., with the steps of material production); (b) including in that chain all the participants in the process, from extractive activities to final consumption; and (c) a "formulary apportionment" instead of the traditional transfer pricing regime. Such premises are acceptable, but the crucial point is still the criterion for quantifying the taxable base corresponding to each state. If we adopt a distribution mechanism of taxable bases other than the arm's length principle, but the apportionment depends on the allocation of assets, the accounting of profits, or any other criterion that ignores labor, the result will be, conceptually speaking, similar. In fact, the new BEPS recommendations lead taxation in that direction.

In that way, although the monetary nature of taxes makes it necessary to start with ordinary corporate financial statements (naturally expressed in monetary units) and end with taxable bases (also expressed in money), there is no obstacle for the apportionment of income to be done according to the working hours actually applied in each country. Consequently, the global net profit of a value chain, calculated under normal accounting rules, would be attributed to each country as a function of the working hours incurred in its territory toward constituting the taxable base for that state's corporate tax.

The rationale for such a system is the labor theory of value and its complement, the concept of surplus: if the total value of a commodity depends on the total labor such commodity incorporates, and all the value exceeding wages is surplus, the latter can only be proportional to the working hours required along the chain.

References

Bértola, Luis. 2017. "Looking at Piketty from the Periphery." In *The Contradictions of Capital in the Twenty-First Century. The Piketty Opportunity*, edited by Pat Hudson and Keith Tribe. Agenda Publishing. https://es.scribd.com/document/351927532/Bertola-Looking-at-Piketty-From-the-Periphery.

Blanco, Andrés. 2022. "International Taxation and the Global Structure of Capitalism: The Influence of the OECD in the Design of the International Tax System." *Review of Radical Political Economics* 51 (2): 218–238. https://doi.org/10.1177/04866134211055871.

Kalecki, Michal. 1971. *Selected Essays on the Dynamics of Capitalist Economy*. Cambridge: Cambridge University Press.

Organisation for Economic Co-operation and Development (OECD). 2020. *Tax Challenges Arising from Digitalisation – Economic Impact Assessment: Inclusive Framework on BEPS*. OECD/G20 Base Erosion and Profit Shifting Project. Paris: OECD Publishing. https://doi.org/10.1787/0e3cc2d4-en; https://www.oecd.org/en/publications/tax

-challenges-arising-from-digitalisation-economic-impact-assessment_0e3cc2d4-en .html.

Piketty, Thomas, and Emmanuel Saez. 2013. "A Theory of Optimal Inheritance Taxation." *Econometrica* 81 (5): 1851–1886.

Piketty, Thomas, and Gabriel Zucman. 2014. "Capital Is Back: Wealth-Income Ratios in Rich Countries, 1700–2010." *Quarterly Journal of Economics* 129 (3): 1256–1310.

Quentin, David. 2017. "Corporate Tax Reform and 'Value Creation': Towards Unfettered Diagonal Re-Allocation Across the Global Inequality Chain." *Accounting, Economics, and Law: A Convivium* 7 (1): 20160020. https://doi.org/10.1515/ael-2016-0020.

United Nations (UN). 2023. "Promotion of inclusive and effective international tax cooperation at the United Nations: Report of the Secretary-General." https://documents .un.org/.

Index

For Product Safety Concerns and Information please contact our EU
representative GPSR@taylorandfrancis.com
Taylor & Francis Verlag GmbH, Kaufingerstraße 24, 80331 München, Germany

www.ingramcontent.com/pod-product-compliance
Ingram Content Group UK Ltd.
Pitfield, Milton Keynes, MK11 3LW, UK
UKHW020004200926
475702UK00015B/2471
* 9 7 8 1 0 3 2 6 0 3 4 7 6 *